TAKE HEART

RECLAIMING YOUR IDENTITY & INHERITANCE

DIANE & NEAL ARNOLD

EVER INCREASING
IMPACT

TAKE HEART:
Reclaiming Your Identity and Inheritance
By Diane and Neal Arnold

Published by Ever Increasing Impact
Charleston, South Carolina 29492

First Printing August 2017
Printed in the USA

ISBN: 978-0-692-90376-6

Editing by Jessica Glasner
Front Cover Heart image by Rosemary Funderburk
Cover Design & Book Layout by Jonathan McGraw

Visit the Arnolds' website at **www.everincreasingimpact.org**

ENDORSEMENTS

"With the world (and much of the church) limping in pain from the effects of fatherlessness and broken families, *Take Heart*—He releases Heaven-sized hope. Diane and Neal's testimony in this book shouts the passion of Jesus to run towards any mess that we find ourselves in. His precious story about redeeming this incredible family is loaded with God's power and His creative presence to 'do it again' in your life and in your family. Get ready to heal your own life and step into the world changing dominion you were designed for!"

DAVE HARVEY
Director of Global Legacy
Bethel Church, Redding CA

"Neal and Diane Arnold are people whose life-experience carries an impartation of love and miracles. These generous, anointed servants are committed to the heart of the Father for His Church and His kingdom. Every page of *Take Heart: Reclaiming Your Identity and Inheritance* is filled with treasure Neal and Diane have unearthed on their personal journey from the deep valley to full restoration and transformative healing. Neal and Diane live the message they share in this beautiful book. *Take Heart* carries practical insight, impartation, and the anointing for you to enter the reality that nothing is impossible with our God! *Take Heart* will draw you upward into new faith, greater freedom, and full joy. Take heart and go after the full inheritance God has for you!"

MAHESH & BONNIE CHAVDA
All Nations Church
Chavda Ministries International

"*Take Heart* is a must read book. Neal and Diane are an amazing couple who really live what they teach. Many times we meet people who have an education, a story, or an anointing. Neal and Diane have all three. When you meet them, they naturally leave a mark on your life that will impact you forever. With the dynamic combination of Neal's business mindset, Diane's passion for counseling families, and their powerful testimony, it is clear to see how God is using them to bring transformation to families. I know this first-hand because they have left a lasting imprint in the life of myself and my wife."

PASTOR JAY KOOPMAN
Young Adult and Youth Pastor
Hrock Church, Pasadena CA

"*Take Heart* encompasses the much-needed message that there are not only numerous biblical truths we must follow but the importance of fully comprehending them if we are to renew our minds and walk in freedom. Neal and Diane have uniquely communicated the importance of comprehending these biblical principles, as well as the significance they bring to an authentic relationship with Christ. The unique approach utilized throughout the book incorporates and integrates how to keep a proper perspective so that we can flourish in healing and freedom, as well as find a pathway of breakthrough and deeper understanding of how to enter your promised land. This book will definitely be an important resource to assist you if prayerfully processed and applied in your life."

DOUG STRINGER
Founder / President
Somebody Cares America / International
Turning Point Ministries International
Houston, Texas

"Without question, for such a time as this God has raised up Neal and Diane Arnold. Like a voice in the wilderness bringing healing, hope, and wholeness, *Take Heart* is a powerful message of how Neal and Diane have walked through the dark valley of pain and brokenness and into the light of forgiveness, grace, and renewal. As their pastor for several years, I have walked with them through some of the most trying times of their marriage. To see them emerge on the other side with victory in every sense of the word is an amazing testimony to the power of God's grace and the reward of a teachable spirit. I cannot be more excited about their growing ministry, their impactful testimony, and this incredibly timely book that will certainly bring hope and help to thousands.

PASTOR RANDY D. RICE
LifeChurch West Church

"With an amazing blend of vulnerability and wisdom, the Arnolds go after the reclaiming of our hearts. The topics of insecurity and intimacy are addressed with precision through personal stories and the impact of encounters with our loving God. Through loving insights, this book stirs emotions and feelings that are often ignored or silenced. Even though there are other books on identity, this book captures the destiny that is found in generosity that can only flow out of being a loved son or daughter of the King. I highly recommend this book for not only your own personal transformation but to assist others in reclaiming their true purpose and calling."

DR. MARK TUBBS
Harvest International Ministries Missions Apostle

"The message communicated by Neal and Diane Arnold in this book is a 'now word' for not only the Body of Christ but for anyone who is struggling to find hope. Many people need a tremendous amount of encouragement and guidance to buckle-down and reclaim their identity and inheritance after experiencing devastating situations. With every chapter, this inspiring couple beautifully integrates their transparency of personal situations with vital truths from the Word of God, which can truly set people free to live their God-Called destiny. I was especially impressed with how each writer successfully communicated their journey and their willingness to expose personal vulnerabilities for the glory of God. Since I have known Neal and Diane, I have grown to admire their professionalism and deep commitment to God. I had the privilege of spending two weeks with them on the mission field in Mozambique with their three boys; they were an incredible blessing to all who connected with their life-message—Take Heart—God is working on your behalf. I strongly recommend this book of revelation and instruction for those who desire to find their way to the Father's Love and experience the covenant that Jesus has provided for All those who will believe. As I read this book, my heart was touched and empowered to experience *all* that God has for me; I am more determined to live my life in the abundance of God's provision."

BRENDA JONES, PHD
Life Givers International Ministries

"For a world living in an identity crisis and consistently missing the fullness of God's best, *Take Heart*, offers real life answers along with a road map to relational transformation. Neal and Diane pull back the curtains and share openly and honestly about failures, hurts and the discoveries made in finding a way back to wholeness. As their pastors, we see the living results of the words written on the pages of this book. For everyone who wants to live life full of abundance and free of shame and despair, *Take Heart* is a must read."

MARK AND PATRICIA ESTES
Senior Leaders North Palm Church

"When one life is all that you have to live, we have chosen to live in such a way that makes sense in the light of eternity. Over 2000 years ago Jesus Christ hung on a bloody cross and He looked out into the future to this present hour, He saw you and your need for the ultimate heart transplant and the free gift of salvation for as many as would receive and follow Him. Jesus came to give us new hearts and a new identity in Him. Jesus never had a goal as he hung on the cross to fill seats in churches. His goal was to fill and transform hearts by encountering His love. We can't afford to convince a person that going to church is the pinnacle of the Christian life. Jesus came to fill our hearts with His spirit in order to transform the world around us. A transformed heart seeks to please the one that gave him a new heart.

"*Take Heart* is about living with the heart of God and allowing Jesus the author and finisher of your faith to transform you and to complete the work that He has started in you. There is something great about each and every one of your lives, and when you give yourself a hard time you're really giving God a hard time because He now lives in you. Take Heart and be free from shame, live with the understanding that you are loved by God and by His mercy and Grace you have been given a new heart to live passionately for Jesus. I believe you are a part of the generation that knows who they are and who they are in Christ Jesus. As you read *Take Heart* I encourage you to read with hope, knowing that what God did to Neal and Diane he can do in you."

CHRIS OVERSTREET
Bethel Church, Redding CA

ACKNOWLEDGEMENTS

Diane and I would like to dedicate this book to the most important inheritance God has given us; our three amazing young men—Matt, Zach, and Jake. They are our pride and joy and continue to amaze us with their dedication to impact others with His presence.

We want to honor our parents, Bill and Joann Gregory and Dean and Carol Arnold. We were richly blessed growing up under your godly influence. We also want to honor our church leaders, Apostles Mark and Patricia Estes. They have modeled being spiritual parents with grace, love, and power.

Many thanks to the young adults at North Palm Church. Your individual testimonies are incredible and encourage everyone who hears them. God has brought many of you into His kingdom from unimaginable early life challenges and now you are 'on fire' revivalists in North Charleston. You inspire us.

Diane and I would like to acknowledge the incredible assistance of Jess Glasner who has been our editor in our first book project. We could not have done this without her amazing help. She guided us through each step of the process, provided encouragement when we became unsure and was a wonderful sounding board for several key parts of this message.

We are grateful for the able help with the graphic arts talents of Jonathan McGraw and Rosemary Funderburk, the critical review and proofreading assistance by Emily Glasner and Alyssa Hughey, the professional review by Dr. Jeanne D. Brooks, and the audio book recording by Matt Ciclone.

Finally, I (Neal) have to honor my incredible wife Diane, whose greatest passion is to be in and carry God's presence. I love you. I (Diane) want to honor my brave husband, Neal for having the courage to share his weakest season to restore others and to bring Glory to God. I love you back.

DISCLAIMER

To protect the privacy of all individuals, all examples used in this book are the blending of different events from various locations and organizations. All names and identifying details have been changed, altered and combined with fictional material. Any resemblance to actual persons, living or dead, or actual events is purely coincidental.

The information contained in this book is intended for your encouragement and educational purposes. It is not intended to be a substitute for professional counseling or advice. Do not use this information to diagnose any mental or physical problems without consulting a professional counselor, psychologist or medical health care provider.

Please seek help from qualified sources with any questions or concerns you have regarding the mental, emotional, physical or spiritual health of yourself or your loved ones. If you need help finding a Bible Based Church or Christian Counseling Services, please visit us at *www.everincreasingimpact.org*.

CONTENTS

Foreword: Dr. Ché Ahn..15

Chapter 1: The Path from Disillusionment to Destiny.................17

Chapter 2: Are You Insecure?...29

Chapter 3: The Father's Love 43

Chapter 4: The Covenant Keeper: One with Him.......................57

Chapter 5: Transformed and Renewed 71

Chapter 6: Like Father, Like Son..87

Chapter 7: Flesh and Spirit...99

Chapter 8: Steadfast Love: While We Were Yet Sinners.............109

Chapter 9: Allowed to Feel...123

Chapter 10: The Path to the Promised Land...............................137

Chapter 11: Something's Gotta Go...151

Chapter 12: Yes and Amen...165

Chapter 13: Discovering the Abundance of God: What's in Your Checkbook?......177

Chapter 14: God's Economy: Where True Wealth is Multiplied..................189

Chapter 15: Occupying the Land: Your Place of Destiny............................201

Chapter 16: Milk and Honey: Fruitfulness in Christ 211

Appendix: More Information on Healing from Traumatic Emotional Experiences..217

Works Cited..219

About the Authors...225

FOREWORD

I have had the privilege of getting to know Neal and Diane Arnold over the last several years, and I've seen how their marriage communicates a beautiful testimony of supernatural redemptive healing. The Arnolds have a passion for families, and in *Take Heart* they share their raw and compelling story. The knowledge found in the pages of this book is meant to help you experience personal restoration and growth, but also godly transformation in your relationships with others.

Diane is a professional licensed counselor. For many years, she has brought the Lord's hope and healing to families who were previously in crisis, trauma, and tragedy. Neal is a seasoned corporate and financial services industry executive with experience in corporate turnarounds and leading publicly traded companies. They are both humble servants of faith, seasoned in leading individuals and companies through restorative transformations. Their book shares over a decade of revelation the Lord has given them surrounding the Scriptures and the heart of the Father on this issue.

Take Heart is not another self-help book offering a 10-step program to becoming a better you. Rather, it is the Arnolds' living testimony of how the Lord restored their marriage and family, following a crisis that nearly ruined their lives. This book is an invitation to be inspired by the testimony of the miracle that occurs when the Great Physician ministers psychological healing to people who've reached the end of their ability to do it themselves.

Through their own struggles, the Arnolds discovered keys to becoming free from unhealthy fear and shame. When we find and utilize these same keys, the Lord will enable us to find strategies for healing the shattered and broken places of our hearts. These tools for cultivating wholeness and identity will help us grasp who God created us to be in ways that make the entire Body of Christ stronger.

Neal and Diane often say that we need to first acknowledge our vulnerabilities and weaknesses in our healing process. While this is not easy for any of us to do, the good news is this recognition of our personal shortcomings never lessens who we are in Christ. We will not see complete victory at home, within our churches, or our places of influence without transparency and honesty. This book presents us with a timely challenge for each of us to share our testimonies, to release hope, courage, and the faithfulness of our Savior to a hurting world.

At times the pressures and issues of life can push people into dark corners of despair, inaction, and insecurity. These challenges can feel like they follow us everywhere, bringing emotional and spiritual weariness. However, as the title reminds us, Take Heart! We must always remember that God is for us and He is greater than any and all of our circumstances!

Our hope is in the victory He has already won. *Take Heart* is a book filled with wisdom garnered through the suffering and obedience of a couple who teach us vital lessons about laying hold of the inheritance Christ died to give us all.

Their candid story inspires hope, as it illuminates God's desire for us to cross the Jordan into our Promised Land. I believe you will be encouraged, encounter healing as you read, be changed, and in turn, bless others from your breakthroughs with the Lord.

DR. CHÉ AHN
President, Harvest International Ministry
Founding Pastor, HROCK Church, Pasadena, CA International
Chancellor, Wagner University

CHAPTER ONE
The Path From Disillusionment to Destiny

"I have told you these things, so that in Me you may have peace.
In this world you will have trouble. But take heart! I have
overcome the world."[1]

CREATED FOR IMPACT, NOT INSECURITY

The Church is desperate for a cure for insecurity, complacency, and a lack of power. The sad truth is that many born-again believers accept Jesus with great anticipation of transformation, but fail to find breakthrough. Even though they faithfully attend a congregation, read their Bibles, and routinely pray, community and covenant relationships remain out of reach. Fear and hopelessness can become constant companions. Truly feeling loved and accepted eludes many. Research tells us that Christians suffer depression and anxiety to the same degree as non-believers.[2] Divorce runs rampant in our society. Most people struggle with seasons that feel far from victorious.

We have all experienced self-doubt and known that uncomfortable feeling of uncertainty and anxiety the moment our confidence plummets.

1: John 16:33

2: Simpson, A. *Troubled Minds: Mental Illness and the Church's Mission.* Downers Grove: InterVarsity Press, 2013.

Insecurity traps us into *feeling* unprotected and vulnerable. These feelings manifest in tangible human ways and can powerfully affect our decision-making processes.

Fear can keep us from asking that great girl out.

Self-doubt can keep us from pressing "send" on that honest email.

Our insecurities can trick us out of opening our hearts to others, blocking us from letting them know that we are experiencing love or even remorse.

Our lack of confidence argues we must dress or act a certain way because the "real us" wouldn't be acceptable or lovable.

Shame keeps us home when we should be in community. It urges us to stay isolated, determined to keep us from reaching our full potential and our God given destiny.

We have all been there. Every single one of us.

But *take heart!* God desires that you fully occupy the "Promised Land" now, here on earth.

And what is the "Promised Land"? Thousands of years ago, it was the tangible fulfillment of God's promise to provide a homeland flowing with milk and honey for His people. For us today, the "Promised Land" symbolizes the abundant lives we are meant to live on earth, the lives Jesus paid for on the Cross.[3]

In this book, we want to share our journey into our Promised Land. His abundant blessings are meant to spill over into every area of our lives, emotional, spiritual, and physical. Our goal is to inspire you and release you to pursue the glorious riches He has in store.

3: John 10:10

Just like the Jewish people, it is our destiny for God to lead us on a journey to the Promised Land. He wants us to walk in ever-increasing freedom, power, and fruitfulness.

God does not want us to be anything less than secure.

Why?

Because we only fully fulfill His call on our lives out of a place of security in Him.

FRUITFULNESS, FREEDOM, AND FAITH

It was with some trepidation we decided to share our story. Failure is never fun. We overcame one of the most difficult marriage challenges. Our for better or worse was a heart-breaking crisis. We believe God has shown us how our story may help give you victory in your own valley. Or it may even provide you with the courage to share your own scars.

It is possible that, like us, you have been duped. We both bought into the lies of the enemy. We languished between a place of hiddenness and doubt for much of our Christian lives. God wanted so much more for us.

As believers, we know deep down that we are called to be fruitful and multiply.[4]

We understand, from a cerebral perspective, that Jesus died so that we might have freedom; freedom from sin and freedom to live life with abundant joy. But very few of us ever taste the fruit of this promised freedom in our daily lives.

After I, Neal, tried to destroy our marriage, God miraculously healed both our covenant and our family. At times it was an uphill battle, but He was faithful to see us through to the end. What's more, our lives are currently

---

4: God's first command to Adam and Eve in Genesis 1:28.

more full of His joy and Presence than we ever knew was possible. He let us taste the fruit of freedom and latch on to His Promise in the wake of trauma.

All that aside, my failure was not something I wanted to talk about. It still hurt. By not sharing the triumph God brought about in our marriage, we recognized we were also keeping others from their own success. We were, in essence, reducing the power of our testimony.

There is power in remembering what God has done for each one of us. If we want to see fruit in our lives and experience total freedom from guilt and shame, it means we must embrace honesty and full vulnerability with Him. If we are afraid to speak out, if we still keep dark secrets hidden from those we love or from God, we are not living fully surrendered. We are living in bondage and compromise, refusing the precious gift of freedom Jesus died to give us.

The extent to which we settle for less is directly related to the extent we live in peace and rest. The more we compromise, the less free we become, the less secure. Conversely, the more steadfast and focused we are to "walk the walk and talk the talk," the more we experience the glorious freedom, security, and power of the love of God. Our stories of overcoming drive out doubt in ourselves and others. In the same way the Book of Acts builds up our faith, so do our miraculous personal histories.

The Church that proclaims the testimony is the Church moving in power, encouraging and delivering those trapped in bondage. His redemption in our lives paves the way for victories in theirs, and on and on. The testimony bears endless fruit. What greater glory and worship can we give our Savior than to parade His triumphs before others in order that they may share in the victory themselves? Without our testimonies, we each run the risk of not fully maturing in the Kingdom. He wants us to flourish so that we can rule and reign with Him.

Trust the Lord to see you through, and don't worry about what other people think. Trade your hiding for honesty and your doubt for faith. Receive the inheritance He planned for you from the beginning of time.

It is imperative that we recognize the value and nature of our inheritance as sons and daughters of God. If we don't, we are forced into a radical and tragic life-detour. One that leads straight into the bitter, inner wilderness of insecurity. In this state, we live a double life. The real, everyday struggle sharply contrasts with the obligatory suit-and-tie Sunday smile.

We get stuck in the mud and mire.

We settle for rituals without *power*.

At times, the lie that the God we serve is not really willing to engage in our lives seems true.

In a place of insecurity and hiddenness, we struggle with a lack of victory or increasing hopelessness. This, in turn, tempts us to doubt God's truth and goodness. It is the same tactic satan tried to use on Jesus in the wilderness.[5] The end result is that God becomes a set of rules or rituals rather than the "friend who sticks closer than a brother."[6]

Jesus overcame these lies with the power of the truth of the Word and His deep intimate relationship with His Father. We can do the same!

We've seen restored confidence in our own lives. His faithfulness carried us through the wilderness to His Promised Land. We learned to trust Him in circumstances where it did not look like victory was possible. We no longer doubt that He is faithful or powerful. We can honestly say today that we would rather trust Him than ourselves.

HE HAS OVERCOME

"I have told you these things, so that in Me you may have peace. In this world you will have trouble. But take heart! I have overcome the world."[7]

5: Matthew 4:1-11
6: Proverbs 18:24
7: John 16:33

Even though you may not have experienced the abundant life yet, take heart, Jesus has overcome the world. He warned us that we would have trouble, but that in Him, there is peace.

The Greek root for the phrase, "that in me you may have" is *echō*[8]. It means to lay hold of, take possession of, or to clothe one's self in. When we lay ahold of, take possession of, and clothe ourselves in Him, we experience peace. In Christ, our peace is not based on our circumstances or understanding, or the heavenly status of our hopes and prayers. Instead, our trust is in Jesus, *who has already overcome.*

We do not stand on our own victory; we stand on the victory of Christ.

This is an essential fact to remember, especially when satan tempts us with doubt or fear.[9] We are called to "take heart" because our Father has already won the victory. In this place of trust, He leads us to eternal triumph and fulfills our every need. He becomes our unshakeable rock in seasons of struggle and uncertainty. He is our security in times of wilderness wandering.

CROSSING OVER

The Israelites wandered in the desert for forty years before entering the Promised Land of Israel.[10] Sadly, believers in Jesus may also wander around in the desert for decades, not getting any closer to receiving their promise. They know the land exists, but like the Israelites, actually living there seems like a pipe dream. Entering the abundant life looks like an insurmountable challenge.

We've been there. We lived in a cycle of *believing for* God's Promises without ever *receiving them.* But God through His mercy ended that horrible pattern for good. With the Israelites as our example, we learned that leaving the wilderness behind and entering the Promised Land requires *crossing* over something significant.

8: "G2192 - echō - Strong's Greek Lexicon (ESV)." *Blue Letter Bible.* Web. 25 May, 2017.

9: Revelation 12:10

10: Numbers 32:13

God's chosen people crossed the Red Sea when God delivered them from slavery to freedom.[11] This is the "crossing" of salvation every believer makes when they accept Jesus.

The second crossing, however, was over the Jordan River from the wilderness to the Promised Land.[12] This is the crossing not all believers dare to brave; *the crossing of sanctification and inheritance,* moving from flesh-led lives to Spirit-led lives.

The Jordan River is time and time again the place of separation. Immersion in its waters becomes the ultimate symbol of transitioning from being led by the flesh to led by *His Spirit.* It is the place where the old man is drowned and the new man is brought to life.

It was the Jordan that separated Lot, a man of the flesh, from Abraham, the man of the Spirit and Promise. It was on the banks of the Jordan that Jacob, Abraham's grandson, wrestled with God and was blessed with the new name of Israel. On the same shore, Elisha used Elijah's cloak to possess and walk in the double portion anointing of Elijah.[13] This action resulted in the passing of Elijah's mantle.[14] Finally, Jesus was baptized in the Jordan. When He came out of the water, "a voice from Heaven said, 'This is my Son, whom I love; with him I am well pleased.'"[15]

To fully embrace life as the "new man," we too must submissively go through the waters and enter in. Our true ministry will not start until we've been fully submerged, have died with Christ, and come out clean, alive in Him on the other side.[16]

11: Exodus 14:21-22
12: Joshua 3:17
13: Genesis 32:22-31
14: 2 Kings 2:13
15: Matthew 3:17
16: Romans 6:11

TAKING THE PLUNGE

Everyone has hidden *something* at some point in their lives. Whether it is secret sin, fear of judgment, past abuse, or addictions. We often fear that if brought into the open and dealt with, we will not be accepted by God or by our community. These hidden areas keep us from healthy relationships. This lack of connectedness can result in debilitating levels of shame and insecurity, wreaking havoc in our lives. Living hidden is the polar opposite of living secure. In darkness, we stumble through life, desperately trying to stay afloat in our own strength amidst the waves of adversity.

In contrast, the secure do not ride the waves. They are safely attached to their God and the community of believers. No matter what comes their way, their house will stand. You can easily spot a secure person. They are marked by trusting, long-term, intimate relationships, high self-esteem, and an ability to openly share their feelings with other people.[17] They are free, healthy, and whole. They trust their Father to see them through.

When our lack of trust towards God or others keeps us from total honesty, we distance ourselves from the very thing that will set us free. Insecurity and fear build walls around our hearts, barring us from the very relationships that will bring us healing and safety. This is a dangerous catch-22. Self-doubt and uncertainty keep us from getting the comfort we need to become confident and whole. In short, insecurity is what keeps us from embracing the cure for insecurity!

Thankfully, we have the cure. His name is Jesus! A healthy relationship with our Messiah opens the door to complete freedom and wholeness. You never have to struggle with self-doubt or hiddenness again, when you are secure in Him. In addition, healthy relationships that prove to be consistent and safe over time will also serve to heal our insecurities.[18]

17: Kirkpatrick, L., Hazan, C. "Attachment Styles and Close Relationships: A Four Year Prospective Study." *Personal Relationships*, 1, 1994. 123–142.
18: Clinton, T., Sibcy, G. *Why You Do the Things You Do: The Secret to Healthy Relationships.* Nashville: Integrity, 2006.

In other words, security breeds more security. Healthy relationships can *literally influence the way we relate to God, others and ourselves. Healing allows us to move from unhealthy to healthy, from insecure to secure.*

The greatest longing of the human heart is to be fully known and loved. To be confident in who we are and who He made us to be. When this longing is met by our Heavenly Father, nothing is impossible.

Some may argue against this, feeling that they are relatively healthy and secure adults without God. However, at the end of the day, the fullness of what He promised us is only experienced through relationship with Him, and Him alone. He is the Tree of Life.

It is important to see our feelings as an opportunity to steer toward the arms of God. Appearances can be deceiving. Feelings can lie. And left to our own devices, we may trust in just about anything *but* God to find a semblance of value. Our parents, our spouses, our work, our diets, our doctors, our talent, and even ourselves; will ultimately fail us.

The more time you spend with the most secure man ever born, Jesus, the more confident you will become. Our complete and perfect identity is only found in the transformative power of His Presence. Romans 8:15-16 in the *Passion Translation* perfectly relates that truth to us where it tells us,

> *"For you have received the Holy Spirit who has enfolded you into God's family, chosen and adopted as His very own child. And the Holy Spirit will never make you feel orphaned, or cause you to fear that God will abandon you. You are free from all bondage and no longer a mere servant. For the Holy Spirit inside your heart cries out, "You are His child, and He is your Father! The Holy Spirit living inside your spirit is the divine proof that you are God's child!"* [19]

God does not want us to feel anything less than whole and secure. Why? Because we fulfill His call on our lives fully only out of a place of intimacy

---

19: "Romans 8:15-16," Simmons, B. *The Passion Translation.* BroadStreet Publishing Group, LLC, 2015.

and safety in Him. When we live in and are consumed with this state of love and safety, we naturally start to feel good about ourselves.

We stand taller, with the assurance of knowing deep inside that we have value.

We believe in ourselves.

We have trust in our decisions.

We no longer need to project a false picture to the outside world.

And, we also have more confidence in our relationships with each other. Our insecurities and hang-ups fade as we experience more completeness and "enter that rest," learning to live in increasing *shalom*.[20]

The safety you experience in Father God opens doors to a whole new way of living. You will no longer be held captive by your past, but will instead courageously step into God's plan for your life. You will be known by your joy and peace, and you will reproduce His healing touch in the lives of those around you.

THRIVING, NOT JUST SURVIVING

We carry real redemptive power to free the captives and lift up the broken-hearted. We are called to demonstrate God's love, wisdom, and strength through our lives, not just by our words. The Gospel without power is no Gospel at all. If we do not believe that He will do what He said He will do, we have become powerless to solve today's greatest societal challenges.

Paul put it clearly in 1 Corinthians 2:3-5, "I was with you in weakness, in fear, and in much trembling. And my speech and my preaching [were] not with persuasive words of human wisdom, but in demonstration of the Spirit and of power, that your faith should not be in the wisdom of men but in the power of God."

20: Hebrews 4:11

We long to see *real* supernatural healing power flowing into and through us and our churches. We are determined to actually step into everything He's prepared for us on *earth*.

Why? Because when we are healed and whole, we can fully partner with the Holy Spirit to release His destiny for ourselves and those around us, allowing us to actually experience life in the Promised Land, to be the City on the Hill. This was His plan from the beginning.

"On that day I swore to them that I would bring them out of Egypt into a land I had searched out for them, a land flowing with milk and honey, the most beautiful of all lands."[21]

"You are about to cross the Jordan to enter and take possession of the land the LORD your God is giving you."[22]

We want to infuse you with hope right now and encourage you to *take heart*.

We have experienced the "Jordan Crossing" in our relationships, emotions, finances, and health, and long for you to experience it, too!

With Him in control, and each of us in His arms, we will bear more amazing fruit than we could ever hope for or imagine.[23]

If we had the honor of speaking and praying with you right now, we would tell you this: *you are not relegated to a life of insecurity, hiddenness, powerlessness, and shame.*

Your heavenly Father wants you confident, encouraged, and full of life. As you continue with us on our journey in the following chapters, we ask you to open both your minds and your hearts. If you do, you will experience God as we have, as a reliable and dependable Father.

21: Ezekiel 20:6
22: Deuteronomy 11:31
23: John 15:5, Ephesians 3:20

Let us bless you along with Paul,

> *"We ask that the God of our Lord Jesus Christ, the glorious Father, may give you the spirit of wisdom and revelation, so that you may know Him better. We pray that the eyes of your heart may be enlightened in order that you may know the hope to which He has called you. Amen."* [24]

24: Ephesians 1:17-18

CHAPTER TWO

Are You Insecure?

"You will be secure, because there is hope; you will look about you and take your rest in safety."[25]

God gives mankind all revelation; in fact, all truth is God's truth.[26] Any truth we gain through our education and life experiences ultimately has its source in God. His Word is the final authority. When society is functioning in a healthy, productive way, we find that His truth has been worked into the culture. When there is a convergence of the Word of God and various cultural, educational, and physical disciplines it will bear great fruit. We can be assured that any discipline that aligns with Scripture will result in positive outcomes for our lives.

I, Diane, have found this to be true in my career as a professional counselor and marriage therapist. I have realized that, when applied in partnership with Biblical principles and the guidance of the Holy Spirit, psychology comes to life. When we choose to filter psychology through a Biblical lens, we have a contemporary useful tool. This partnership provides us with a

25: John 11:18

26: McMinn, M., Phillips, T. *Care For The Soul: Exploring the Intersection of Psychology & Theology*. Downers Grove: InterVarsity Press, 2001.

powerful, relevant restoration model that sets people free to receive every-thing Jesus redeemed with His precious blood.[27]

Over the last several years, we have watched this integration create power-ful experiences in people's lives. In my counseling practice and our ministry center, we are witnessing tremendous results by combining these disci-plines. Human hearts are being restored. People are finding hope again, as they become not only healed but healers. It is also a journey the Lord took us on personally many years ago when He rescued our marriage.

We are longing for that same personal experience of freedom to be im-parted to you. As you read, we pray that you will acquire more than infor-mation for your brain files. It is our desire that your heart connects with the message, and that you allow God to reveal and release you into your unique Kingdom destiny.

We begin the journey in the 1940s. At this time, a piece of research was de-veloped by a psychologist named John Bowlby. His mission was to under-stand why children experience anxiety and distress when separated from their primary caregivers. His work inspired what psychology has named "attachment theory." This theory describes the forming of and security about our early relationships.[28]

We believe that Bowlby's findings have provided one of our most effective and successful tools. Why? Because when we understand our attachment or relating needs, we open a door to healing. It can change us personally as well as relationally with God and with others. We were made for relationship.

Interestingly enough, this theory can begin to explain why we respond certain ways when we are hurt or separated from loved ones. This research tells us that children must develop a positive relationship with at least one primary caregiver to ensure healthy social and emotional development.[29]

27: 1 Peter 18-19
28: Bowlby, J. *A Secure Base*. New York: Basic Books, 1988.
29: Ibid.

How the caregiver answers the child's heart question, "are you there for me?" decides whether a secure or insecure attachment will form.[30]

Another researcher, named Mary Ainsworth, discovered that a secure primary relationship produces deep feelings of trust and love in a child. If our childhood experiences were more positive, they become our source of safety, stability, and confidence. On the other hand, if they were more hurtful, they become the source of anxiety, self-doubt, and mistrust. She suggested that behaviors, such as crying or ignoring, can be responses from children that they are feeling "disconnected" from their caregivers.[31]

Perfect parents do not exist. It is impossible to be physically or emotionally there one hundred percent of the time for your children. Even the most sensitive of caregivers get it right only fifty percent of the time.[32] At this point, you may be asking yourself how your primary caregivers measured up to Ainsworth's and Bowlby's standards (or how you measure up, for that matter).

Answer this fundamental question to find out: was your caregiver nearby, accessible, and attentive?[33,34]

If the answer to this question is perceived as "yes," the result is often feeling loved, secure, and confident. A person who is able to answer yes holds a more positive view of themselves and others. They believe they are worthy of being loved and are comfortable with both closeness and independence.[35] They are labeled as secure.

30: Ainsworth, M. "Attachment Across The Lifespan." *Bulletin of New York Academy of Medicine, 61*. 1985. 792-812.

31: Ainsworth, M. *Attachment & Human Development, 1* (2), 1999. 217-228.

32: Howe, D. *Attachment Across the Lifecourse: A Brief Introduction.* London: Palgrave, 2011.

33: Bowlby, J. *Attachment and Loss, Vol. 1. Attachment.* New York: Basic Books, 1969.

34: Ainsworth, M. *Attachment Across The Lifespan.* Bulletin of New York Academy of Medicine, 61, 1985. 792-812.

35: Clinton, T., Sibcy, G. *Why You Do the Things You Do: The Secret to Healthy Relationships.* Nashville: Integrity, 2006.

If, however, the answer to this question is "no," the person tends to doubt their self-worth and will probably not expect their community to be there for them. These types of uncertain experiences can result in everything from minor anxiety to extreme despair and depression.[36] People who have had these types of experiences are, essentially, described as insecure.

WHERE IS THIS GOING?

This information becomes useful to us along with another piece of research. In the late 1980s, Cindy Hazan and Phillip Shaver studied attachment styles in adults. They categorized people into four general styles of attachment (or relating) behavior: secure, anxious-ambivalent, anxious avoidant, and fearful.[37] Their research is important because it revealed how our childhood *relating styles* continue to influence our thoughts, feelings, and behaviors well into adulthood.[38] Our early childhood experiences actually affect the way our brain will try to understand how to navigate our future adult relationships.[39] Our first encounters and perceptions are powerful lenses through which we will view future relationship development.

It is exciting to know that our attachment styles are always under construction. They are continually being shaped and molded by our life circumstances and our relationship interactions.[40] The nature of our adult friendships and romantic relationships can help solidify or change our early relating styles.[41] In other words, we can be simultaneously wounded by *and* healed with relationships.[42]

36: Ibid.

37: Hazan, C., Shaver, P. "Conceptualizing Romantic Love as an Attachment Process." *Journal of Personality and Social Psychology*, 52, 1987. 511-524.

38: Waters, E., Weinfield, N., Hamilton, C. "The Stability of Attachment Styles From Infancy to Adolescence and Early Adulthood: General Discussion." *Child Development, 71*, 2000. 703–706.

39: Siegel, D.J. *The Developing Mind: How Relationships and the Brain Interact to Shape Who We Are.* New York: Guilford Press, 2015.

40: Clinton, T., Sibcy, G. *Healthy Relationships.*

41: Johnson, S. *The Practice of Emotionally Focused Couple Therapy: Creating Connection.* New York: Brunner-Routledge, 2004.

42: Clinton, T., Sibcy, G. *Healthy Relationships.*

WHAT'S YOUR STYLE?

Knowing your adult attachment relating style will help you understand the ways you may defend yourself. Or it may help you make sense of the walls you may have built around your heart. Most importantly, understanding how you *relate* could help you better emotionally connect to the important people in your life.

Don't be discouraged or alarmed if you do not see yourself fitting into only one of the four categories. Many people find themselves with traits from more than one style.

See if you identify with one or more of the attachment (relating) styles listed below:

Secure attachment styles have a positive view of themselves and others. They are comfortable with intimacy and don't fear the rejection of others. In relationships, they report greater satisfaction and vulnerability.[43] Essentially, a securely attached person is one who is healthy, happy, and whole.

A secure style of relating usually results from a history of warm and responsive interactions from infancy to the first significant relationships as an adult.[44] These children know their caregivers will provide reassurance and support, so they are comfortable seeking them out in times of need. Children with a secure style of relating see their parents as a safe base from which they can venture out and independently explore the world.[45]

A secure adult shows a similar pattern with their relationships and will allow his or her spouse or close friends the freedom to make independent choices.[46] A secure attachment style is comfortable with the idea that they need support from others and others will need their support at times.[47]

Secure people are at peace when they are alone and are not afraid of rela-

---

43: Kirkpatrick, L., Hazan, C.. *Attachment Styles*.
44: Clinton, T., Sibcy, G. *Healthy Relationships*.
45: Ainsworth, M. *Attachment*.
46: Johnson, S. *Creating Connection*.
47: Johnson, S. *Creating Connection*.

tionship rejection. Their associations tend to be honest, open, and equal.

Jesus is the exact representation of someone with a secure relating style. He was not afraid to make the hard call, even when it meant He wouldn't be accepted by the ruling social group. He didn't seek the approval of man. He never doubted who He was. He was in perfect relationship with His Father. In fact, there wasn't a moment He felt rejection or disapproval from God. They were in perfect unity, and He continually sought opportunities to spend time in His Father's Presence.

This is the attachment style that God has planned for each one of us. Our earthly parents are meant to mirror the ultimate security that God demonstrates towards us. However, we live in an imperfect world. Our families may have fallen short of emulating God's character in some way or another. The result? It is possible that other forms of attachment styles were established in us. These could be; *anxious-ambivalent attachment, anxious avoidant attachment*, and *fearful attachment*.

An **anxious-ambivalent attachment** is driven by fear of rejection and abandonment, with feelings of low self-worth. Because of their need to be liked, people with this style of attachment seek high levels of approval from their relationships.[48] A person with an ambivalent relating style senses fear that only recedes when they experience intimacy and connection.[49]

When faced with a relationship loss, they will fight for connection. You will often see this style get louder and louder to get the attention of their significant attachments.

Their biggest fear is having no interaction at all. As a result, they may inadvertently settle for negative attention, poking and prodding until a fight breaks out, in a desperate attempt to interact. You may hear them say things like, "I hate being without close relationships," or, "I am worried that others don't value me as much as I value them."

48: Clinton, T., Sibcy, G. *Healthy Relationships*.
49: Hazan, C., Shaver, P. "Attachment As An Organizational Framework for Research on Close Relationships." *Psychological Inquiry, 5*, 1994. 1–22.

Their fear of rejection drives the ambivalent adult to try to get their arms around situations that cause them anxiety.[50] They desperately need details regarding all of the "who, what, when, and where's of life," in their attempt to make sense of any situation that triggers feelings of rejection or disconnection. This relating style is vulnerable to perceived criticism and experiences a deep fear that they aren't competent enough to make it on their own.[51]

The Gospels give us a strong candidate for an ambivalent attachment style: the Apostle Peter. Before he could get to work building the Church, his relational style had to heal and change. In the book of Matthew, we learn of the beautiful instance where Jesus healed Peter by developing an intimate relationship with him.

The healing began on a stormy night as the disciples fought against a strong wind and heavy waves to return to the safety of the shoreline. Out of nowhere, Jesus came into sight, and He appeared walking on the water!

When the disciples saw Him walking on the lake, they were terrified.

"It's a ghost," they said and cried out in fear. But Jesus immediately said to them: "Take courage! It is I. Don't be afraid."

"Lord, if it's You," Peter replied, "tell me to come to You on the water."

"Come," He said.[52]

Peter stepped out in courage. Or did he? For the purpose of our study we would like to propose this: if Peter displayed an ambivalent attachment style, this moment may illustrate the embodiment Peter's insecurity. He was trying to find well-being and approval outside of himself.

50: Johnson, S. *Creating Connection.*
51: Clinton, T., Straub, J. God Attachment: *Why You Believe, Act, and Feel the Way You Do About God.* New York: Howard Books, 2014.
52: Matthew 14:26-29

In fact, the story continues: "But when he saw the wind, he was afraid and, beginning to sink, cried out, 'Lord, save me!' Immediately Jesus reached out His hand and caught him. 'You of little faith,' He said, 'why did you doubt?'"[53]

Jesus had faith that if His Father told Him to walk on water, He could. On the other hand, Peter leaned on the faith of Jesus instead of building his own secure relationship with God the Father. Peter illustrates how insecurity creates doubt and fear that can cause us to sink. Although he was bold, he struggled because he needed someone else to affirm his safety.

If you resonate with this attachment style, it's okay. Thankfully, Peter's issues (and ours) are not stronger than God's power. Jesus was right there to catch Peter from drowning. He reached out and caught Peter in His arms. He will reach out and catch me and you, too.

There, on the water, face to face with Jesus, a miracle occurred.

Imagine Peter, grasping the hand of Jesus, fearing for his life. Picture that when he focused in on Jesus' expression, he could even see the little flecks of gold in His eyes.

Look into those eyes with Peter.

When you are face to face you can feel His breath on your forehead.

You can hear His beating heart.

In that intimate space, Peter suddenly found himself able to do the impossible: he could walk on water, too. His secure relationship with his friend, Jesus, paved the way towards developing a deeper trust in God and walking in the miraculous.

That is the power of finding security in the arms of Jesus, the most intimate relationship we can have.

53: Matthew 14:30-31

An **anxious avoidant attachment** is driven by a fear of closeness and intimacy and a worry of failure in relationships.[54] For this relating style, being vulnerable does not come easily. An avoidant relating style may altogether deny the need for close relationships. They often consider themselves self-reliant islands. People with this attachment style often desire a high level of autonomy and tend to lead inward lives.[55] Unfortunately, this independence can often look like they are self-centered and overly attentive to their own habits or comforts.

As children, they are often known as those who are good at playing by themselves. They may seek isolation and feel pseudo-independent, taking on the role of parenting themselves.[56]

In adults, the avoidant style shows distress by going away, shutting down, or needing space to figure out what is happening. They are driven by a need to "fix it" in their relationships, dealing with rejection by distancing themselves from the source of pain.[57] In heated or emotional situations, they can often choose to turn off their feelings and not "react."

Deceivingly, this relating style appears calm on the outside and is seen as generally experiencing low levels of anxiety in their relationships.[58] However, if their close people continue to poke and prod, they can usually be forced to engage. And when they do, they will probably come out fighting.

Consider Jonah, a classic avoidant. In the Old Testament, God gives Jonah the assignment to, "Go to the great city of Nineveh and preach against it, because its wickedness has come up before Me."[59]

The story becomes interesting because of one small detail: Jonah didn't have Father God's heart for the people of Nineveh. In fact, he believed

54: Johnson, S.M. *Creating Connection.*
55: Clinton, T., Sibcy, G. *Healthy Relationships.*
56: Ainsworth, M. *Attachment.*
57: Hazan, C., Shaver, P. "Organizational Framework."
58: Clinton, T., Straub, J. *God Attachment.*
59: Jonah 1:2

they were a hopeless cause not worth his time and that they should be destroyed for their sins.

Using Jonah as our Biblical example of an avoidant, his next step makes perfect sense. Instead of running towards the emotional conflict, like most avoidants, he runs in the opposite direction: "But Jonah ran away from the Lord and headed for Tarshish." Notice the Scriptures tell us that he ran not only from the assignment but *from the Lord.*

Because his heart was not the heart of the Father, I believe that Jonah ran away from the shame of being exposed. He went down to the port of Joppa, where he found a ship leaving for Tarshish in his effort to escape God and his assignment.

As the story goes, the crew agreed that in order to save their ship from certain destruction, they must throw Jonah overboard. Jonah, knowing he had failed and there was nothing he could do to fix it, surrendered to the crew and plunged over the side into the dark icy waters.

Jonah 1:17 tells us, "Now the Lord provided a huge fish to swallow Jonah, and Jonah was in the belly of the fish three days and three nights."

The three days in the fish's belly radically changed Jonah's identity. His first response was willful disobedience, but how? "But I, with shouts of grateful praise, will sacrifice to You. What I have vowed I will make good. I will say, 'Salvation comes from the Lord.'"[60] In the confines of the fish's belly, Jonah renews his relationship with God. When he steps into a place of intimacy, Father God offers mercy, comfort, and security in return.

In this time with the Lord, Jonah learns the extreme measures God will take to show how much He loved him; enough to send a giant fish to save him from certain death. The fruit of this intimacy? The salvation of a nation. Jonah 3:5 says that "the people of Nineveh believed God's message, and from the greatest to the least, they declared a fast and put on burlap to

---

60: Jonah 2:9

show their sorrow." Jonah's change not only caused him to trust God in a different way but his new identity carried the assignment and authority to help start a revival in a city.

Many of us find parts of our assignment or identity unacceptable or unforgivable. We pronounce our own judgment on our character. In an effort to avoid shame or rejection, we run away from God's love rather than into His arms. Yet, our Father loves us so much that even in the middle of the ocean, He will find a way for us to encounter His Presence.

A **fearful attachment** is driven by a dual fear of rejection and intimacy that may have developed out of extreme loss or trauma in childhood or adolescence.[61]

People with this relating style have mixed feelings about both trust and intimacy in relationships. On the one hand, they desire connection. On the other hand, they feel uncomfortable with closeness. For example, they will ask you to come near because they need to feel loved, but then push you away because they don't trust you.[62]

When in conflict, this relating style will freeze, or fluctuate between flight or fight.[63] The fearful style is fragile, easily shattered, and vulnerable to any perceived offense.[64] As an adult, try as they might to keep their feelings at bay, they can't. Instead, life is one big emotional storm.[65]

Judas Iscariot displayed some of the characteristics of this style. He kept the cash. Perhaps he was always drawn toward carrying responsibility and proving himself through performing well? He wanted others to know that he was "working for the Kingdom." However, we also know that Judas was fairly independent, and the enemy always goes for the isolated and lonely. Isolation creates a fertile environment to get picked off by the devil.

61: Johnson, S., Williams-Keeler, L. "Creating Healing Relationships For Couples Dealing With Trauma: The Use of Emotionally Focused Marital Therapy." *Journal of Marital and Family Therapy, 24*, 1998. 25-40.

62: Johnson, S. *Creating Connection.*

63: Clinton, T., Sibcy, G. *Healthy Relationships.*

64: Clinton, T., Straub, J. *God Attachment.*

65: Clinton, T., Sibcy, G. *Healthy Relationships.*

When Judas led the wild mob of Jewish officers to the Garden, he identified Christ with a kiss. After the kiss, Jesus looked into Judas' eyes and said, "Judas, are you betraying the Son of Man with a kiss?"[66] He was saying, "Is that how you would betray Me, Judas? With a kiss, a sign of affection?"

Traitors are those who once were loyal to the one they betray. Only *those within the camp* can be traitors. We can clearly see that Judas was conflicted in his loyalty and affections to Jesus. We can only assume his emotional life was in an uproar.

In the end, Judas was caught in the enemy's trap and was so filled with shame and remorse that he hung himself on a tree. This tragedy shows that when an individual remains distant from God, the healing so desperately needed never has a chance to take place. Unfortunately, they have blocked the only interaction that could transform them: the Lord's Presence.

NOW WHAT?

God does not want us to have anything less than a secure attachment style. Why? Because we fulfill His call on our lives fully only out of a place of security in Him.

For three and half years, the disciples spent time in the Presence of Jesus. A continuous intimate relationship with Him resulted for most of them in the confidence, security, and boldness they needed for their mission to spread the Gospel.

Healthy attachments that prove consistent and safe will over time help heal insecurity in our relating styles.[67] In other words, *healthy relationships with others, with God, and even with yourself can literally help to change your attachment style from unhealthy to healthy, from insecure to secure.*

What was the key that Judas refused? Abiding in Him, *trusting in Him.*

66: Luke 22:48
67: Kirkpatrick, L., Hazan, C. "Attachment Styles."

Like Peter and Jonah, the closer we move towards intimacy with our Father, the more secure we become; the closer we move toward Jesus, the more we become like Him.

To believe that God created you is good.

To believe He loves you is even better!

But…

If you struggle with insecure thought patterns and negative self-talk, or if fear and shame are constant companions, it is a clear sign that there is room for healing and growth. We all need a deep restoration in the spirit that God created in us. When love is allowed to reclaim and renew our minds, we are brought into a place of being transformed.[68] Allow the healing Presence of God to come on you. He wants to touch you and to know you.

Let us share with you how our insecure attachments have faded in the light of His Presence. We believe and declare, that you too can break through into your Promised Land of freedom through His love!

Let's pray,

> *"Jesus, I ask You to reveal the Father to me.[69] I believe You are saying to me right now, 'Come, you who are blessed by My Father; take your inheritance, the Kingdom prepared for you since the creation of the world.'[70] Jesus, I am under Your leadership and know that You take care of me like a shepherd and hold me close to Your heart.[71] Amen and Amen!"*

68: Romans 12:2
69: Luke 10:22
70: Matthew 25:34
71: Isaiah 40:11

CHAPTER THREE
The Father's Love

"Whoever does not love does not know God,
because God is love."[72]

The common understanding of the Hebrew term *shalom* is "peace." However, in the Scriptures, *shalom* means more. It means to be "safe or complete." It provides more than a state of mind or a state of being. Rather, it is a word describing *warmth* and *friendliness*, nothing broken, nothing missing. *Shalom* encompasses the state of deeply knowing, "all is well with the world."[73] All of us want to feel that *shalom*.

However, real life doesn't always facilitate feelings of perfect safety, completeness, or wholeness. Actually, it is *impossible* to achieve this *shalom* on our own. This is because human beings are only truly safe when they are in God Himself. By living a life of believing in God and abiding in Him, we are complete and whole and have the power to live in *shalom*.[74] To walk face to face with God, holding nothing back, and hiding nothing produces that *shalom*. This is because God's nature is perfect love.

72: 1 John 4:8
73: "H7965 - shalom - Strong's Hebrew Lexicon (NLT)." *Blue Letter Bible*. Web. 8 June, 2017.
74: Hebrews 4:3

What's amazing is that God so desires our lives to be permeated with His relational *shalom*, that He gave us the Gospel provision—the suffering, death, and resurrection of His Son, Jesus. All so we could be *in Him*.

It is in this place, the place of face to face with God in the Spirit, where we begin to know we are wanted and safe. The Bible teaches us that, "whoever is united with the Lord is one with Him in spirit."[75]

When we are united with God's Spirit, we are open and fully seen. This vulnerability and trust open the door in our hearts for the Holy Spirit to rush into our lives. We never have to be afraid, or hesitant of His Spirit because God is love.[76] Jesus teaches that the places where we feel robbed, dead, or torn-down were never instigated by Him. John 10:10 assures us of this, where it says, "the thief comes only to steal and kill and destroy." But, on the other hand, Jesus says, "I have come that they may have life, and have it to the full."

When we live in or are consumed with, this state of love and safety, we *naturally* start to feel good about ourselves. We stand taller, in the confidence of knowing deep inside that we have value. We have confidence in ourselves. We have confidence in our decisions. And finally, we also have confidence in our relationships with each other. Our insecurities and hang-ups fade as we experience more completeness and, "enter that rest." When we learn to live in increasing *shalom*[77], we no longer need to project a false picture to the outside world.

THE REST OF TRUST

The unsettling truth is that even the most wonderful earthly father cannot truly help us reach our full potential. This can create an internal tension that only one thing can resolve: *God's grace.*

75: 1 Corinthians 6:17
76: 1 John 4:8
77: Hebrews 4:11

Only God's grace can carry us into the fullness of His abundant favor and blessing. It is in this place of experiencing His grace that our nature begins to transform into one that is more healthy and secure.

Trust is powerful. One beautiful example of this is found in our nine-pound Morkie, Toby. He exhibits all the qualities and characteristics of a secure being and has never met someone he didn't greet with enthusiasm. However, he also sometimes struggles with trust and rest. We see Toby become an absolute mess whenever a little thunderstorm threatens his peace. Like most of us, Toby does not like storms. It is sad to see him in such an out-of-control state, shaking like a leaf.

However, there is one thing that will calm him down and help him experience *shalom*, even in the midst of the storm.

When one of us picks him up, looks him in the eyes, and speak words of comfort over him, an amazing thing happens: he stops shaking. Slowly, he nestles into our arms, his breathing returns to normal, and he falls into a peaceful sleep. Toby knows he can trust us to take care of him. In our arms, safe and secure, he finds perfect peace.

It's the exact same way with God and us.

Unfortunately, many of us have not had the same experience with our earthly fathers. One of the worst effects of a painful father relationship is that it can make it difficult to trust God as our good Father. Sadly, it can also hinder our understanding of how to deepen our relationship with Him.

SAFE FATHER

Statistically, the presence or lack of a father makes a significant difference in the family home. One study from the National Center for Fathering reports that the presence of a father in the home leads to, "better school performance, reduced substance abuse, less crime and delinquency, fewer emotional and behavioral problems, less risk of abuse or neglect, and lower risk of teen suicide."[78] In addition, in a thirty-year study, researchers at Johns Hopkins discovered that the most significant predictor of mental health problems was a lack of closeness to one's parents, especially the father.[79] In short, the presence of a father can be a matter of hope and safety or discouragement and distress.

A national poll commissioned by Lee Strobel on fatherhood and faith revealed that among adults aged 18-30, more had difficult relationships with their fathers than ever before. Interestingly enough, this age group also represents the highest percentage of people who struggle with a belief in God.[80] We believe these two trends are intrinsically interrelated.

Another recent article by the Census Bureau states, "If it were classified as a disease, fatherlessness would be an epidemic worthy of attention as a national emergency." An estimated 24.7 million children (33%) live in absence of their biological fathers.[81]

Now, don't lose hope! There is a solution! Through His death and resurrection, Jesus gives us access to our Heavenly Father. Now we can "approach God's throne of grace with confidence" and receive the fathering that we so desperately need.[82]

During Jesus' time on earth, He displayed the perfect Father/Son relationship for us to follow. He loved to spend time with His Heavenly Dad. The Gospels are full of examples of Jesus faithfully spending time with God

---

78: National Center for Fathering. Osborne, C., McLanahan, S. "Partnership Instability and Child Well-Being." *Journal of Marriage and Family, 69*, 2007. 1065-1083. 2012. Retrieved March 21, 2017. http://www.fathers.com/statistics-and-research/the-consequences-of-fatherlessness.

79: Thomas, C.B., Dudzynski, K. "Closeness to Parents and the Family Constellation in a Prospective Study of Five Disease States: Suicide, Mental Illness, Malignant Tumor, Hypertension, and Coronary Heart Disease," *Johns Hopkins Medical Journal*, 134 (5), 1974. 251-270.

80: Rau, A. *Fathers & Faith: New Poll on Struggles with Dads and God.* Bible Gateway, 2015. www.biblegateway.com/blog/2015/02/fathers-faith-new-poll-on-struggles-with-dads-and-god/.

81: U.S. Census Bureau, Current Population Survey. *Living Arrangements of Children under 18 Years/1 and Marital Status of Parents by Age, Sex, Race, and Hispanic Origin/2 and Selected Characteristics of the Child for all Children 2010*, 2010.

82: Hebrews 4:16

in prayer. In fact, Luke 5:16 says He, "often withdrew to lonely places and prayed."

In the lonely place of prayer, Jesus received His identity, assignments, and security straight from the source of life. God wants us to utilize our access to Him in that same way.

He longs to repair and restore us. He can take care of all of the negative effects of a fallen world which have created insecurity in our lives. Whether it was caused by a lack of a healthy father figure or any other factor. He wants you to let Him be the father you have always longed for.

NEAL'S STORY

For years, I "stuffed" my feelings, not allowing anyone to meet my heart's desires, including God. It was just too risky to trust anyone. Relationships appeared too dangerous, so I decided I could only trust myself to meet my needs.

I played basketball in high school and later in college. I remember one game where I was kneed in the thigh driving to the basket. Our team was headed to the end of the year tournament, and we didn't have enough guards to have me out of the game with an injury.

The diagnosis from the trainer told me that I was definitely headed for the bench. But inside my head was the familiar, "Neal, put away any feelings, silence the pain. You have to find a way to play through it." I knew our team needed me. I had learned to feed on the satisfaction of believing people counted on me and they were proud of my dedication.

So, we taped my leg tighter. I popped some aspirin, stood to my feet, and got back on the floor.

With every step, a throbbing pain shot through my leg, but I couldn't face the shame and weakness of the dreaded bench or letting others down. The discomfort was strong, but my determination was stronger.

I was born a strong-willed person, but my tenacity and self-reliance intensified during my childhood. I grew up as the only boy among four sisters, though my parents adopted my brother after I left home. We learned responsibility early.

By the time I was five, I was driving tractors on our farm in the Midwest. This was largely because we all had to do our part to run that size of an operation. Before starting in school each day, I knew the weight of daily responsibility that fell on my shoulders, and I learned the strength that it would take to bear up under these expectations. We were conditioned to work hard and taught to "grit" our way through tough situations.

I know that my father loved me deeply, but there was no room for emotions in the serious work of running a large family business.

We avoided discussing subjects touching the deep honesty of heart-felt issues. There just never seemed to be any time for "that."

I knew and felt on a personal level as a child that something was wrong. I could see my parents struggling to communicate their own emotions. Later on, I learned they had adopted these difficulties from their own families. Their inner problems always simmered just below the surface, hidden in plain sight.

Sadly, my awareness of the trouble was not enough to cure the generational pain. Unfortunately, like my forefathers, I fell right in line. I kept my emotions to myself and kept up what I thought was a tough and resilient exterior.

The world of sports compounded my "strong man" persona. I immersed myself into the life of a driven, dedicated competitor. The more I embraced this self-dependency in athletics, the more it carried over into every single area of my life.

Looking back, I was developing into a classic avoidant attachment style. I secretly knew I greatly needed to be cared for and nurtured. However, I was not open to being vulnerable with those feelings to those who would attempt to love and support me.

My coping mechanism? Guard myself against any sign of brokenness by shutting down and working harder on my next goal or accomplishment.

The avoidant relating style is where someone *acts* like they don't have any needs because they believe their needs will *never be met*. Deep down, the only person they believe could meet their needs (which they deny having!) is themselves.

The problem with this thought is that there is only one who is wholly trustworthy.

Jesus.

Trusting in anything or anyone else is a straight road to striving and destruction.

Fast forward, and I am a married, successful career man. My nickname at work was Mr. Spock, which I considered a compliment. After all, this was the mark of a strong, analytical leader, right? Who needs other people when they will only let you down?

Like in basketball, my career in business soon scored goal after goal, as I never seemed to need to "sit on the bench." Willing to carry the load, my success soared. But it was only my flesh, or self-capabilities, that I leaned on. I ignored my spirit and my heart. I soon found myself measuring my value as a human being solely on my accomplishments.

I used my own measure of value to guide others, too. Since strength was found in concealing the heart, I knew I had success. I wanted everyone in my life to learn from my celebrated example, especially the gorgeous girl I married. But she operated differently than I did. I knew there had to be something wrong with Diane. To me, her issues were obvious. My unprofessional diagnosis?

Overly emotional.

Needy.

Dependent.

These labels kept even my wife at a safe distance. Relationship, even in marriage, was too emotionally confusing and scary for me to navigate. Retreat became my go-to play.

THE BREAKING POINT

To facilitate covering up my heart pain, just like a strained muscle, I worked more. The more I worked, the more I kept people at a distance. The more I kept people at a distance, the less I had to focus on my real relationships or my own heart.

I was running, *and fast.*

As one might suspect, when my carefully constructed world started to unravel, I had to find more counterfeit acceptance.

My breaking point hit in the workforce, but when aspirin was not enough, I sought something more extreme.

The pain killer I chose, however, was severe. And had severe after-effects that could have cost me everything I treasured and held dear.

In a last ditch effort to "feel" anything other than the pressure of failure, I betrayed myself and my family and had a secret affair.

I was at a point of inconceivable destruction of everything I had worked for in my life.

At this juncture in the story, you should know that I was raised knowing all the Bible stories and the basic requirements of a good Christian walk.

Along with my career success, I prided myself on looking like a perfect Christian husband and father. I was doing my job to provide responsibly. On the outside, I was doing all I knew (or had time) to do.

Just like my learned childhood experiences, discussing subjects that touched the deep honesty of heart-felt issues was avoided. There just never seemed to be any time for that. Like my early family life, these experiences were exactly what was missing. I was always isolated, because the isolation was relational, and rooted deep inside of me. Even with my wife, and my children around me, I felt alone. In fact, I even isolated myself from myself.

The worst of it though, was that I isolated myself from God.

I know some reading right now will resonate with what I am saying to you. Let me tell you now, there is hope. You can experience healing and *shalom*. I did, and I believe anyone who leans into God can too.

I had to recognize that my failure, while startling, was nothing to be ashamed of with Christ. Now, there is nothing more precious than knowing that I am dependent on my Father.

Despite what I projected on the outside, I was just like everyone else. I was broken and needed restoration.

For me, the realization of this was deeply painful. I am choosing to share this with you because I believe you're worth it. Your future is worth my being open and honest with you right now. Learn from my mistakes. Don't learn the hard way, but if you already have, don't worry. God is stronger than any pain or shame or mistake we have made.

For me, my wake up call was public and painful.

But it was also transformational because it taught me the secret to life.

It's this: the one person I can truly trust is Christ himself. It was a severe mercy, but a mercy indeed.

I wish that I could turn back the clock and see what a difference that would have made in the middle of the mess. I wish that I could tell my depressed, hopeless self that my freedom was on its way. I wish I would have known that *shalom* was available in a deeper way before I made my biggest mistakes.

So there I was. My marriage on the rocks, my relationships with my sons on the line, sitting in the office of a counselor. The "need-nobody man" was brought to his knees.

But it opened the door to a miracle.

OVERCOMING: HIS WORK OR YOURS?

"You have a marine complex," she said simply.

"Finally, someone understands me," I thought as I considered the counselor's diagnosis a compliment.

She sensed my relieved response and clarified. "No, Neal, that's not a good thing."

She continued, "Your problem is that your head and your heart have been disconnected. And, that's dangerous." She waited and then asked, "How do you feel right now?"

I sat speechless for a moment, totally stunned.

All I could muster up was, "I have no idea what you are asking me."

She prodded, "Think about what emotion you are having as we talk."

Nothing. She continued, "Can you name a feeling?"

Again, nothing. Confused, I shook my head.

She understood I was stuck and reached to help me, "Happy? Sad?"

Still nothing. At this point, I felt cornered. As an extreme avoidant, I didn't do emotions. I endured and ignored pain. But something in this moment struck me deep within the recesses of my very being.

I fell on my knees in a desperate cry. I had reached the end of me. I thought I had to do the overcoming work. But now, I literally had no one left to turn to except for God. *I could never make it without Him.*

It was a light bulb moment. I would soon be totally free.

The weight I had carried from my early childhood, the weight of holding it all together and always having to be the guy others could count on literally fell off my shoulders.

Instantly His healing Presence assured me that as I trusted fully in Him, I would be safe. For the first time, "Mr. Spock" acknowledged something was wrong, and that he had to go the bench, and heal. That was a bigger success and *stronger* win than hiding in the shame of not being perfect. For the first time, I allowed myself to release the pressure of carrying the team. For the first time I knew, God was carrying them, and me.

From there I learned something beautiful. God as our Father has given us the provisions to enter into total security, complete healing, and *shalom*. Unlike the coping mechanisms I developed in sports, emotions could be a sign of health and security. After all, Jesus was the most influential leader to walk the earth. He showed a full range of emotions, from anger (turning over the tables at the Temple)[83], to sadness (His tears over Lazarus' death)[84], to even exuberant joy (when He praises His Father)[85]. He illustrated that the emotional center of our hearts *need* to connect to Him. We need relationship with others, and we need to be aware of how to walk in relationship with others.

83: John 2:15
84: John 11:35
85: Luke 10:21

Maybe you're like me and you cope by masking your pain because life has taught you not to trust anyone. Believe me, friend, it was never God who taught you that. You can trust Him. He has your best in mind, all the time. He has patiently pursued you because He deems you worth it.

THE TRANSFORMATIVE POWER OF
GOD'S GRACE AND PEACE

Completeness is not always measured by how things look. People need to grow on the inside as well as the outside. Thankfully, because of a special covenant with God, established with Jesus' death on the Cross, we can.

Jesus wants us saved, set free, and living out our calling. I love Brian Simmons' *Passion Translation* of the Bible. He teaches that Jesus' last words on the Cross express Jesus desire for our freedom, as His church, the Bride.[86] Brian shares that this last word, *kallah*, in Aramaic means, "It is finished." However, *kallah* in Hebrew means "bride."

With His last breath, Jesus finished His assignment and paved the way for His Bride to join the family of God and fully share in the Kingdom of Heaven. Not only are we accepted, but we are commissioned. He wants us to take up His mission, and "do the works" He did. Even better, He wants us to actually, "do even greater things."[87] He is faithful to do all He promises. He heals us, delivers us, and fills us with peace and joy, no matter what circumstance we face. But it starts on the inside.

I had to admit that He had to do the work to make me whole. It was not up to me. I used to get stuck because I didn't totally believe I could receive all that Jesus' blood paid for. In my natural man, I believed that being dependent on someone else was a lack of wholeness. But in Christ, restoration comes when we learn to cultivate a healthy dependency on Him and others.

86: Simmons, B. *The Passion Translation*. BroadStreet Publishing Group, LLC, 2015.
87: John 14:12

The world tries to sell us the self-fix package, and often times, their do-it-yourself plan is appealingly straightforward. But it is an utter lie. All they provide is a wide spectrum of counterfeit ways to meet our needs of acceptance, fulfillment, and completeness. However, anytime we look to ourselves or the world for these needs to be met, we wind up in bondage.

We gain strength by growing in dependency on our Heavenly Father. Jesus teaches us this where He says, "I am the vine; you are the branches. If you remain in Me and I in you, you will bear much fruit; apart from Me you can do nothing."[88] He wants something stronger than being "acquaintances" with us. He wants our relationship with Him to be more than skin deep; He wants a *covenant relationship*. This is where my journey led me, and as I entered into a covenant relationship with Him, my life slowly began to heal.

Let me pray for you,

> *"Jesus, I thank You for the power of Your healing Presence that touched my life, saved my marriage, and restored my relationships with my children, my community, and ultimately, with You. Father, I thank You that You are using my mess as an opportunity to extend Your Kingdom through my life. As my friends read these words, I thank You, Holy Spirit, that You are touching their hearts and beginning to show them things about themselves and their past that You want to heal. And God, I thank You that Your will is being done in their lives and mine as You establish a covenant with us, Your Bride, the Church. I know the restoration You provided for me is available for all who come to You for help. We love You, Jesus. Amen."*

88: John 15:5

CHAPTER FOUR

The Covenant Keeper: One with Him

"I will remain in the world no longer, but they are still in the world, and I am coming to You. Holy Father, protect them by the power of Your name, the name You gave Me, so that they may be one as We are one."[89]

PERFECT LOVE

"The answer to your question is easy," my grandfather said with a smile as he sat across from me, Diane, and my grandmother, Sarah.

My question was why, after fifty-four years of marriage, did they want to talk about their relationship with me!

He continued with a smile, "I am not perfect in love yet."

What did he mean?, I thought.

"You see, I love your grandmother greatly. But, I want to see her as a beautiful, finished work. I want to see her the way the Father sees her."

89: John 17:11

It was quite a different answer than I expected. Grandpa Harold completely embraced the fact that he was put on this earth to learn how to love well, his wife included. He wanted to see her with the same grace and love that the Lord did.

I knew I was in the presence of a great man. A man who understood *covenant*.

I believe that one of the most important and foundational teachings for the Body of Christ to understand today is the covenant that God has made with us. Many understand that word to mean an exchange of promises, but that is a better example of the word *contract*, not *covenant*.

A covenant is an exchange of *people*.

People become intertwined in a covenant relationship. Once they enter this state, they are no longer their own. They become one in God's eyes. We see this illustrated in the marriage covenant, between a man and a woman.

In the *Passion Translation*, Brian Simmons tells us that Eve was not taken out of the rib of Adam, as most of us learned in Sunday School. Rather, God *split Adam in half* to form Eve.[90] In marriage, we are joined not only in the flesh but in every dimension of our being. We become indivisible. If you are married, odds are that you have some understanding of what it means to hurt when your spouse is suffering.

I think when God looks down at married couples, He sees one unit, instead of two people. He wants us to do more than just tolerate our differences in marriage. He intends that we are more fully like Him when we are together.

Grandpa Harold understood covenant. My admiration of him continued to grow as we resumed our conversation. He didn't tell me about him and my grandmother's trouble communicating or their difficulties with finances throughout the years, or even if their marriage was ever in danger of failing. He wanted to process the goal of learning how to love unconditionally. He was mature enough to not point fingers at other people's problems.

90: Simmons, B. *The Passion Translation*. BroadStreet Publishing Group, LLC, 2015.

Grandpa also wasn't in a hurry. He understood that covenant meant he was to treat his wife the same way he would like someone to treat him. What a challenge to all of us walking in covenant relationships. What sacrificial, selfless love!

Covenant necessitates dying to ourselves, but the rewards are well worth it. This understanding starts at home with ourselves, then leaks out onto other relationships. It is essential that we understand covenant and embrace it in the body of Christ. We are to be the shining example of selfless love for others.

Our God is a covenant-making King. He holds himself to His Promises even when we do not. Covenant is a different kind of bond. When we begin to focus on it, it unlocks for us a better understanding of who He is and how His Promises have been established for the Kingdom. It is the basis of our unbreakable security in Him.

In Hebrew, the word for covenant is *berith*, which means "to cut," as in circumcision.[91] A covenant always involves a *sacrifice* or the shedding of blood.

In Latin, the word for covenant is *sacrament,* meaning "a religious ceremony or act of the Christian Church. An act that is regarded as an outward and visible sign of inward and spiritual divine grace."[92] Our covenant with God is one sealed in His own blood. This is evidenced by inward and outward spiritual, divine grace. This is the ultimate security of covenant.

A DIFFERENT KIND OF PROMISE

God never goes back on His word. We see His examples of covenant with the Jewish people, and these covenants are still in effect to this day because of His faithfulness. "Then God said, 'Yes, but your wife Sarah will bear you a son, and you will call him Isaac. I will establish My covenant with him

---

91: Easton, M. "Entry for Covenant." "Easton's Bible Dictionary." Web. June 19, 2017.
92: "Sacrament." *www.oxfordreference.com.* The Oxford Dictionary of Phrase and Fable, 2005. Web. June 8, 2017.

as an everlasting covenant for his descendants after him.'"[93] Again, "Know therefore that the Lord your God is God; He is the faithful God, keeping His covenant of love to a thousand generations of those who love Him and keep His commandments."[94]

He also established a covenant with those who bless His people: "I will bless those who bless you, and whoever curses you I will curse; and all peoples on earth will be blessed through you."[95]

This is a key point: when we understand God's covenant pattern and bless those He blesses, we participate in *their* inheritance. In other words, we become family with His family. This is what it means to be "grafted in."

Joining God's family has even greater significance in the larger scheme of things. *God's government is based on family.* His government, and His alone, is the only power that will transform the world.

The structure for this family was established in the Old Testament with His covenantal people, the Jews. Jewish history, identity, and heritage display God's heart for his chosen people. His covenants with the Jews reveal His desires, His nature, and His values, for them. This same covenant is meant for us today, regardless of any failings or disobedience.

From the covenants, we can trace man's journey from marriage, to the fall, to the promise of restoration. They extend from fatherhood to extended family, from tribes, to priests, and eventually, to God's Kingdom. These biblical, historical covenants become the outline for our lives. We are transformed from a sinner to a saint, from isolation to a family, from an orphan to a son, and from a homeless wanderer to a ruler!

The persecution of the Jewish people through the ages reveals the hatred that resided in their enemies. Unfortunately, many still struggle with knowing how to understand God's chosen people. Feelings of offense, prejudice,

---

93: Genesis 17:19
94: Deuteronomy 7:9
95: Genesis 12:3

or "uncomfortableness" that many feel towards Jews may find their roots in generational strongholds.

Sadly, many of us don't recognize our prejudices as destructive and we choose to live in bondage. These preconceptions may cause us to miss the blessings promised to those who bless God's people. But God loves breaking chains off of people's lives. He wants all His kids free! If you relate to this, don't fall into the trap of self-condemnation. Just tell God you're sorry and ask Him to change your heart. He will. In addition to the freedom, you'll get in on the blessings.

THE COVENANT

God made seven unique covenants with man. Each of these covenants has different elements. From the first to the last, they form the foundation of our faith. By taking just a cursory glance at these covenants, we can trace our journey with God and discover His plans.

In the first covenant, God establishes that family is defined by marriage between a man and a woman.[96] He essentially changes their names from Adam and Eve to Husband and Wife. And He gives them their assignment: become a father and mother!

In the second covenant, established after the Fall, God reminds us that all is not lost.[97] He has a plan to redeem and restore all that was destroyed in Adam and Eve's disobedience.

In the third covenant, God vows to never again to destroy the world by flood.[98] And He gives them a rainbow to seal the Promise.

96: Genesis 1:26-2:3
97: Genesis 3:14-19
98: Genesis 9:8-17

In the fourth covenant, God swears to give Abraham a great land and to bless his descendants. His lineage will become a great nation, and through them bless all the nations of the earth.[99]

In the fifth covenant, the covenant of Moses[100], God's family assumes the form of "a kingdom of priests and a holy nation."[101]

In the sixth covenant, God promises to establish David's kingdom forever.[102]

The prophets, especially Isaiah and Jeremiah, taught Israel to hope for a Messiah who would bring "a new covenant." This is the bond through which God's law would be written on men and women's hearts.[103]

This was completed in the seventh and final covenant, the "new covenant," sealed by Jesus' death on the Cross.[104] After His resurrection, He assumed the role of Royal High Priest and fulfilled all the promises God made in the previous covenants.[105]

All that had been lost in the fall of man was restored when Jesus called out "Bride" on the Cross. We can once again return to the Garden as the Bride, the slate is washed clean.

THE KALLAH OF CRISTOS

Now that we, as the Body of Christ, are joined with Jesus, we are no longer our own. Romans 7:4 teaches, "So, my brothers and sisters, you also died to the Law through the body of Christ, that you might belong to another, to Him who was raised from the dead, in order that we might bear fruit for God."

99: Genesis 12:1-3, 17:1-14, 22:16-18
100: Exodus 19:5-6, 3:4-10, 6:7
101: Exodus 19:6
102: 2 Samuel 7:8-19
103: Jeremiah 31:31-34, Hebrews 8:8-12
104: Matthew 26:28
105: Hebrews 4:15

This relationship extends to the entire body of Christ. God did not call us to an association or denomination; He called us to family. Families are to be built on an unbreakable covenantal bond as well. But this is not easy. To walk in covenant with one another can be difficult, especially if we don't view other believers as true brothers and sisters.

We believe one of the main reasons our churches don't move in power is because we've settled for something more like a club than a covenant. Unfortunately, I know many will understand this feeling from their own experience. They may have wondered why "church" hasn't truly helped their lives in any significant way.

Our son, Jake, demonstrated a beautiful example of respecting covenant relationships years ago. Both he and one of his older brothers thought it would be great to join a campus organization. They had a fun experience in it the year before, and were excited to have another year with their friends. Membership displayed a certain social status, and offered extracurricular activities.

Finally, the acceptance day came. Jake was welcomed with open arms, but sadly his brother was not! It took Jake all of one minute to make his decision.

Since his brother didn't get in, he chose to skip out, too. His brother and his brother's feelings were way more important than being in the group. For Jake, it was easy because *he belonged to a family*.

In covenant, your suffering becomes my suffering, and your joy becomes my joy. Why wouldn't it? We are family. However, we cannot do this in the natural, at least not authentically. We are called to walk in covenant with the Church in the same way we are now in covenant with Jesus. "Just as a body, though one, has many parts, but all its many parts form one body, so it is with Christ."[106]

106: 1 Corinthians 12:12

Unity is very different than covenant. If you are in unity, you are often still focused on your individual needs or agenda. In covenant, you are forced to think about everyone's needs. There is greater purpose beyond yourself.

Collaboration still leaves you with the option to leave when it no longer feels productive to be a part of the group. In a covenant, you have to stay and work it out, just like in marriage. There is no other alternative. You cannot get rid of your brother or sister.

When I know who I am, and I take on the responsibility as a son or daughter of God, I am able to provide what my family needs. They will always need my best, my care, and my choice to engage and connect with them. Apathy and indifference towards my closest relationships is the fast-track to an unsuccessful family life.

God has called you to be in covenant with certain people. These are the people who will sharpen you and will have the courage to speak boldly into your life. Most of the time, they will be those with whom you live and do ministry.

Though messy and painful, people's choices to step out in love and speak truth to us is powerful.[107] Proverbs 27:6 says, "Wounds from a friend can be trusted, but an enemy multiplies kisses." God wants His children to have good friends, not friends who are only interested in being popular. Actually, God calls those people *enemies*, not friends.

ME? OFFENDED?

Offense causes us to take a look, a word, or a moment, twist it and magnify it to extreme proportions. Before we know it, we break the bond of one of our vital covenant relationships. Do not fall victim to the spirit of offense! God asks us to live as covenant *partners* with the Body. Not as bitter, jealous acquaintances, who can only connect at an entertainment-deep level.

107: Ephesians 4:15

All of us have experienced times when a seemingly insignificant event can exhaust our emotional capacity. When this happens, we allow the effects of hurt feelings to damage other areas in our lives.

How does this happen? How do we get side-tracked and offended by the small looks or words?

The enemy does not want us to have close families. He does not want the body operating in covenant. Doesn't it make sense that we experience these feelings strongest from interactions with the *ones we love the most?*

Offense is out to strike at the heart of walking in covenant with others. Remember the dangers of isolation that Judas fell into? Remember the self-protection that Neal relied on instead of God?

The enemy wants you isolated. It is much easier to devour the isolated animal, rather than the one in the center of the pack. The next time your spouse, child, or best friend says something that offends you or hurts your feelings, stop a moment and ask yourself an important question. Are you partnering with Holy Spirit, or are you are partnering with the spirit of offense? Our agreement has great power. "Again, truly I tell you that if two of you on earth agree about anything they ask for, it will be done for them by my Father in Heaven." [108] If you are partnering with offense, forgive, and get back on board with God.

One of the greatest threats to God's Kingdom is offense and divisiveness. The more we become bitter from the pain of past hurts, the more easily we succumb to subsequent offenses. It is a vicious cycle, but for the Body of Christ, *offense is not an option in covenant.*

Like my Grandpa Harold, we all need to look at our covenant relationships through the lens of the loving Father. We need to allow God to change the way we see people.

108: Matthew 18:19

Covenant happens when we truly carry one another's burdens because we have removed the masks and we appreciate the diversity of the body of Christ.[109] This appreciation naturally happens when we seek to validate and encourage rather than change or compare each other's calling and gifts. In this place, we can grow and develop together as family, and each be launched into our unique places of ministry.

As believers, we are to carry the spirit of restoration and healing. We are to love steadily through any hurt, rejection, backstabbing, gossip, or any slight, no matter how minor.

In His Kingdom, love is the ultimate weapon to destroy the enemy. Love conquers all and love drives out fear. And through Christ, we can do all things and love through any circumstance, in the same way that Christ does with us. Philippians 4:13 says, "I can do all this through Him who gives me strength."

JUST LIKE JESUS

Ephesians 1:6 says that God has "made us accepted in the Beloved."[110]

Consider Jesus, the most secure Man to walk the earth. He experienced the deepest rejection known to man, and He bore it all so that we might be saved, healed, and restored. An exchange has taken place: we are accepted because of His rejection. We are "accepted in the Beloved."

Our identity begins to change from insecure to secure as it mirrors that of our grace-filled heavenly Father. What do we do with this new identity that looks like our Father?

We begin to relate to others out of His perfect nature. We will not only be loved, but we will feel loved and be motivated to give it away to others. This is the natural outgrowth of security.

109: Galatians 6:2

110: "Ephesians 1 (KJV) - Paul an apostle of Jesus." *Blue Letter Bible.* Web. 8 June, 2017.

There is nothing that you can say or do to make the Father love you any less than He does now. His love is unconditional and results in healing on a deep level. Especially when it is experienced and applied to life's hurts and wounds. It is worth repeating Romans 8:15-16 in the *Passion Translation*:

> *And you did not receive the "spirit of religious duty leading you back to the fear of never being good enough." But, you have received the spirit of "full acceptance" enfolding you into the family of God. And you will never feel orphaned, for as He rises up within us, our spirits join Him in saying the words of tender affection, "Beloved Father." For the Holy Spirit makes God's fatherhood real to us as He whispers into our innermost being, "You are God's beloved child."*

Sometimes there are problems with earthly parents that can never be resolved. However, in the Lord, it doesn't matter if nobody wanted you, nobody loved you, or your parents were unmarried or worse. When you come to God through Jesus Christ, you become a member of the greatest family in the universe. God has no second-class kids!

RECOVER ALL—TRUST HIM

After I, Neal, nearly lost everything, then in Christ discovered all that I ever needed, there was still an aftermath of emotion that had to be dealt with. I was done ignoring my wounds. I wanted healing in every area of my life. After the encounter with God's love, our marriage entered into a state of repair by God's miraculous grace. However, there were many fears that I found trying to hang on to my life that I had to lay on the altar.

Even after experiencing His tenderness towards me, I had questions. My exposure to the way a fallen world works caused me to try to measure God's grace by human standards. I started to get nervous.

How could God fully forgive me?

How would God trust me to serve, now that everyone knew I had failed so miserably?

But perhaps worst of all was the fear that threatened my most vital covenant in the Body of Christ.

How could Diane ever be able to trust me again?

The battles became constant in my mind. But, I remembered His tenderness, and clung to one of our faith's most amazing provisions, that "we have the mind of Christ,"[111] and that "there is now no condemnation for those who are in Christ Jesus."[112] In Christ, Father God was working on my own healing. Yes, I took a risk with my life when I chose to be vulnerable and trust Him, but I reaped a huge reward of freedom. I can tell you now that it was worth it.

As it turns out, all my fears were lies.

Diane also chose to trust.

Diane also chose to be vulnerable.

Diane chose to understand that she also owned a part of our difficulties.

We both chose the Father's words over the world's opinion. "Be kind and compassionate to one another, forgiving each other, just as in Christ God forgave you."[113] We both chose to stop offense in its tracks and throw it out of our house for good.

Because we chose this road, our marriage was restored. Neither of us have to live in the pain and frustration of fear or rejection. This is because God's family is whole, complete, healthy, and secure. There's no family equal to it.

111: 1 Corinthians 2:16
112: Romans 8:1
113: Ephesians 4:32

BECOMING FEARLESS

When we strive to serve God for any other reason than our love for Him or love for others, we are working out of fear of punishment or rejection. What we need is the obedience that flows from knowing His goodness.

In Jack Frost's life-changing book, *Experiencing the Father's Embrace*, he relays how God set him free from the pressures of living an extremely, self-dependent and destructive lifestyle. He shares his first-hand experience:

> *When we begin to serve God for the praise of man or to find identity in what we do, no matter how great the call of God is on our lives, no matter how powerful the gifts or the anointing flow in our ministry, that underlying attitude of self-love can begin to produce a hidden resentment and anger, fueled by a fear of rejection and a fear of failure. In this dangerous place, only an encounter with the love of God can lead us into transformation.*[114]

Rejection is a killer. Because man was created to have fellowship with God, it is one of the most painful human experiences. Feelings of rejection can inspire us to hide in self-protection or attempt to control our environment to create the appearance of being OK. However, when we do this, we become the ones trying to *look* perfect. Oddly, we then become the ones rejecting others who are humanly flawed. None of us want to be in that cycle. Thankfully God is a good God, and He doesn't want that for any of us.

For Diane and me, fear and shame were indicative of a larger problem: not fully knowing or trusting God's nature. Have you experienced the same thing? These emotions could be the sign that you have lost your connection with Father God. Like us, you may have forgot that He is in control of the universe. Remember, you are in a covenant relationship, an exchange of people; His whole being, for your whole being, brokenness for wholeness.

This battle for the heart of man is basically the determination of whether fear or faith will rule in our lives. Faith begins by knowing God's accep-

---

114: Frost, J. *Experiencing the Father's Embrace.* Lake Mary: Charisma House, 2002.

tance of us through the Cross. This acceptance has nothing to do with what we have done or have not done, but on what Jesus did for us.

If we embrace His love, we won't fear the approval of people and can instead focus on loving them. In a place of security, we are able to understand Jesus' command to love others as we love ourselves. This shifts our focus from our insecurities to the needs of others in our lives.[115]

Don't lose hope before crossing over from pain into gain and victory in Him. Don't buy into the lie that God has turned His back on you. His word tells us clearly, "Never will I leave you; never will I forsake you."[116] We must choose to press on to the beauty that lies beyond ourselves. We must choose to believe that His covenants with us are unfailing. When we do, we will find Him, and when we find Him, we find who He made us to be.

Let's pray,

"Lord, You are the Maker of covenant for all of us. You paid the price with the precious blood and the willing complete sacrifice of Your Son. We walk in freedom because of what He did, not what we do. We ask You to lead us into relationship according to Your plan. Help us to be covenant keepers. May we become the united Body of Christ that You intended. May we walk in restoration and forgiveness just as You first forgave us. We place our trust and confidence in You to make us into kings and priests to release Your shalom. Thank You, Lord. Amen."

115: Mark 12:31
116: Hebrews 13:5

CHAPTER FIVE
Transformed and Renewed

"But you are a chosen people, a royal priesthood,
a holy nation, God's special possession, that you may declare
the praises of Him who called you out of darkness into
His wonderful light."[117]

CALLED

My grade school friend, Ryan, was visiting us and came to meet me, Diane over lunch not long ago. We hadn't talked in a long time and we had a lot to catch up on. Abandoned by his parents and his last girlfriend, Ryan's past was defined by trauma, exclusion, and deep emotional pain. Though he longed for acceptance and love, his fear of rejection manifested in his life in explosively negative ways. Unable to watch his destructive patterns for long, one person after another dropped out of his life, which only affirmed what he believed deep down inside. Nobody wanted him.

It seemed Ryan was determined to stay stuck in the past. He told me stories where his self-pitying mindset caused him to stop and tell anyone who would listen all about his latest troubles. As his story unfolded, it seemed

---

117: 1 Peter 2:9

that he often chose the most inopportune times to participate or draw attention to himself.

Would I, he wondered, be willing to mentor him?

As much as I desired to see Ryan succeed, I wasn't sure I was up to the task. What could I provide Ryan that all his counselors and pastors hadn't already offered?

Just as I was about to say, "I'll be praying for you…" The Holy Spirit stopped me. He spoke these words in my spirit, "He needs to belong. He needs to be affirmed as My son and an heir."

WHAT WERE YOU CHRISTENED?

Most people do not choose their names. On the whole, names are "bestowed" at birth. Or, in some cultures, as the child grows up and moves through various rites of passage, they will receive a name.

Names are not only written on your birth certificate. As we journey through life, more names are "bestowed," designating the plot points of our lives. Take for example the bullet points on your resume, your experiences, your community, or even your bank account. These things work to harmonize the description of who you are as a whole person. Your personality, your future, and even your past.

However, we all know what it feels like to experience the darker side coined by these names. Certain names sting. Some of these "stingers" are pretty sticky, too. If left unchallenged, the damaging names we heard as children can stay with us into our adulthood. For example, some children very early heard names like *poor, spoiled, uneducated, troublemaker, loud,* or *shy.* These names followed them as they grew and matured, ultimately becoming a part of their identity. Negative labels are inherently dangerous.

The harmful labels of life, even if they've stuck for most of your years, are not stronger than God's unlimited power. As soon as we tune into the

Father's voice, we can allow the limitations of those names to be removed. God can and will heal the hurt and damage caused by them as He roots them out of our identity.

WHAT'S YOUR TESTIMONY?

Have you ever experienced your mind insisting that God created you and loves you, but your heart seems to tell you a different story? I've been there.

Your emotions seem to say, "What's wrong with me?"

"Am I lovable?"

"Why can't I ever do anything right?"

"I am a disappointment," and on and on.

When thoughts and emotions loom larger than the Promises of God, they can fool us into missing God's truth about who we are. Don't let that be you. These labels are only tricks, fooling us into aborting our passions and God-given destinies. Negative labels, as you probably know from experience, stop us from pursuing the plan God has in mind for us. They fool us into confusing the purpose He has had for us since the beginning of time.

As with the negative labels, we often are unsure about who we are because we use performance and expectations as a reference.

"My parents say I'm nice…"

"Everyone at school says I'm sharp…"

"My friends say I'm gifted…"

"My coworkers say I'm a hard-worker…"

You may be thinking, "So what? Aren't those good things?"

Well, yes…and no.

When we allow the measurements and judgments of others to define our lives, we put ourselves in a position we were *never meant to be in*. You put yourself in the bleachers with the spectators, when God wants you in the game. He not only wants you in the game but carrying the ball and making the plays. You are His star performer and it is His desire to show you off to the world!

Any voice you allow to define yourself that is not the Father's can create a faulty foundation in your life.

God feels nothing but perfect love when He thinks about you. Our Heavenly Father is perfect love and His Word tells us He can think no evil of us: *"[love] thinketh no evil."*[118] He defines us as good, acceptable, and lovable. That might not be the way He defines our behavior, but that is how He defines us! And as we become more secure in His Presence, the more our thoughts and behavior will begin to align with what He deems as good, acceptable, and perfect.

RYAN'S TIPPING POINT

As Ryan and I sat there, our lunch long since eaten, I had to take a moment to decide what to do about my marching orders from Holy Spirit.

"You want me to tell him, he needs to belong, and is already affirmed as Your son and an heir? I thought we tried that!"

However, the Holy Spirit continued, "Diane, I want you to love him as you would like to be loved. I want you to tell him that he is important and wanted. Tell him I approve of him and have a wonderful purpose for his life. But, right now, he can't hear Me above the noise of his lecturing and attention-getting. Ryan is not his behavior. He is worth so much more than only his performance."

118: "1 Corinthians 13:5 (KJV)" *Blue Letter Bible.* Web. 8 June, 2017.

I thought for a moment. This *was* a new approach.

Instead of trying to deal with Ryan's past and trying to "fix" his behavior, God wanted me to speak blessing over his life and call him up and beyond his insecurity. *I was to call Ryan by the names he had received from God, not from his past or his behavior.*

At the same time, the Lord told me that His compassionate love for Ryan included boundaries around some of his difficult habits. The things that didn't line up with Father's standards had to be developed into new patterns of thoughts and behaviors for him. So, I smiled and decided to give Holy Spirit's process a try.

The day before he left town, I found an opportunity and everything changed.

After listening to Ryan lecture for ten minutes on the value of "loving others," I felt prompted to ask him a very important question. Gently placing a hand on his shoulder, I quietly asked, "Ryan, do you feel loved?"

I continued, "If you have some time, can we look up a couple of those Scriptures you were talking about?"

He stopped, looked down, and stood still without talking for minutes that felt like hours. As I not-so-patiently waited for an answer, Ryan finally glanced up at me and softly confessed that he couldn't read one word of what was on the page.

He told me he accumulated his material by listening to sermons online, memorizing the thoughts, and repeating them as quickly as he could to the nearest person. Ryan had never learned to read.

A pain went through my heart. That explained a lot. Ryan was trying so desperately to fit in, to be loved, and to be accepted.

"Ryan," I continued, truly awed by the wisdom of the Father, "You are needed and wanted. You have a powerful testimony, and you love the Lord. He wants to use you to bring hope and healing to others. You are worth way more than your performance. I need you to see yourself as greater than how you see yourself now. But, there are ground rules for what that looks like. For instance, you cannot keep acting the way you are acting. You are not making friends with your behavior right now. If you really want to touch people's lives, some things need to change."

His eyes lit up; Holy Spirit had begun His work.

Over that short weekend, Ryan began to see himself as God saw him: as beloved, as precious, as accepted. His journey is not over yet. But he *chose* to take the road to healing and wholeness. He *chose* to submit his will to the Father's, to allow the Lord to do a good work in him.[119] After that day, I watched in amazement as Ryan's security continued to grow by leaps and bounds. His confidence in God's love was working its way into his identity.

Ryan now accepts and loves himself, and in return, more people accept and love him. New healthy relationships are forming.

It's amazing what a name can do.

What name will you choose to answer to?

FREEDOM JOURNEY

Because we all have different relating styles, the way each of us grows in security will be different as well. For some, it is a speedy process. For others, it will take a little longer.

For instance, a more avoidant attachment style often struggles with trusting God's *willingness* to love them, because their confidence lies more within themselves.[120] They often feel, "God isn't there for me when I need Him. I will have to go at life alone and I don't really *need* Him anyway." They tend

---

119: Philippians 1:6

120: Clinton, T., Straub, J. *God Attachment: Why You Believe, Act, and Feel the Way You Do About God.* New York: Howard Books, 2014.

to have an arm's length relationship with God, focusing more on duty than on a relationship with Him.[121]

For this sort of person, it is difficult to believe the Lord won't disappoint them. Healing may come slowly, or, like Neal, possibly the result of a painful "valley" experience. However, when their trust in themselves has proven false, the healing Presence of God has room to work.

On the other hand, a person with a more ambivalent relating style is easily upset when they don't see God working in their lives.[122] They crave the reassurance that God is pleased with them and are constantly looking for the next intimate encounter with Him.[123] Their desire to please God is so strong, they are the first to sign up for volunteer programs at church. This relating style may take many trips to the Salvation alter just to be sure they are *really* right with God.

With true experiences in His Presence, they too will be fully transformed into a person who feels loved, affirmed and secure with God. They won't doubt that they are accepted; they will know it.

Whether our restoration comes in stages or instantly, healing happens when we immerse ourselves in His love and step into our identities as His sons and daughters. In this place, we will look like His Son, accepted and beloved.

GIVE LOVE A CHANCE

"You also, like living stones, are being built into a spiritual house to be a holy priesthood, offering spiritual sacrifices acceptable to God through Jesus Christ."[124]

121: Ibid.
122: Ibid.
123: Ibid.
124: 1 Peter 2:5

One of the foremost names God calls us by is a "holy priesthood," those who offer spiritual sacrifices. Worshipers.

You were created to worship.

Whether you dance, sing, read Scripture, pray, whether you cook, paint, or write, an *attitude* of humble worship makes room for God to show up in big ways in your life.

In exchange for our worship, God assures us of our value and acceptance in tangible emotional, physical, and spiritual ways. His Presence overshadows us and we become the heavenly offering of praise that brings healing to ourselves, and even to the nations. What's even better, the more secure we become in Him, the more you are able to look beyond your immediate concerns to the needs of your families and neighbors. We become healing agents in the hands of the Restorer.

We simply have to lay down our plans and thoughts to put first the exaltation of our Heavenly Father. In this place, we will truly answer to our name as 'worshiper.' It is a heart posture that covers all areas of life, from relationships, to your job, to a traditional praise service. 1 Corinthians 10:31 says, "So whether you eat or drink or whatever you do, do it all for the glory of God."

In this place, we spend time experiencing the love of the Father and allow those encounters to define our lives. Here, we fully submit to the Lord's agenda.

It is in this place that we come face to face with our Father.

It is the only place where we are healed, transformed, and made secure in who He called us to be!

It is the place where we receive the identity we were meant to have from the beginning of time. The only cost is an exchange of submitting our will to "His good, pleasing and perfect will."[125]

125: Romans 12:2

TRANSFORMATION

Worship is a mind, body, spirit experience. From a psychological stand-point[126], the act of worship engages the emotional places of our brains in a way that causes positive physical results in our bodies, not to mention our spirits and minds. Worship opens the door to total life transformation.

I quoted the end of Romans 12:2 above, but now I want you to take a moment and meditate on the whole verse in the *Passion Translation*: "Stop imitating the ideals and opinions of the culture around you, but be inwardly transformed by the Holy Spirit through a total reformation of how you think. This will empower you to discern God's will as you live a beautiful life, satisfying, and perfect in His eyes."

Metamorphóō is the Greek word where we get *transformed*, and means "to change into another form."[127] It's where we get our English word metamorphosis. *Morphe* stresses inward change as an ongoing process.

What are we transforming into? A renewed, better us? No, we are transforming to look more like our Father. 2 Corinthians 3:18 affirms that, "… We all, who with unveiled faces contemplate the Lord's glory, are being transformed into His image with ever-increasing glory, which comes from the Lord, who is the Spirit."

Vine's Expository Dictionary goes on to further describe a transformation that is a complete inward change "under the power of God."[128] It demonstrates a new character and conduct affected by none other than the Holy Spirit. Transformation through renewed minds comes as believers *expose themselves to the very Presence of God.*

How to we get there?

126: We will cover this in greater depth in Chapter 8.

127: "G3339 - metamorphoō - Strong's Greek Lexicon (NIV)." *Blue Letter Bible*. Web. 2 June, 2017

128: Vine, W. "Transfigure - Vine's Expository Dictionary of New Testament Words." *Blue Letter Bible*. 24 June, 1996. Web. 2 June, 2017..

Well, there are many ways that we each experience His Presence. Some worship, some read the word, some pray, some dance, some write. The list could go on and on. What is important to understand is that if we spend time in His Presence, in intimacy with Him, we *will* be changed.

JACK'S STORY

Before I share about my cousin Jack, once more take a moment between you and God to meditate on Romans 12:2: "Stop imitating the ideals and opinions of the culture around you, but be inwardly transformed by the Holy Spirit through a total reformation of how you think. This will empower you to discern God's perfect plan for you, living a beautiful life, satisfying and perfect in His eyes."

Jack was suffering when I, Diane, spoke with him about his recent (almost) wedding. He had experienced a horrible betrayal that the world comically calls a "Runaway Bride." His fabulous destination wedding in Paris had been canceled. Jack did not think it was funny. The bridal party was there. But, Sue, his ex-fiance, was a no-show.

It was humiliating and painful, so he reached out for some advice. After three or four weeks of calls, emails and some tears, Jack decided he was done working through the event.

Was he going to be alright? At first, I was concerned. Had he really faced the grief of such a terrible betrayal? It was such an unexpected and painful event. The counselor in me didn't want him to spend time suffering from one ounce of shame or rejection. I wanted Jack assured that God accepted him fully and had awesome plans for his future.

As I prayed and talked with Jack, we discussed the importance of him understanding the Father's love and safety during this season. I felt honored to support Jack as he discovered how to enter into his personal, worship place. Amazingly, in these quiet times, the Holy Spirit began transforming Jack's heart. Over the next few months, Jack explained to me that he had come to realize that his ex-fiancé was not in a healthy place.[129] He told me he was determined to keep working through forgiveness, even though it would be hard.

My cousin said he was assured that his heavenly Father loved him and hated to see him go through such a hurtful event. He had also found an amazing support group to hold him accountable to continue working through his grief. Jack thanked me for loving him well and explained he was ready to release everything to God. His heart was getting strong and *healthy*. He was transforming into someone like Jesus.

JUST LIKE JESUS

In the light of the secure relationship style that Jesus provides in the Scriptures, let's see how Jack experienced breakthrough by following His example.

First of all, Jack affirmed my help in his healing process. Jack was able to put *value in our time together*, able to look outside of his immediate problem and explore the worth of growth.

Second, my cousin was able to have empathy for his ex-fiancé and realize *she* was in an emotionally unhealthy place. Again, he was able to look beyond his own pain and understand that people make poor choices and sometimes these choices hurt others who are innocent.

Next, Jack relied on God for the strength to forgive, specifically, those who did not deserve forgiveness. He was also able to comprehend that this process could take some *time*.

Importantly, Jack reached for the security of his heavenly Father in the middle of his distress. Jack had laid his head on his Father's chest and he

---

129: A helpful key for all of us dealing with rejection: not everyone is healthy emotionally, and this causes pain to innocent bystanders.

had found peace. In this place of perfect *shalom*, he believed that God's plans for him were to prosper him and to do him good.[130]

Lastly, he came to understand the importance of other secure people in his life, people who were able to walk with him day in day out while he healed.

For anyone counseling or mentoring someone through their hurt, this is the response we long to hear.

I was both excited for him as well as surprised at how fast Jack worked through the process. It was clear to me, Jack had received hope, healing, and revelation through his time with the Holy Spirit. For my cousin, the move from a place insecurity to security happened very quickly. It served as a clear example of God's sovereign power. Something much more powerful than my flawed wisdom had worked in his life. It was God.

The Father had totally transformed and renewed Jack's heart.

How? Through the overwhelming healing glory of His Presence.

GOD'S GOOD AND PLEASING WILL

Sometimes, when you are in His Presence, things happen that are unexplainable. The word "renewed" comes from the Greek word *anakainōsis*, meaning a change of heart and life.[131] This is an important point. Renewal is a life change, not just a mind change. Every part of our being is affected by the dual process of transformation and renewal. It is not only our thoughts that are renewed in His Presence. Our entire life will be a new development, achieved by God's power, not through our effort.[132]

130: Jeremiah 29:11

131: "G342 - anakainōsis - Strong's Greek Lexicon (NIV)." *Blue Letter Bible*. Web. 13 June, 2017.

132: "G342 - anakainōsis."

LETTING GO, AND LETTING GOD

We live in the southern United States, a region marked throughout history by a cacophony of racial and social discord. These historical influences continue to affect the health of relationships between the people and even our local churches.

Several years ago, I, Neal, had an experience that marked my life forever. It was during the preparation for the first visit by Ché Ahn, the head pastor of Harvest Rock Church in Pasadena, California. A group of us had been faithfully praying for God to move in our city, to bring healing and restoration. During a worship and prayer session, I began to physically shake nonstop. This was more than a small quiver, yet I was not alarmed. I knew it was God. However, it continued after the service and lasted for three days!

When I laid down to sleep that night I continued to tremble. This was by no means a normal "church" experience. The shaking was so intense at times that I could literally do nothing but rest. You might be wondering what I was thinking during this time!

During this experience, it was my spirit that was overwhelmed, not my mind. Remember where God brought me from? The mind-only existence? While I was still aware of all the usual activity buzzing around me, my heart was elsewhere. It was with Him. I had never felt so close to Him in my life! I share this experience not to seem super spiritual, but to let you know God wants you and me to know Him in more than just our minds. He wants us to experience Him. It was joyous and awe-inspiring and beyond my understanding. I had no teaching for this.

I've met success. I know what it feels like to be at the top of the pile, or the front of the class, or the MVP.

This was different. Better than all the accolades combined. This was extraordinarily precious and I never wanted to leave. It was utterly fulfilling.

And it had absolutely nothing to do with my own effort. All I could do was receive. When it was over, I was a new man and held a new vision for what the Father desired for me, our family and our region.

In those three days, God set my heart on fire to see our region made whole. The old man was self-serving. The new man cared about much more!

HITTING THE DECK

For years I, Diane, struggled with 2 Corinthians 3:18, which teaches, "And we all, who with unveiled faces contemplate the Lord's glory, are being transformed into his image with ever-increasing glory, which comes from the Lord, who is the Spirit."

I believed that if I could just figure out how to get my thoughts right, I would wake up one morning a much better version of myself.

However, one experience marked my life forever.

I was in a sweaty, hot building with a red dirt floor in the African country of Mozambique. Neal and I and our boys were on a missions trip to visit Heidi Baker's widely acclaimed IRIS ministry base. We took adventures with her ministry team out into the wild of the African "bush-bush." The believers there see life changing miracles all the time, and we witnessed many.

The tent's atmosphere was heavy with expectancy because God's life-changing might and power commonly manifest themselves at their meetings and outreaches. Our family was sitting in the midst of the gathering when local pastors invited us up to the front to pray for us.

As they began to pray for me, an immediate change happened in my spirit. It felt like an explosion of God's Presence deep inside, and I ended up face-down in the dirt. Laying there, I heard the Holy Spirit tell me I was ushered into Heaven's "Throne Room." I knew that I was in the actual Presence of God. I have no perfect words to describe the experience. In

God's Presence, I was marked by waves of deep inner love and at the same time, an emotion of *reverent* fear.

In the African mud, my life became so clear, so simple! All God wanted for me was to intimately be with Him, in the Throne Room. There I was changed and renewed forever.

When I finally stood up and dusted myself off, I was not the old Diane. I was transformed into a new Diane, the daughter of God! Like Jack, I was overwhelmed with Daddy's love. I was a part of His family, His covenant with me was sure, my future was secure. It was a memorial stone experience, my life was changed forever.

INVITING THE HOLY SPIRIT

Maybe you are not familiar with the powerful, life-changing Presence of God that we have encountered. However, it is undeniable that these experiences have changed us into different, new people.

Perhaps you have known the Lord Jesus for a long time, but have been left feeling that something was missing. You are missing a love experience with the Holy Spirit! You need him just like we did.

Let's pray,

> *"Jesus, I know Your Word teaches me that You sent Holy Spirit to come and help me through this life. I want to invite Him to come and fill me with His love and power. Take me beyond my understanding and my life experiences. Give me a picture of who You are without my boundaries. Show me truth through Your Word about Holy Spirit. Thank You, Father! Amen."*

CHAPTER SIX
Like Father, Like Son

"For those whom He foreknew He also predestined to be conformed to the image of His Son, in order that He might be the firstborn among many brothers."[133]

THE POWER OF THE PAST

Not one of us can deny our earthly roots. At some level, we look like our physical parents because we share their DNA. You may share your dad's curly brown hair and your mother's sense of humor. You may love cheese, or rocky road ice cream, just like Grandpa, or struggle with your temper, just like him.

Are you a perfectionist, like your mother? Or perhaps, in an attempt to not be like her, you ran in the polar opposite direction and are the sloppiest person on the planet. Still, you can't get around the fact that you and her share an uncanny ability to argue your points to death, and you both have the exact same shade of green eyes.

Sharing traits with our parents can be a good thing if you are blessed with good parents. It can also be damaging, especially in cases where parents

133: Romans 8:29

were abusive or absent. Regardless, even if you had the best parents on earth, they were not perfect. We all enter adulthood with some amount of baggage from our natural family's genes.

What does this say about your earthly family? Does your physical lineage matter to the Lord? Yes, your heritage matters. God traces all the key figures of the Bible through a physical family lineage, even Jesus.

Have you read one of the Biblical genealogies before? Well, all of those "begats" serve a purpose to help us gain an understanding of how He sees us and how we occupy the Promises of God for our lives. The Jewish people are the spiritual forefathers of the Body of Christ. Romans 11 talks about how we are "grafted" into the promises of Abraham, Isaac and Jacob, so now they are a part of your spiritual bloodline. If you want to receive your spiritual inheritance, you must seek to honor and understand where you spiritually come from.

Paul explains how God's Promises were originally made to the Jews, the cultivated olive tree. It makes sense then that most of the main characters in the Bible are Jewish. What's amazing is that when you embrace God's plans and purposes, as demonstrated by the Jewish people, you embrace God's plans and purposes for your own life.

The sad alternative is visible throughout the history of the entire world. Look at the nations who have chosen to extricate the Jews from their societies, and their global social status today. Feeding and watering these prejudices or strongholds in our lives is like fertilizing a weed. It will brutally limit the fruitfulness of the healthy parts of growth, and potentially even kill growth altogether.

FACE THE FACTS

The Jewish spiritual lineage is filled with people just like you and me. They were blends of potential and failure, victories and losses, lovers and destroyers. Face the facts: families are messy business. But this didn't disqualify them in God's eyes. He never turned His back on the Jews throughout

Scripture, and He still loves them today. It is this same faithfulness that He extends to you. He never disqualified you. He has never rejected you throughout your life, and He still loves you today.

God disclosed the imperfections of the heroes in the Bible to let us know that He is more than able to use us and heal us in the midst of our failures. More importantly, that He will use our problems for our good.

Genesis 50:20, tells us the story of Joseph's brothers who had betrayed him so brutally when they sold him into slavery. The verse tells us, "You intended to harm me, but God intended it for good to accomplish what is now being done, the saving of many lives."

God's desire for Joseph is the same as God's desire for you and me. It is meant to help us keep moving towards the goal without getting sidetracked by our own sin or the sin of our families. Remember, Jesus taught us that the enemy is the one who will "steal and kill and destroy."[134] Do not let anyone tell you that your past limits you and therefore devours your destiny. God has a better strategy and the power to accomplish what He planned from the beginning *if we let Him.*

Need an example? How about the fact that Neal and I are enjoying a happy marriage filled with beauty and trust, instead of staying stuck in the pain and regrets of the past!

Without God's redemption and healing, we would be divorced and possibly still broken. Instead, out of the ashes of the betrayal, God created something remarkable. Now, we are able to bring hope and healing to countless marriages suffering similar distance and discord. This is real Kingdom multiplication! God exchanges our junk for gold every day.

Here's the trick. Don't accept your baggage as your identity. Don't allow the negative to define you.

134: John 10:10

Pressing into our heavenly Father breaks us free from our baggage and pushes us towards our ultimate goal, which is to look more and more like Jesus.

In Christ, we can conquer whatever tries to hold us back from receiving everything He has in store for us. Romans 8:37 confirms this where it tells us "in all these things we are more than conquerors through Him who loved us."

As we become more like Christ, we will experience more grace, peace, freedom, and unmerited favor. As we continue to rest in His perfect peace, we will grow in our understanding of God's love and acceptance. Our inheritance is that we are sons and daughters of God.

The only thing He asks of us to receive this inheritance is to trust Him to heal us and transform us.

CALLED

In the last chapter, we talked about both the negative and positive consequences that names play in our lives. They are truly powerful and impactful. Our family name influences both our identities and destinies. In regions of the United States, parents will commonly give their children a first name after the mother's family name. In that way, they keep alive both husband and wife's family heritage.

When you joined God's family, you received a new name. You became one of the righteous and redeemed. Your adoption into His family means that you are now identified with His Son. This is why we are called "Christians," i.e. "little Christs." You ceased to be identified as lost or forgotten.

Not only are we now included in His family, but God views us as His most precious treasure, the first fruit of His creation. And through you, God is doing His mighty work to bring restoration and healing to the nations.

This is not some hoped-for future state or a work for the heroes of Bible times. It is a covenant made by God and sealed by the blood of His Son, and it is His deepest desire. He is using you and me to accomplish His perfect purposes to free those around us from the bondages of sin and evil. James 1:18 tells us "He chose to give us birth through the word of truth, that we might be a kind of firstfruits of all he created."

Our new name establishes that we belong to the tribe. Our Father is the God of Abraham, Isaac and Jacob. We get to partake in the beautiful history of the Bible. The story of the Jewish people is now our story.

What's more, our new name establishes that we are known and know each other *because* we share the same Heavenly Father. *We are literally family.* We share in the inheritance. As it goes, sharing in the family inheritance also means sharing the family responsibility. We are called to take ownership of the Kingdom, to plow the fields, to bear good fruit!

However, with the position comes certain expectations. Don't worry though, because, in the end, God's plans are always more fun than our plans!

Once we become sons and daughters, the standard goes up. We also see this in earthly examples. For instance, when a homeless child is adopted and must then conform to the new family's home rules. With higher standards come higher positions. Why is the bar higher? Because God, in His mercy, wants to teach us to rule and reign with Him. The new expectations have to do with living as sons and daughters of light. Once adopted, you can't live like a street child anymore. As princes, all "pauper" behavior must disappear. It is simply inappropriate when you are born again into His family.

THE FAMILY

Who do you think carries the most influence in the world for change? Governments? Organizations with impersonal plans, strategies, and budgets? The media?

While these structures certainly have their place, they are not God's structure of choice when it comes to global impact.

His structure of choice is His family.

1 Corinthians 12:12 affirms this unity by stating, "Just as a body, though one, has many parts, but all its many parts form one body, so it is with Christ."

Any program or ministry within the church cannot be sustained without a healthy family structure as a foundation. "Programs" do not and will not replace healthy family environments that reproduce healthy, fruitful sons, daughters, and grandchildren.

In addition, just because learned traits have become familiar behavioral norms, it doesn't mean they're correct. We have to submit to God's design for families, not our past experiences or expectations. We believe we all must live honestly enough to ask hard questions about these family habits. If they don't work, don't teach them to your kids or community! Change them to God's patterns.

For our family, it meant giving up some habits, people, and places, and exchanging them for Kingdom living. Sound difficult? It's not! Just let Holy Spirit lead. In the end, we exchanged learned behaviors that could have destroyed our lives, for God's beautiful standards of love and trust. God's response: we are thriving.

Let go and let God is our new theme. Trust us, it's much more fun on the other side of pain and shame!

BORN AGAIN

We often speak of being "born again" in evangelical circles. In the mystery of our spiritual rebirth, we gain access to the Kingdom. John 3:3-5 illustrates a relevant story here:

Jesus replied, "Very truly I tell you, no one can see the Kingdom of God unless they are born again."

"How can someone be born when they are old?" Nicodemus asked. "Surely they cannot enter a second time into their mother's womb to be born!"

Jesus answered, "Very truly I tell you, no one can enter the Kingdom of God unless they are born of water and the Spirit."

We are born again into a family, a royal family, the first family. In this mysterious process of spiritual rebirth, we are totally reconciled to God. This was the purpose of the Cross: "For God was pleased to have all His fullness dwell in Him, and through Him to reconcile to Himself all things, whether things on earth or things in Heaven, by making peace through His Blood, shed on the Cross."[135]

Out of this place of complete reconciliation, we are transformed into a "first fruit," a holy offering to God.[136] Our lives become a living demonstration of the Father's heart of reconciliation for the entire universe, providing hope, bringing healing, peace, and joy.

This is an incredible mission. The act of being born again is an invitation to co-labor with the King of Kings. We are to be a partner in setting right all things that went wrong in the Fall, to free those under the bondage of sin, death, and discord. God uses family as His form of government in establishing His Kingdom.

What will that look like in your life?

What will that look like in your family?

135: Colossians 1:19-20
136: James 1:18

RIPE AND READY

A healthy family consists of mothers and fathers who bear good fruit. As these men and women grow in security, assured they are loved by God, an amazing metamorphosis happens. This is one of the most important messages this whole book will teach you.

Healing and health produce more healing and health.

Our healing has been contagious for others! When God is on the move in your own life, your transformation will be rubbing off on everyone who will let it.

We have seen those who form secure relationship styles naturally begin to mentor new believers, assuring the young in the faith that they too share in the royal lineage. As they mature, these "children" (in maturity, not age) go on to become healthy parents in their church family.

Supported by a mature and healthy family, Christians are launched into their individual and collective destiny. The cycle continues, the Kingdom expands.

And what is this collective destiny?

To establish and expand the Kingdom of God!

One of the perks of receiving your new name as a believer is that you become a part of the team. You all share the same name, the same goals, the same mission. Here's our mission as a team: "Therefore go and make disciples of all nations, baptizing them in the name of the Father and of the Son and of the Holy Spirit."[137]

137: Matthew 28:19

Jesus calls us to be priests and kings, to take territory and use our special talents to become part of the family government of His Kingdom.[138] We model God's perfect plan in our territory.

However, we also have a *specific* assignment for our time and our region. Jeremiah 1:5 reads, "Before I formed you in the womb I knew you, before you were born I set you apart; I appointed you as a prophet to the nations."

You have a calling specifically designed for you by your heavenly Father. God imagined your assignment and your destiny before you breathed your first breath.

NAME CHANGER, GAME CHANGER

In Genesis 17:5, God changed Abram's name, which meant "exalted father," to Abraham, which means "father of many nations." His new name carried not only Abraham's new assignment but also the foundation for God's Promise. Because of his and Sarah's history of infertility, it was naturally impossible for them to become the parents of many nations without the Lord's help.

The Lord is faithful to His Promises, though. The choice to trust God is never a mistake. During Abraham's time, there was a lot of shame attached to being childless. However, because of his choice to trust, he and his wife got to experience the healing power of God too. He went from a desert nomad and son of an idol merchant to a son of God. He went from a childless old man to the father of the chosen people! His heritage passed from one kingdom, marked by futility and barrenness, into a new Kingdom, marked by fruitfulness and victory.

Going from "Abram" to "Abraham" dramatically marked the change in the status of his citizenship. Biblical names carry significance beyond modern

---

138: This was known as the ekklēsia. For more information, see: "G1577 - ekklēsia - Strong's Greek Lexicon (NIV)" *Blue Letter Bible*. Web. 2 June, 2017. www.blueletterbible.org//lang/lexicon/lexicon.cfm?Strongs=G1577&t=NIV

Western cultural norms for names. Throughout the Bible, parents named their children prophetically.

What we mean by this is that God inspired parents to choose certain names for their babies that would prove to be an accurate "God Label" for the child's future and destiny. Long before they could possibly know what the future held, Moses' adopted mother named him a name that literally means "deliverer."[139] From birth, God paved the way for Moses every time someone said his name. In this example, every time they called out for him, they declared his destiny and purpose straight to him!

The prophetic names continue through the Bible,

Adam, the first man, means "of the dust or earth."[140]

Isaac, Abraham's son, means "he will rejoice."[141]

Jacob, Isaac's son, means "deceiver" or "supplanted."[142]

David, the popular historical king of Israel, means "beloved."[143]

Check these out in the Bible for yourself and see how prophetic they are!

A good New Testament example is found in the life of John the Baptist. He was born to Zacharias, whose name means "Yahweh remembers,"[144] and Elizabeth, "my God is an oath or the fullness of God."[145] Like Abraham and Sarah, this couple waited decades for a child.

Then, there is the story of Ruth and Naomi, found in the book of Ruth.

139: "Moses." *www.behindthename.com*. Behind the Name, 2017. Web. July 8, 2017.
140: "Adam." *www.behindthename.com*. Behind the Name, 2017. Web. July 8, 2017.
141: "Isaac." *www.behindthename.com*. Behind the Name, 2017. Web. July 8, 2017.
142: "Jacob." *www.behindthename.com*. Behind the Name, 2017. Web. July 8, 2017.
143: "David." *www.behindthename.com*. Behind the Name, 2017. Web. July 8, 2017.
144: "Zechariah." *www.behindthename.com*. Behind the Name, 2017. Web. July 8, 2017.
145: "Elizabeth." *www.behindthename.com*. Behind the Name, 2017. Web. July 8, 2017.

Naomi, which means "sweetness," left Judea with her husband and two sons in a time of famine.[146] The family wound up in Moab, where tragically, her husband and sons died. With her new daughter-in-law Ruth, she returned to Bethlehem. There, Naomi told everyone to call her *Mara*, which means "bitterness."[147] Everything sweet from her life was missing. She was a widow, childless, and living with her childless, widowed daughter-in-law.

However, Mara is not the name God gave her; He saw her life as one of sweetness. Through Ruth, God brought hope and restoration back to Naomi's life with a beautiful baby boy. She became a living example of the sweetness of restoration.

Interestingly, my middle name is Elizabeth also which means "covenant restored." It constantly reminds me that God keeps His promises and I will experience His fullness. Who knew my name would have such prophetic significance over my life! What comfort my name brought me when Neal and I began to piece our lives back together.

When we become members of God's family, we become a part of the legacy that gives new significance to our names. Why is this important? If we live with an awareness of the legacy of our family's destiny or assignment, it will be harder to fall into some of the lies of the enemy's attack.

Let's pray,

> *"Holy Spirit, thank You for coming now and removing the negative labels that this world and the enemy have tried to place on me. I'm sorry for letting them stick in the past, and I release them now to You. I am letting go. Come, Holy Spirit. Place Your seal on me, and mark me as Your child. I now know that in Christ, You see me as a Priest, a Royal Heir, and an Adopted Child. This is my inheritance. This is who I am. This is my new name. Amen."*

146: "Naomi-1." *www.behindthename.com*. Behind the Name, 2017. Web. July 8, 2017.
147: "Mara-1." *www.behindthename.com*. Behind the Name, 2017. Web. July 8, 2017.

CHAPTER SEVEN

Flesh and Spirit

"The mind governed by the flesh is death, but the mind governed by the Spirit is life and peace."[148]

"No one can serve two masters. Either you will hate the one and love the other, or you will be devoted to the one and despise the other. You cannot serve both God and money."[149]

THE POWER OF THE PAST

Human beings have an incredible ability to hurt one another, even Christians. When we operate out of our own strength or flesh, without submitting to God, we have the power to negatively impact the inheritance of our family's bloodline for generations.

The good news is that if we trust Him and submit our flesh to the work of His Holy Spirit, our spirit will completely overshadow our flesh.

148: Romans 8:6
149: Matthew 6:24

As Christians, we have an inherited "birthright" status through Jesus Christ as the firstborn Son of God.[150] As God's only begotten Son, Jesus received the Kingdom from His Father and is Lord of all.[151] Christ has promised to share with us the same Kingdom and inheritance.[152] Through Him, we join Jacob in the triumph of spirit over flesh, "God raised him from the dead so that he will never be subject to decay. As God has said, *'I will give you the holy and sure blessings promised to David.'*"[153]

However, in order to transfer our inheritance from one of the flesh to one of the Spirit, it requires a change or circumcision of our heart. This is the circumcision that removes our flesh and gives us His Spirit as our sustaining strength.[154] The only thing that really matters is living by the transforming power of this wonderful "new creation" life. And all those who live in agreement with this standard will experience true peace and God's delight.

Nevertheless, like Jacob, we have all experienced these two inheritances at war with each other. We all resonate with Paul when he wrote, "I do not understand what I do. For what I want to do I do not do, but what I hate I do,"[155] and "for the flesh desires what is contrary to the Spirit, and the Spirit what is contrary to the flesh. They are in conflict with each other, so that you are not to do whatever you want."[156]

At this point, you may be thinking: "But I thought the old nature was crucified with Christ. Why must I die daily? This does not sound fun."

It's true, it does not sound fun. And it is true that the old nature was crucified with Christ. However, that does not necessarily mean that our transformation is instantaneous or fully completed in us.

150: Romans 8:29, Colossians 1:15, Revelation 1:5
151: Acts 2:36, Philippians 2:9-11, Revelation 19:16
152: Romans 4:13, Galatians 3:29, Ephesians 1:18, Hebrews 11:16
153: Acts 13:34
154: Colossians 2:11
155: Romans 7:15
156: Galatians 5:17

If we are going to fully walk in the freedom and the inheritance He intends, it requires our active participation. The process of becoming a new man takes time. It requires making Spirit-led decisions, every single day.

THE MOUNTAIN OF DECISION

"When the LORD your God has brought you into the land you are entering to possess, you are to proclaim on Mount Gerizim the blessings, and on Mount Ebal the curses."[157]

Abraham's first trip to Canaan, the land between Mount Gerizim and Mount Ebal, is recorded in Genesis 12:6-7. It is here God tells Abraham this was the land that He would give to Abraham's descendants.

God told Moses to bless Mount Gerizim, the green and verdant mountain, and curse Mount Ebal, the dry and barren mountain. It was on Mount Ebal that Joshua made an altar. He was sacrificing burnt offerings and peace offerings to God after suffering defeat to Ai due to the sin of Achan. Upon their repentance, God once again delivered His people. Here, Joshua wrote the laws of Moses as a remembrance of God's holy standard upon the Mount's uncut stones.

In between these two mountains, God offered His people a choice: "This day I call the heavens and the earth as witnesses against you that I have set before you life and death, blessings and curses. Now choose life, so that you and your children may live."[158] Living in the shadow of the mountain of blessings and the mountain of curses, the Israelites were constantly reminded they had the freedom to choose, even within the Promised Land.

Blessings? Or curses? The choice was theirs.

Likewise, the choice is ours.

157: Deuteronomy 11:29
158: Deuteronomy 30:19

You and I have the freedom to choose blessings or curses. We have the power to choose which birthright will have preeminence in our lives.

While we may not have the mountains looking down on us reminding us of our freedom to choose life or death, we each have our conscience and our free will. These both serve as the "place of decision" for us here on earth.

OUR SPIRITUAL INHERITANCE

In ancient times, genealogies contained a family's history. The bloodline detailed the triumphs and failures, the blessings and curses, passed through the generations. If anyone wanted to know why they were where they were, or why they became who they became, all they had to do was work their way up the bloodline.

Jesus' family history is outlined through the genealogies and listed in the Gospels of Matthew and Luke. The first one, in Matthew, traces His lineage from Abraham and through Mary.[159] This is important because it shows us His *spiritual* bloodline of Promise and supernatural "belonging."

On the other hand, the lineage in Luke traces Jesus' bloodline from Adam to Joseph.[160] This heritage plays out the *natural* bloodline of His family, filled with sin, corruption, and pain.

These two bloodlines are very significant. Why? Because we all have two bloodlines, a natural one and a spiritual one. We are all born from the seed of the first son; Adam. But when we are born again, we receive a spiritual bloodline of restoration and victory. This bloodline is born out of the reach of the curse of sin and death.

159: Matthew 1:1-17
160: Luke 3:24-38

TWO BIRTHRIGHTS

With our two bloodlines and our two natures, come two birthrights: our natural birthright and our spiritual birthright. These two birthrights, or natures, are constantly at war with one another. Who will win? The flesh or the spirit?

The Bible is filled with stories surrounding this ongoing war. Consider the first family crisis in history, the enmity of Cain against Abel in Genesis 4.

Cain was the firstborn son of Adam and Eve. Firstborn sons assumed the father's authority, received a double portion of the inheritance as well as responsibility for the family upon the father's death. As the story goes, God asks Cain and his younger brother Abel to bring Him the first fruits of their labor. Abel obeyed, Cain did not. The result? God received Abel's gift, and He rejected Cain's. The aftermath was horrendous.

Cain allowed jealousy in his flesh to override what he knew was right in his spirit. The flesh won. In his anger, he committed the first murder, killing his brother.[161]

Next, consider the story surrounding Ishmael's birth.

Abraham and Sarah were finished waiting for the child that God had promised them so many years before.[162] It was time, they reasoned, to take matters into their own hands. They would get their inheritance at all costs, following the flesh; no need to wait on God and the Holy Spirit. And so, they contrived of a way to "make" a baby on their own through Sarah's servant, Hagar.[163] Maybe God would bless their conceived plan?

The baby that Abraham fathered with Hagar was born from a seed of rebellion that has continued up to this day. This decision has caused great pain, death, and devastation; for both Ishmael's descendants and God's

---

161: Genesis 4:8
162: Genesis 16:2
163: Genesis 16:4

chosen people the Jews. This enmity continues to play out even today as the nation of Israel continues to be in strife with the followers of Islam.

When the flesh overrides the spirit, the tragedy is tremendous, sometimes lasting for thousands of years.

It goes on.

Esau, Isaac's first son, sold his birthright for a momentary pleasure, a bowl of stew, satisfying the flesh.[164] Not comprehending the value of God's Promises and the power of his inheritance, Esau rejected what was good and righteous in his choice for a spouse as well.[165] The outcome? All of his descendants became pagans, the Edomites. Not only were they pagans, but they joined the side of the enemy, continually attacking God's people up until the time of King David.[166]

Perhaps the most significant example of the war between our two birthrights is the one that takes place inside of Jacob.

In the early stages of his journey, it appeared as though Jacob's flesh would triumph. He deceived his father and took his brother's inheritance.[167] The name his natural parents gave him was fitting, as Jacob literally means "supplanter." But then, Jacob's heart began to change. A wrestling match with an angel at Bethel ended when Jacob's flesh submitted to God's Spirit.[168]

His reward for the Spirit's victory?

A new name, one that fit his new spirit-man. He was now called Israel, the one who is "Triumphant with God."[169]

164: Genesis 25:33

165: Genesis 26:34

166: "Edom." *www.jewishvirtuallibrary.com*. Jewish Virtual Library, 2017. Web. July 8, 2017.

167: Genesis 27

168: Genesis 32

169: Boyd, J. *Bible Dictionary*. Ottenheimer Publishers, 1958.

Unfortunately, many of us have not finished our wrestling match. We don't understand the very thing that may hold us back may be invisible, possibly even in our bloodline.[170] We have all seen where choosing the flesh creates havoc in lives and church communities. These choices sometimes extend for generations, take, for instance, abandonment or addictions. Thankfully, we have a God who gives new names to us and our life situations!

THE POWER OF WORDS

The flesh and the spirit both carry blessings and curses. Both matter. Derek Prince wrote one of his best books specifically about this topic. It is called, not surprisingly, *Blessings and Curses*. In it, he teaches that blessings and curses are mentioned over 640 times in the Bible.[171]

However, what exactly are blessings and curses? They seem both inanimate and animate all at the same time! Many of us think this type of thing only exists in third world countries.

The answer is that blessings and curses belong to both the invisible and spiritual realm. Yet, Derek Prince tells us, they have control over the physical realm. They usually impact more than an individual. They typically extend through families, tribes, regions and nations and are passed down through generations, *unless broken*. They may have a significant impact on our identities and inheritances. We learn from Paul in Galatians 6:7-9;

> *"Do not be deceived: God cannot be mocked. A man reaps what he sows. Whoever sows to please their flesh, from the flesh will reap destruction; whoever sows to please the Spirit, from the Spirit will reap eternal life. Let us not become weary in doing good, for at the proper time we will reap a harvest if we do not give up."*

The good news is that we do not have to repeat the patterns of our earthly fathers and mothers. Under the blood of Jesus, every curse in broken. And

---

170: This is what the Bible refers to as "iniquities."

171: Prince, D. *Blessing Or Curse: You Can Choose.* Grand Rapids: Chosen Books, 2006.

through His word, every blessing is ours to receive. What matters is whether we choose to agree with the curse or agree with the blessing.

Our words and thoughts matter! Again, we learn in Matthew 12:35-36, "A good man brings good things out of the good stored up in him, and an evil man brings evil things out of the evil stored up in him. But I tell you that everyone will have to give account on the day of judgment for every empty word they have spoken."

What we say has great power to affect our lives, and our kids' and grandkids' lives, either positively or negatively. Why? Because, "The tongue has the power of life and death, and those who love it will eat its fruit."[172]

Negative labels that people or the enemy have spoken may try to stick to our identities as curses. Often unwittingly, we repeat these curses over ourselves without understanding the impact of our actions. Then we are surprised and disappointed when our situations do not improve.

Consider the impact of words like,

"I'll never be successful."

"I'll never lose weight."

"I'll never find the right person to marry."

"It's too late for me…"

Each of these words affirms fear and add fuel to the fire. They continue the vicious cycle where we unconsciously put our "yes and amen" on stuff we actually hate! Is it any surprise that we are not successful, we don't lose weight, and we perpetually date around if we are telling ourselves to keep doing just that?

172: Proverbs 18:21

We have prayed with lots of people that needed to break agreement with the lies spoken over them as children like;

"You will *never* amount to anything."

"You are worthless *like your father.*"

"You'll be *lucky* if any man will want you."

These words, tragically, form a part of people's identity. On the other hand, our kingdom words have just as much power to impart life. As children of the King, we can now choose to speak blessing over our lives and the lives of our family and regions.

Abraham and Moses could have easily gotten stuck in their early life situations. One came from an idol worshiping family and the other was abandoned by his mother. They both made serious wrong choices along the way. But God's spoken Promises over their lives proved more powerful than their circumstances or decisions along the road to their destiny. The same is true for you and me.

God wants you to walk in your spiritual inheritance more than your past challenges. He wants you to lead a people group out of the bondage of life's struggles.

An excellent place to start is Numbers 6:23-27. Though it may sound awkward, speak this verse over yourself, over your family, your job, and your church. Take a leap of faith and say it *out loud.*

> *Tell Aaron and his sons, "This is how you are to bless the Israelites. Say to them: 'The Lord bless you and keep you; the Lord make his face shine on you and be gracious to you; the Lord turn his face toward you and give you peace.' So they will put my name on the Israelites, and I will bless them."*

Remind yourself each day you have a great Promise over your life and carry the favor of the Lord. We can create Kingdom realities with the words we declare. As His disciples, our words carry the power of creation, much like our heavenly Father. We are more powerful in the unseen Kingdom than we know.

Jesus taught Peter in Matthew 16:19, "I will give you the keys of the Kingdom of heaven; whatever you bind on earth will be bound in heaven, and whatever you loose on earth will be loosed in heaven."

God expects that we bless others out of the blessing that rests on us. Romans 15:27 assures us that, "They were pleased to do it, and indeed they owe it to them. For if the Gentiles have shared in the Jews' spiritual blessings, they owe it to the Jews to share with them their material blessings." We have the privilege and a responsibility to steward the blessings passed down to us and to those who will go on after us.

The Lord sees us through time into all generations. It is vital therefore that we not only receive our own healing and promises but also pass the torch. Our family line carries God's purposes and inheritance. John 15:16 declares, "You did not choose me, but I chose you and appointed you so that you might go and bear fruit, fruit that will last, and so that whatever you ask in my name the Father will give you."

May we step more fully into the Kingdom of victory and set aside all the things that seek to steal and rob us of an eternal inheritance. The choice is ours.

Let's pray,

"Jesus, I ask You to give me wisdom. I love the way You created me, my family and the world. Help me to see from Your perspective and truly love others well. I declare according to Your Promises that my family will learn to fully rule and reign with You. May we no longer see our circumstances as limitations, but rather, as victories of the Righteous King. Please teach me to take up my assignment to shift the atmosphere in the territory You have given me to be one of blessing and favor. Come, Lord, and drive out the giants in this Land. Lord, I thank You that You have a plan, a purpose, and call on my life. Your will be done! Your Kingdom come, on earth as it is in Heaven![173] Amen."

173: Matthew 6:10

CHAPTER EIGHT

Steadfast Love: While We Were Yet Sinners

"The Lord is not slow in keeping His promise, as some
understand slowness. Instead He is patient with you, not wanting
anyone to perish, but everyone to come to repentance."[174]

"The Lord is compassionate and gracious, slow to anger,
abounding in love. He will not always accuse, nor will He harbor
His anger forever; He does not treat us as our sins deserve or
repay us according to our iniquities. For as high as the heavens
are above the earth, so great is His love for those who fear Him;
as far as the east is from the west, so far has He removed
our transgressions from us."[175]

DAVID

There is no end to the lengths broken people will go to fix themselves
before they turn to the only One who can bring total wholeness. Our souls
try to handle our problems our own way. Take King David for example,
whose trouble began one evening when he caught a glimpse of Bathsheba

---

174: 2 Peter 3:9
175: Psalm 103:8-12

taking a bath. He lusted over her, and as the well-known story goes, acted on his feelings.[176] He had her brought to the castle and there he took her into his private chambers. Not long after, she found out she was pregnant.

This episode was highly problematic. First of all, they were not married to each other. In fact, they were both married to *other* people. And while men were permitted more than one wife, to forcefully take another man's wife was 'very wrong' in God's Laws.

David chose not to repent of his sin, attempting to clean up his own mess. His misguided efforts resulted in the murder of Bathsheba's husband.

Let's back up. Before this event, David's life was marked by a devout connection to God, what we would call a secure attachment style. This beautiful and intimate friendship is recorded in many of the Psalms.

God saw David "a man after my own heart."[177] However, Samuel 11:27 tells us "the thing David had done displeased the Lord." Now they were simply out of tune, and David let the discord linger on and on until their disconnection pinnacled into a major confrontation.

David created distance between himself and God the moment he looked dishonorably upon Bathsheba. The gap grew wider and wider until it ended in the tragic death of an innocent victim. His sin without repentance led to more sin. The same principle holds true with us today.

Even at our best, sometimes we give victory to the flesh instead of the spirit. In this case, David went after instant gratification of the flesh, instead of going after God's heart in his spirit. Most of us can agree that at some point in our lives, we have said or done something that we were not very proud of. We have all felt the sting of shame and the lure of hiddenness.

176: 2 Samuel 11
177: Acts 13:22

Our Biblical predecessors were no different. Moses committed murder.[178] Abraham lied.[179] So did Jacob.[180] Peter had anger issues.[181] Paul said he was "the worst" of sinners.[182]

Yet, in these Biblical examples, each worked through their own process of restoration, leading to a place of peace and closeness with God. What's more, God used their lowest points to reveal His plan of grace and healing for all of us, no matter how deep our shame goes.

LET'S TALK ABOUT SHAME

In the Garden of Eden, "Adam and his wife were both naked, and they felt no shame."[183] Their nakedness was a symbol of genuineness and vulnerability. Sadly, after the Fall, vulnerability became intrinsically linked to a distinctive feeling.

Shame.

Webster's Dictionary defines shame as "a feeling of guilt, regret, or sadness that you have because you know you have done something wrong, or a feeling of dishonor or disgrace."[184]

Shame is a normal human emotion and can be categorized as healthy or unhealthy. Healthy shame is understood as conviction or boundaries that are given to us to keep us safe and humble before God.

Brené Brown is one of the best minds currently exploring the effects of shame. She has published works that have been listed on the *New York Times Best Seller's list*. Brown describes healthy shame as the feeling that, "I

178: Exodus 2:12

179: Genesis 20:1

180: Genesis 27:19

181: John 18:10

182: 1 Timothy 1:15

183: Genesis 2:25

184: "Shame." *www.merriam-webster.com*. Merriam-Webster, n.d. Web. 13 June 2017.

have done something that goes against my core values and beliefs, and I feel badly about that."[185] In contrast, toxic shame describes the feeling of, "I am inherently flawed and defective and therefore unworthy of love and belonging."[185]

When we are open and vulnerable before our Father God, healthy shame causes us to understand that we are dependent on His grace. Healthy shame is a source of humility in our lives reminding us that we are not perfect and will make mistakes that require repentance and forgiveness. Jack Frost reminds us that, "it is in this place that the bondages begin to be broken that may have hindered the flow of intimacy for a lifetime."[187]

However, on the other side, unhealthy shame is an attack on our whole identity or our worthiness as a person. Basically, this is the difference between "I *did* something bad" and "I *am* bad."[188] And when shame becomes your identity, when you believe that you are fatally flawed, or defective, you become dehumanized and toxic to yourself and those around you.

WHY ARE YOU HIDING?

In the Garden, Adam desired to go beyond the boundaries of safety erected by God. Essentially, Adam chose to decide what was "safe" for himself, instead of trusting God. In that moment he relied on his own judgment over God's,

> *Then the eyes of both of them were opened, and they realized they were na-ked; so they sewed fig leaves together and made coverings for themselves. Then the man and his wife heard the sound of the Lord God as he was walking in the garden in the cool of the day, and they hid from the Lord God among the trees of the garden. But the Lord God called to the man, "Where are*

185: Brown, Brené . "Listening to Shame." TED. March 2012. Lecture.
186: Bradshaw, J. *Healing The Shame That Binds You*. Deerfield Beach: Health Communications, 2005.
187: Frost, J. *Experiencing the Father's Embrace*. Lake Mary: Charisma House, 2002.
188: Bradshaw, J. *Healing The Shame That Binds You*. Deerfield Beach: Health Communications, 2005.

you?" He answered, "I heard you in the garden, and I was afraid because I was naked; so I hid."[189]

Why do we hide when God calls us? For the same reasons, we hide from vulnerable relationships. We are terrified that people, or God, will find out how broken and damaged we really are. We believe the lie that "hiddenness" is our best protection from the shame and pain. That is what unhealthy shame does; it produces feelings of fear and a desire for isolation.

Healthy shame produces repentance, hope, and healing. Unhealthy shame makes us run *away* rather than face possible rejection. Healthy shame encourages us to run *towards*; to reconnect and reset what was broken.

An avoidant attachment style would present itself in this Genesis account by asking; "Hey honey? How about we run and hide over there? Maybe under that bush? No one will see us there."

On the other hand, an ambivalent attachment style might respond: "How about we take some of these itchy fig leaves to cover up? No one will ever notice, right? Do you think He still loves us?"

A more avoidant style reduces shame by retreating or reacting defensively in painful situations.[190] Judgmentalism and deflection are mechanisms that attempt to keep shame at bay with thoughts like, "Maybe I'll be okay if I can take the attention off of me." Or, "Maybe I will feel better if I can blame someone else for my hurt." Adam tried this by blaming God and Eve. Fearing intimacy, true avoidants can maintain a tough exterior and potentially reject love and feelings of comfort from people and God.[191]

In order to escape from negative feelings, some can easily find themselves in the temporary relief of alcohol, drugs, pornography or work addictions.

189: Genesis 3:7-10
190: Clinton, T., Straub, J. *God Attachment: Why You Believe, Act, and Feel the Way You Do About God.* New York: Howard Books, 2014.
191: Ibid.

These are distractions that fill the emotional void of living on the island of self-sufficiency.[192]

More ambivalent attachment styles find themselves growing more self-critical and may use passive or subservient behavior to avoid potential shame.[193] They can also have a tendency to spend great amounts of time and effort resisting what they perceive as unfavorable comments in their relationships.[194] True ambivalent styles can find themselves becoming hypersensitive to the approval of both God and others. They can get stuck thinking things like "I can't hear God, even He doesn't want to spend time with me," or, "I'm not good enough so I guess I'm just doomed to do everything alone."

In the end, it doesn't matter whether you deal with shame by running from it, ignoring it, or deflecting it by blaming others. What does matter is that we take our shame to our heavenly Father. If we don't, the negative feelings we develop toward ourselves may become a deeply embedded part of who we think we are.

Our heavenly Father is someone who's always ready to share a laugh or wipe a tear. His children are always safe with Him. His love "always protects, always trusts, always hopes, always perseveres" for our benefit.[195]

Problems arise when unhealthy shame becomes a part of our identity. When this happens and someone, God included, tells us they love us and accept us, we experience an internal conflict, often reacting with suspicion.

"They can't really mean that, right?"

"If they really knew me, they wouldn't believe that."

192: Ibid.

193: Cassidy, J., Shaver, P.R. *Handbook of Attachment: Theory, Research, and Clinical Applications*. New York: Guilford Press, 2008.

194: Clinton, T., Straub, J. *God Attachment*.

195: 1 Corinthians 13:7

"Oh boy, now I had better not be vulnerable or show them any negative parts of me."

I assure you, God does mean it. Numbers 23:19 tells us, "God is not human, that He should lie, not a human being, that He should change his mind. Does He speak and then not act? Does He promise and not fulfill?"

What's more, He is infinitely more trustworthy than we are. *What He says about us is what is true.* We need to consider, *what we say about ourselves or believe about ourselves may not be true. In fact, it might be 100% false, literally, a lie from the pit of hell.*

Lamentations 3:22-23 tells us, "Because of the Lord's great love we are not consumed, for His compassions never fail. They are new every morning; great is Your faithfulness." When Jeremiah wrote these verses, Babylon had just conquered and burned Jerusalem, his home. It doesn't make sense that he would write "great is Your faithfulness" in the middle of loss, fear, and uncertainty. However, Jeremiah viewed the loss through the lens of God's steadfast love despite the circumstances. We know that Jeremiah felt loved and secure with Father God.

RECEIVING CORRECTION

Unconfessed sin will quickly catch up with us. In David's case, he pushed God away and finally was confronted by the prophet Nathan.[196]

What if you were David?

How would you feel if your most shameful sin was supernaturally disclosed to a man of God, who showed up at your front door with some bad news?

Then, how would you feel if he proceeded to tell you that what you did was going to be broadcast on every major news channel?

196: 2 Samuel 12

Adam and Eve chose the "duck and cover" fig leaf approach, which was unfruitful. They seemed to have quickly forgotten God is omnipresent.

David's original response was trying to conceal the event by murdering the one man who might discover his secret. However, God intervened and sent a prophet with a serious wake-up call. At the height of this prophetic confrontation, we are given a breakthrough example of how to deal with shame in a healthy manner.

David chose the pain of correction at the hand of God in order to be restored in relationship, instead of trying to continue to hide or remain in rebellion to God's requirements. David responded, "I have sinned against the LORD."[197]

Like David, we need to fear the Lord. It is important to have a high regard for God and His Word.[198] We cannot fear God and love evil.[199]

David *knew* his Father as good and feared His approval more than the thoughts of men. He didn't let shame hold him back!

Shame tells us the bridge back to God is unsafe and too far to reach. Shame makes our problems seem bigger than they really are and we feel smaller and more alone than we truly are. Shame makes us want to hide from the problem rather than move toward the Problem Solver, God. There is nothing that will make us more insecure than hiding our sin or not dealing with shame.

Avoiding repentance by wallowing in shame or ignoring our issues does not cancel our sin. It actually forfeits the great gift of grace and the peace that flows from it that Jesus gave to us on the Cross. Because it is God's nature to love and forgive, repentance always brings us closer to Him and makes us more secure.

197: 2 Samuel 12:13
198: Psalm 119:9
199: Romans 12:9

Repentance of our sin goes much further than feeling bad about it or expecting God's goodness to cover it. It actually means to change our mind.[200] God does not get in the way of our ability to choose our own will. He will not compete with our choice to make His will a priority in our lives.

Revelation 3:19 reads, "Those whom I love I rebuke and discipline. So be earnest and repent." Correction and discipline are actually signs of His love. Our Father loves us enough to help us change, to help us transform, and to steer us away from our destruction.

After the fire of David's sin and repentance had died down, there was still a mess left to clean up. Consequences are a reality. Even though David was fully forgiven and restored to right relationship with God the instant he repented, he still would have to bear the consequences of his sin.

Because David showed contempt for the Lord, Bathsheba's son died. David pleaded with God for a week for the child's life, but in the end, the baby went home to Heaven. When David heard the news, he stopped fasting and returned to his life and responsibilities in the palace. 2 Samuel 12:20 tells us, "Then David got up from the ground. After he had washed, put on lotions and changed his clothes, he went into the house of the LORD and worshiped. Then he went to his own house, and at his request, they served him food, and he ate."

David didn't stay angry at God or get offended at how things turned out. He knew His Father was good, that his Father loved him, and that his Father always wanted the best for him.

Many of us get stuck at this point. If the consequences are a result of our disobedience, we may get offended and angry at God. We wonder at how broken we've become. But remember, brokenness is not the end unless we choose to stay there.

200: "G3340 - metanoeō - Strong's Greek Lexicon (NIV)." *Blue Letter Bible*. Web. 13 June, 2017.

Even though our Father may not deny the consequences of sin in our lives, He loves us perfectly and is faithful to heal our wounds. The resulting fragrance is one of lasting peace and rest.

In 2 Samuel 12, this healing grace manifested when Bathsheba bore another son, Solomon, meaning "peaceable."[201] Nathan the prophet came back under the command of God to give the child a second name, Jedediah, which means "beloved of the LORD."[202] God's plan for David's son became a beautiful picture of Heaven's wisdom displayed here on earth. What a stunning example of the profound grace and peace the Lord extends to those who repent, submit to His will, and accept His love and kindness!

JULIE'S STORY

My college roommate, Julie, grew up in a house where her mother warned her that "boys were bad." The result was that Julie was always afraid that men were going to physically or emotionally harm her. From the time she was a little girl, Julie subconsciously denied her need for relationship and connection in an effort to protect herself from all of the world's "dangerous" men.

As she proceeded through life, it seemed her relationships never flourished. The men she did risk going out with told her repeatedly that she was nice but impossible to get to know. She admitted she never gave them a chance to get close, quickly ending the relationship before she might have to trust or get too vulnerable.

For Julie, it was not uncommon to withdraw, numb her feelings, or try to portray a specific image to avoid pain. Subsequently, many of us struggle to be honest with the people in our lives. We are afraid if our brokenness is actually revealed, we will not be loved.[203] For Julie, one stuffed feeling after another resulted in her turning to pornography to feel some sort of

---

201: "Solomon." *www.behindthename.com*. Behind the Name, 2017. Web. July 8, 2017.
202: "Jedediah." *www.behindthename.com*. Behind the Name, 2017. Web. July 8, 2017.
203: Clinton, T., Straub, J. *God Attachment*.

emotional connection. This secret kept her from being too susceptible to a real human being.

Julie told me she was just trying to figure out how to feel something, anything.

However, not surprisingly, pornography only compounded her deeper shame issue. Julie was embarrassed, lonely, and depressed. Humiliation had kept her under lock and key for so long that healthy human connection was out of reach.

As Julie confided in me about this problem in her life, the story unfolded even further. She was miserable and trapped in a vicious cycle.

Julie hated herself.

Her mentor had informed her that she simply "needed to repent, change her behavior and get some accountability."

I agreed. Julie did need to work on all of those things. But, I knew there was another major issue at hand that could not remain unaddressed.

She needed to know that God truly loved her.

She slowly began to open her heart as I spoke the truth of God's love for her. I continued to assure her that His plans for her life were good, and that healing was hers if she would trust Him.

Right before she hung up, Julie stopped a moment and began to say one last thing.

"You know Diane, this conversation was my final attempt to try to figure out my life. I think if I hadn't been able to feel that God even cares… well…"

"Well, what?" I asked, curious of where she was going.

"I had considered taking my life tonight."

Her words hit my heart. The Julie I knew was a beautiful woman, whose breakthrough, future and destiny were already bought on the Cross. She just needed to let God in. I told her how glad I was she had called, silently thanking God for His incredible timing.

That day, the Holy Spirit triumphed over the spirit of shame. It is a spirit that seeks to isolate, paralyze, and finally, to kill.[204] God had much more in store for His precious daughter Julie. Her life was just beginning!

THE TICKET TO GLORY

"At that time the disciples came to Jesus and asked, 'Who, then, is the greatest in the Kingdom of Heaven?' He called a little child to Him, and placed the child among them. And He said: 'Truly I tell you, unless you change and become like little children, you will never enter the Kingdom of Heaven. Therefore, whoever takes the lowly position of this child is the greatest in the Kingdom of Heaven.'"[205]

Humility is the condition to enter the Kingdom of Heaven. Jesus taught his followers about this character principle, by pointing them to the most obvious example of weakness and humility: a child.

Children, by nature, are dependent; they know their needs. Children are also teachable, constantly learning and responding positively to correction. When we humbly admit our needs to the Father and respond positively to correction like a little child, we will be met with understanding and care. This is the most secure place to be.

David modeled true humility. In the end, he was not willing for anything to come between him and his connection with his heavenly Father. David came to a place of true repentance over his sin. He was teachable.

204: John 10:10
205: Matthew 18:1-4

If we do mess up, and we all will, we must humbly and quickly move toward Father's heart in repentance and invite Him in to bring us to a place of healing in our hearts and souls. This is where we find true rest and peace. This is where we will be transformed. This is where we will find true security and acceptance. When God says that we are accepted, it does not mean that we are tolerated. It means that we could never bother, upset, or disturb Him. We are all His favorites!

It is impossible for us to take too much of His time, to annoy Him, or cause Him to reject us. He wants nothing more than for us to be *close* to Him. He never pushes us off into a corner and says, "Wait, I'm too busy. I don't have time for you." No, He says, "I'm interested in you. I want you. You're welcome here. Come in. I've been waiting a long time for you." He longs for us to be with Him.

However, there is one thing that does upset Him: *when we choose to stay away from Him.*

As Adam demonstrated all too well, one of the largest hindrances to intimacy with both God and others is choosing to stay distant, closed, and refusing total honesty and vulnerability. Yes, it is common for people to think they will be rejected if others know the truth about them. While it may be true that some people may judge us if they knew all the secrets in our closets, this is clearly not the heart of our Father. More importantly, it is not how He wants the body of Christ to operate.

And while we might suffer rejection from those we love, God will never reject us. *He always loves us.*

What's more, there are many more people who will value you because of your open heart and vulnerability. Hiding your junk only puts up walls. Honesty opens the door to healing and relationship.

David wrote a special psalm to God after he sinned against Him. Let's pray along with David,

> *"Have mercy on me, O God, according to Your unfailing love; according to Your great compassion blot out my transgressions. Wash away all my iniquity and cleanse me from my sin....Create in me a pure heart, O God, and renew a steadfast spirit within me. Do not cast me from Your Presence or take Your Holy Spirit from me. Restore to me the joy of Your salvation and grant me a willing spirit, to sustain me.*[206] *Amen.*

206: Psalm 51:1-2, 10-12

CHAPTER NINE
Allowed to Feel

"No longer will they call you Deserted, or name your land
Desolate. But you will be called Hephzibah, and your land
Beulah; for the Lord will take delight in you, and your
land will be married."[207]

IN THE FIRE

When we feel rejected, our natural response is to run for cover and lick our wounds. We become internally focused, and most of the time completely disregard the fact that our offender *may also be in pain.* Jesus, however, gives us a different example. Jesus knew what it felt like to be utterly disdained and shunned, "He was despised and rejected by mankind, a man of suffering, and familiar with pain."[208]

For three and a half years, Jesus gave His life totally to doing good: to forgiving sins, healing sicknesses, delivering the demon-oppressed. He did nothing *but* good. At the end of that period, His people were given a choice to crucify him or Barabbas, a guilty criminal, rebel, robber, and murderer.[209]

207: Isaiah 62:4
208: Isaiah 53:3
209: Matthew 27:17

His rejection was intense. More intense than any other human has ever, or will ever, know. The crowds demanded that Jesus be crucified and Barabbas be released from captivity.

However, instead of retreating to the comforts of Heaven, to focus on receiving His own healing, Jesus prayed to the Father to forgive those who called for His death. He was concerned about what would happen to *them*.

That is the perfect example He left for us to follow.

THE WAY OF JESUS

As a counselor, I am aware that a marriage relationship is often in trouble years before someone calls it quits.

This proved true with my family. I wanted to blame our whole mess on Neal. However, I knew deep inside that *it wasn't true*. We had both contributed to the pile of rubble and destruction in front of us. He had just decided to quit pretending.

I had been married for close to twenty-five years when I heard Neal say the painful words, "I don't love you anymore. I think we need some time apart to sort this out."

Neal had hit rock bottom.

I had been rejected, betrayed.

Everything we had built was in shambles. Shock, followed by confusion and fear, entered my heart for weeks and months to come. My default was to pretend it wasn't happening or lie to myself that it wasn't true, which only left me with a sense of numbness that quickly wore off.

The strange part about this season is that I could honestly look you in the eye and say that we both respected each other, and even more than that, still actually loved each other.

The problem was…we did not like each other.

It was going to take a miracle to put the pieces of our long-neglected marriage back together, and it seemed impossible.

After a period of separation, Neal and I spent time with a few different marriage counselors. Over time, we discovered that our restoration was going to take more than our souls (composed of our minds, wills, and emotions) returning to our marriage covenant. We needed a different sort of help to find our way to healing; we needed deep surgery to remove the shrapnel from the years of emotional distance and bad relationship habits.

For several months, we sought the wisdom of pastors, therapists, close friends, and family. They were supportive and kind, but they couldn't take away the horrible sorrow and distress. Despite all the wise counsel, we often still found ourselves trudging through the torment of indecision and fear.

Why did it still hurt so bad? Should we just figure out how to live apart? Why couldn't we shake off the deep pit in our stomachs? What about the boys?

I remember going to bed, night after night, singing to the Lord. The surrender of the hurt and pain in those moments gave me a very short-lived sense of peace. I would finally drift off to sleep, only to wake up in a start with that feeling of dread in the pit of my stomach. And then my thoughts would clear. I would remember, and my heart would break all over again.

I can honestly say that my reaction to the feelings of rejection was very self-focused. I didn't wonder how much Neal must be hurting inside. I didn't think to ask *why* my husband thought, felt, and behaved the way he did.

I definitely didn't want to admit that *I* could have contributed in any way to the chaos we were both facing.

Without any great options, I would sit and cry. I would pray and then cry some more, trying to make sense of my hurt. I was plagued and overwhelmed with fear and uncertainty. Had I deserved this? Could God hear me? Contemplating the dismal future I imagined for myself and my children, I found plenty of reasons for more and more tears.

But, my greatest fear, was that I was not wanted and not good enough.

At first, I would think this was the most painful wound I would suffer. And then I faced the ultimate embarrassment and humiliation. Soon everyone else also knew that I had been discarded as a wife.

There were many days that my soul screamed to stay angry and get even. I felt like I had a "pass" because I was so hurt.

Yet, slipping into the victim role never gave me the peace that I desired.

Other days, I simply allowed myself to feel down. As a professional, I knew that allowing ourselves to experience feelings is a huge part of the healing process.[210] In my place of sadness, Jesus was sad right along with me; even though He had good things in store for my future, it was important to mourn the loss.

In John 11:1-45, Jesus encountered Mary and Martha deep in sorrow over the death of Lazarus. Jesus responded to their pain by weeping, even though He knew He was about to raise Lazarus from the dead. Why? Because being filled with human compassion, Jesus was able to experience healthy mourning. His secure relating style allowed Him to trust His Father and know that His ways were perfect. "As the heavens are higher than the earth, so are My ways higher than your ways and My thoughts than your thoughts."[211]

God answered my pleas to take away my hurt by calling me to face deeper areas of pain that needed restoration. My foundation and core rejection

---

210: Gray, J. *What You Feel, You Can Heal: A Guide For Enriching Relationships.* Mill Valley, CA: Heart Pub., 1994.
211: Isaiah 55:9

issues had to be addressed before He could reclaim my marriage. For me, that meant a season of learning to understand, heal, and manage my feelings. It wasn't the instant gratification I wanted, but a large part of me knew a bandaid wasn't going to cut it.

Matthew reminds us that as Jesus suffered the ultimate phase of His rejection on the Cross, bloody and bruised, He cried out, "My God, My God, why have You forsaken Me?"[212] And there was no answer from Heaven. For the first time in the history of the universe, the Father turned a deaf ear to the Son's cry. Then Jesus knew that His Father had rejected Him. But, why had He rejected Him?

Jesus was made sin with our sinfulness, and God averted His eyes and stopped His ears to the cry of His Son. "Your eyes are too pure to look on evil…"[213] After that, there was only one more cry that came from the lips of Jesus before He died. It has been said that He died of a broken heart, not from the rejection of His people, but from the rejection of His Father.

For every person who has suffered the agonies of rejection, I want to tell you right now that Jesus experienced the deepest pangs of rejection. He did this so we might be saved and healed of our wounds. So that we will never have to face the rejection of the Father. Nevertheless, that does not mean we will not face rejection from men. In fact, we believe that some wounds are so painful that the mind refuses to acknowledge them.[214] They are there though—deeper than the mind, reason, and memory. They strike at our value as a person. They are a shot from the enemy's arsenal of rejection, fear, shame, hopelessness, and low self-worth.

Like shrapnel, these wounds are sometimes invisible on the surface. However, if left to fester for years, they can change our God-ordained destiny in

---

212: Matthew 27:46

213: Habakkuk 1:13

214: Brewin, C., Andrews, B., Valentine, J. "Meta-Analysis of Risk Factors for Posttraumatic Stress Disorder in Trauma-Exposed Adults." *Journal of Consulting and Clinical Psychology, 68*, 2000. 748-766.

DePrince, A. et. al. "Motivated Forgetting and Misremembering: Perspectives from Betrayal Trauma Theory." Belli, R.F., *True and False Recovered Memories: Toward a Reconciliation of the Debate (Nebraska Symposium on Motivation 58)*, New York: Springer, 2012. 193-243.

the Kingdom. They injure us even deeper as they dislodge from their scar tissue and head straight for the heart during times of stress or pressure. I can promise you the best remedy is dealing with the pain face-to-face with God. If we turn to Him when we are wounded, it allows the Holy Spirit to remove the shrapnel and to guide and support us as we move forward.

GROWING STRONGER

Following a painful or devastating experience, like rejection or abandonment, the body and mind may become disconnected.[215] This survival mechanism helps hurting people cope with unimaginable pain in their lives.

Research in neuroscience suggests that traumatic memories are stored not only in the brain but also in the body.[216] These studies tell us that heartbreaking fear and shame impact every part of the individual: emotionally, physically, and spiritually.[217] Consequently, a complete healing needs to address each of those specific areas.

We understand a personal experience with damaging fear and shame establishes unhealthy emotions in us. Therefore, it makes sense that it will take another healthy personal experience to restore us to a place of wholeness and wellness.[218]

Daniel Siegel is an author, child psychologist, and a Clinical Professor of Psychiatry at the University of California School of Medicine. His work centers on brain function and development. According to Siegel's research, our brains are *social*. They are built for relationship. He tells us that relationships transform neuronal functioning and actually modify how our brains develop as we grow through the years.[219]

215: Siegel, D.J. The Developing Mind: How Relationships and the Brain Interact to Shape Who We Are. New York: Guilford Press, 2015.

216: Van Der Kolk, B. The Body Keeps the Score: Mind, Brain and Body In The Transformation of Trauma. London: Penguin Books, 2015.

217: Siegel, D.J. The Developing Mind.

218: Jennings, T.R. The God-Shaped Brain: How Changing Your View of God Transforms Your Life. Downers Grove: InterVarsity Press, 2017.

219: Siegel, D.J. The Developing Mind.

This is exciting news!

Why? We believe that the positive experience of encountering the love of God can initiate restoration and healing of all types of emotional suffering.

LEFT HEMISPHERE, RIGHT HEMISPHERE

The left and right hemispheres of the brain have distinct functions that become predominant early in life.[220] We know the left and right hemispheres of our brains process information in very different ways.

The capacity to sense and express emotions are mediated initially by the right hemisphere of the brain.[221] This hemisphere is visual, processes information intuitively and simultaneously, and is responsible for recognizing faces; expressing music, color, and image organization; reading social cues; and aspects of our creativity.[222]

Not surprisingly, children start out in life as primarily right hemisphere processors.[223] As infants and children, we tend to learn and experience more often through our five senses.[224]

Meanwhile, the left hemisphere of our brain houses systematic and logical thought.[225] This hemisphere is more adept at verbal tasks involving analytical thinking, numbers, and reasoning.[226] The left tends to see information as patterned, structured, and under control, processing what it hears in a conversation in an orderly fashion.[227]

220: Jennings, T.R. *The God-Shaped Brain.*

221: Siegel, D.J. "Attachment and Self-Understanding: Parenting With The Brain In Mind." *Journal of Prenatal and Perinatal Psychology and Health, 18 (4),* 2004. 273-285.

Siegel, D.J. *The Mindful Therapist: A Clinician's Guide to Mind Sight and Neural Integration.* New York: Norton, 2010.

222: Schore, A.N. "Attachment and Regulation Of The Right Brain." *Attachment and Human Development, 2(1),* 2000. 23-47.

223: Jennings, T.R. *The God-Shaped Brain.*

224: Siegel, D.J. *The Developing Mind.*

225: Siegel, D.J. "Attachment and Self-Understanding." Siegel, D.J. *The Mindful Therapist.*

226: Siegel, D.J. *The Developing Mind.*

227: Guastello et al. *Chaos and Complexity In Psychology: The Theory of Nonlinear Dynamical Systems.* Cambridge: Cambridge University Press, 2009.

In Western culture, where the academic and medical fields are steeped in Greek philosophy, we have been conditioned to value logic over our emotions. We are taught that if something cannot be observed or measured, it cannot be *real.* This idea is drummed into our heads from kindergarten through the rest of our educational training.

The left brain is king!

And the tragic result? We undervalue the encounters that are initiated in the other parts of the brain. And worse, *this can cause us to restrict our experiences about God's Presence to written and logic-based truth alone. Logic and understanding are, at their core, based on man's reasoning alone.*

Jewish thought perceives God as beyond our limited comprehension.[228] In early Jewish culture, God was understood through accounts about His nature passed down through spoken family stories and traditions. Our right hemisphere enables us to be comfortable with unanswered questions and elusive mysteries. The Jewish faith allowed these religious experiences to create a more whole-brain, balanced approach to faith and learning. In a whole-brain approach, you need both right and left hemispheres, both emotion and logic. What these early traditions should reveal to us is that knowing Him involves all of our brain and all of our being.

Through a balanced approach, we are better able to learn, experience, and grow because of who God really is. This is why we remember field trips, role-playing, and hands-on learning, connected to emotion, while we may or may not remember what the English professor lectured on, engaging our logic. When all five of our senses are involved, there is a long lasting memory of our experiences.[229] It makes sense then that our faith encounters will be more full and lasting when we utilize both emotion and logic. To truly know God, we must engage both our feeling and our understanding.

228: Singer, I., Adler, C. *The Jewish Encyclopedia.* London: Funk & Wagnalls, 1902.

229: Brookes, J.D., PhD. *The Neurobiology of Spiritual Warfare.* [Scholarly project], n.d.

Secure relating styles share representational processes from both hemispheres of the brain.[230] That is why a person is able to both feel and understand that they are worthy of love and acceptance.[231] In contrast, the damaged limbic brain, created by brokenness in relationships, stores pain where logic alone cannot reach it.[232]

Encounters with healthy relationships in our lives allow for healing and new connections to be made in both our right and left hemispheres.[233] Since these relational experiences can also include interaction with the Holy Spirit, tools like inner healing prayer, intercession, and worship meet these damaged attachment needs.[234]

Most importantly, these interactions also reach places deep inside and tell us that God not only loves us...*He likes us.*

As an added bonus, these healthy relating experiences and interpersonal connections can result in our whole brain continuing to be shaped all the way into adulthood.[235] In other words, the parts of our brains that may have been hurt by unhealthy encounters can start to be healed by healthy relating experiences. *This complete healing brings restoration to our identity and focus to our destiny.*

So, it seems that science confirms the eternal truth. Spending time in God's Presence has the power to heal our spirits, emotions, as well as the way our physical brains interact, develop, and remember.

230: Siegel, D.J. *The Developing Mind.*

231 Roisman et al. "Earned-Secure Attachment Status in Retrospect and Prospect." *Child Development, 73 (4),* 2002. 1204-1219.

233: Brookes, J.D., PhD. *Spiritual Warfare.*

233: Siegel, D.J. *Mindsight.*

234: Cozolino, L. *The Neuroscience of Psychotherapy: Building and Rebuilding the Human Brain.* New York: W.W. Norton & Co., 2002.

Tronick, E. "Emotions and Emotional Communication In Infants." *American Psychologist, 44 (2),* 1989. 112-9.

235: Siegel, D.J. *The Developing Mind.*

GETTING ALIGNED

It is vitally important to activate the truth of the Word with the experiences of faith. Jesus loved to teach this way. He would often use metaphors while at the same time demonstrate the importance of the sermon with *hands-on learning*. He *preached* the Word[236], *laid His hands* on the sick and they were healed[237], He *fed* the masses.[238] Being in His Presence was the ultimate experience that utilized all of the functions of the brain and the entire physical body.

The Holy Spirit continues this work today. He wants *all* of us involved. He wants our logic functions and our emotional functions working together. He instructs us by saying, "God is spirit, and His worshipers must worship in the Spirit and in truth."[239]

An encounter with His Presence helps us connect both hemispheres of the brain. What's amazing is that God interacts with us in the Spirit, as well as the natural. In His Presence, through worship, our spirits are opened to healing. What this looks like will vary for every individual. Some laugh, some cry, some are extremely expressive, others are filled with solemn peace. No matter what it looks like, experiencing His power and love is indescribable and draws us into the deeper part of God Himself.

We're not sure what season of life you're facing. Maybe it's a marriage where you feel alone, or you're divorced and feel abandoned by the one you loved and trusted. Or, you are fighting a sickness and you feel disconnected from the life you once knew.

Let us assure you that we are all made for a real connection to a heavenly Father who wants to heal our hurting hearts. 2 Corinthians 13:14 states, "May the grace of the Lord Jesus Christ, and the love of God, and the fellowship of the Holy Spirit be with you all." In His Presence, the Lord

---

236: Matthew 4:17
237: Luke 4:40
238: Matthew 14:13-21
239: John 4:24

allows us to experience what the Word told us was available to us: His grace and love. He is healing hearts, souls, bodies, and minds in the river of rest.[240]

LEARNING TO TRUST AGAIN

"Instead of your shame you will receive a double portion, and instead of disgrace you will rejoice in your inheritance. And so you will inherit a double portion in your land, and everlasting joy will be yours."[241]

We must not forget that the story does not end on the Cross. Three days later, Jesus rose from the dead, was restored, made whole, and was seated at the right hand of the Father. Because of what He did, we are now welcome to join Him at the table.

When we are safe and secure in His Presence, there can be no fear or shame. Through Jesus, we are reinstated and restored to relationship with our heavenly Father. In other words, because of what Jesus did on the Cross, we receive our true identity back as the sons and heirs of God.

It took some time, but the Lord resurrected our marriage and our security. Our personal journey consisted of working with different therapists before we found one that could speak into our emotional and spiritual wounds. During that same time, we both submitted ourselves to periods of personal reflection and inner healing. Much of this was spent with trained counselors and mentors that faithfully ministered to us in the Father's Presence.

However, everyone's road to restoration looks different, which is a good thing! God made every human unique. Because of this, we strongly encourage you to seek the Lord and godly counsel in your own reconciliation. Only He knows the future and He Promises it is for your best. Our confidence is not in an outcome; it is in the nature and goodness of God Him-

---

240: Isaiah 66:12
241: Isaiah 61:7-8

self. He says in Isaiah 61:3, He will "bestow on them a crown of beauty instead of ashes, the oil of joy instead of mourning, and a garment of praise instead of a spirit of despair. They will be called oaks of righteousness, a planting of the Lord for the display of His splendor."[242]

Here is the pivotal lesson that we want you to catch. *Our marriage restoration did not make or break His faithfulness.* In fact, no life circumstance can change the fact that God is faithful. The truth is that divorced, widowed, sick, or not, His Promises *are still true.*

THROUGH THE STORMS

> *"Shadrach, Meshach and Abednego replied to him, 'King Nebuchadnezzar, we do not need to defend ourselves before you in this matter. If we are thrown into the blazing furnace, the God we serve is able to deliver us from it, and he will deliver us from Your Majesty's hand. But even if He does not, we want you to know, Your Majesty, that we will not serve your gods or worship the image of gold you have set up.'"*[243]

Lisa, a friend of mine, experienced this truth firsthand as she signed the divorce papers sent to her by her now ex-husband. She had spent close to three years waiting for him to move home and once again make their family complete.

Over those years, Lisa tried marriage counseling, peer mentoring, healing prayer, and declaring truth over their marriage. She had held onto the promises, praised, and pleaded, but in the end, nothing had changed and she was alone. This wasn't the ending that Lisa had hoped and prayed for.

Nevertheless, the time waiting had not been wasted. All the hours in the Father's Presence had caused her to know her Father's heart for her. As she signed her name on the final line, her understandable pain was met with her new trust in God to take care of her. It was a bittersweet moment, one indicative of Lisa's security.

242: Isaiah 61:3
243: Daniel 3:16-18

Today, Lisa has joined one of our local prayer ministries. She spends several hours a week helping broken people and families work to be restored. She says she would have never known her calling without the time she had spent in the wilderness with her Father by her side.

Lisa is okay because she has the Lord; she transferred her hope to Him. He is the Author of perfect victory well beyond what we may understand at the moment.

BEAUTY FOR ASHES

Job 13:15 says, "Though He slay me, yet will I hope in Him; I will surely defend my ways to His face." When I was young, this worried me. Who would sign up to be slain?

What I later came to understand is that Job had faith in God's complete trustworthiness, dependableness, and kindness. Job understood that he as a man could not fathom the mysteries of God's plan. But most importantly, Job knew that no matter what might be in store for him while on the earth, his heavenly Father would not reject him.

Like Job, in my greatest moments of hurt and despair, I knew God was for me and not against me. Inside I was dying, but I knew He carried life and that was exactly what I so desperately needed. I determined to trust in Him, *though He slay me.*

At that point, I had no guarantees. I didn't know that my family would one day be the whole again, but I knew something more important: God held me and the answers for my life. He would take my ashes and make them something beautiful, just as He did for Bathsheba.

Bathsheba means "daughter of the oath" in Hebrew.[244] She was a woman who was horribly abused. Her husband was murdered. Her baby that came

---

244: Easton, M., M.A., D.D., *Illustrated Bible Dictionary, Third Edition.* Public domain: Thomas Nelson, 1897.

from a one-night stand died. She must have felt so alone, so rejected, and so afraid.

But she was the "daughter of the oath," the daughter of the *covenant*. God proved Himself faithful to restore her hope and her future. She bore a son who went on to be one of the most famous kings who ever lived: King Solomon.

It doesn't matter how hopeless or out of control things look. If we can safely turn toward our Father God, there is hope. As long we're living in this world, life's issues are inevitable. Even if there is no divine intervention for your circumstance, you can still find comfort in knowing that you can run to His Presence. Once there, He is faithful to lead you out of the wilderness and into your Promise.

Let's pray,

> *"I ask You to give me wisdom on my journey through healing. Show me the way to go. Lead me by Your love. Bring me into Your Presence. Amen."*

CHAPTER TEN
The Path to the Promised Land

"They are not just idle words for you—they are your life.
By them you will live long in the land you are crossing
the Jordan to possess."[245]

If there was ever a man who needed restoration, it was Moses. Moses was filled with self-doubt, and he suffered from a stutter.[246] He was isolated and nowhere near living out his calling. However, the role that God assigned to him since birth was to deliver the Jewish people from slavery. But how could he do that, Moses reasoned, when he was afraid to talk out loud?

God replied to the complaint by saying, "Who gave human beings their mouths? Who makes them deaf or mute? Who gives them sight or makes them blind? Is it not I, the Lord?[247]

The Bible is not clear why Moses had a fear of talking to people. Who knows, perhaps children made rude or hurtful comments in the palace when he stumbled over a difficult word. Many times, it is the little com-

---

245: Deuteronomy 32:47
246: Exodus 4:10
247: Exodus 4:11

ments or internal doubts that impact us the most. These slights can result in an overwhelming and seemingly unexplainable insecurity.

We know that all Moses' weaknesses and failures didn't change his assignment from God. The Father still chose to use Moses. God didn't rebuke Moses for his unworthiness. Instead, God brought Moses into *His* Presence. And, as Moses encountered the inspiring Presence of God through the burning bush, he began to transform into his new identity as a deliverer.

It is worth noting that Moses did not change his mind on his adequacy or preparedness for the task set before him. Rather, he began to trust God more fully. His sight and thoughts moved from himself to God. Face to face with God, it was no longer unthinkable for him to lead the Israelites from the bonds of slavery in Egypt. This change, also called metamorphosis, began when Moses recognized that what he had encountered in the bush was the Great I Am. God's Presence was the source of his restored identity.

There is a fascinating layer to Moses' story that is not often discussed. *Moses was not cured of his speech impediment.* Why? This seems rather unusual, doesn't it? What did God have in mind?

In my opinion and for the purpose of this study, we can use this as an illustration of how God makes beauty from ashes. Moses' speech impediment forced him into community and reliance on his brother Aaron, the Levite who apparently was a good public speaker. Like Moses, God will bring brothers and sisters alongside us on the journey to strengthen us in our weakness, to speak truth, to help bear our burdens.

While deep roots of insecurity are only fully healed in God's Presence, our Father often uses healthy community to jump start the process. The Church, as a community, has the beautiful privilege of helping one another connect to the Master Restorer. In His Presence, there is no division; it is no longer just about us. In His Presence, we are forced to be aware of and respond to our family's needs. It is God's desire that we cross the desert and enter the Promised Land as community on a collective journey, just as his chosen people did in the Bible. In order to be prepared for this assignment, we all need an unrelenting dedication to wait on the Lord. Remember, our healing takes place on His timeline, not ours.

RISKY BUSINESS

Do you remember Mary? She was the sister who chose to be in the Lord's Presence over helping out in the kitchen.[248]

Her sister, Martha, who was doing all the work, tried to shame Mary into helping her out.[249] Martha emphasized that Mary was wasting her time, *that her performance mattered more than her relationship.*

Relationship with Jesus depends on connection. He was ready and willing to be close to both Mary *and* Martha; however, relationship takes two people who desire to trust and risk. One person constantly striving for approval is not a relationship. It is an actor's performance.

Poor Martha. She must have been quite insecure. Love felt like something to be earned through work, not something given freely out of a covenant relationship. We often fall into the same trap, wanting the approval of man rather than Christ. We want others to acknowledge our sacrifice, expecting people to agree with our scorekeeping. In this, we attempt to try to find significance or acceptance. Of course, it is not fulfilling because it comes from the wrong source: ourselves.

I, Diane, often tell the people whom I mentor that close relationships are a lot like rock climbing.

Imagine yourself after climbing to the top of a rock wall. It's taken everything in you to climb to the top. The wall represents life's difficult journeys. It is marked with your blood, sweat, and tears and pain.

Your partner is on the ground attached to you by a thin rope. Of course, it is your goal to get back down somehow. If you know anything about rock

---

248: Luke 10
249: Luke 10:40

climbing, you know that in order to make it down safely, you have to trust your partner to get you back to the ground. The process involves counter-intuitively leaning away from the wall.

You could cling to the wall, but the risk of falling and getting hurt grows exponentially minute by minute. Another bad option is to stay up at the top. That solution keeps us paralyzed, stuck in a state of confusion, afraid of the journey.

Holding onto the wall is the same thing as holding onto your pain, your shame, and your fears. We experience no vulnerability or trust in this option. Martha operated in a similar manner. Her need to prove her worth through work didn't allow her to experience the genuine acceptance and security of her relationship with Jesus.

Neither holding on or staying at the top is a plan for lasting security. Unfortunately, most of us have tried these options all too often. The only legitimate choice to safely descend is to lean away from the wall, *to risk being seen at your worst*, and trust your partner to get you down. Fear and shame are barriers that can keep us from leaning out away from the wall. Fear of not being liked or a fear of feeling rejected are examples of our fears. Shame of failing or shame of letting everyone down are additional barriers we may encounter. Regardless, if our ultimate goal is experiencing that connection with others and God, *it will take some risk on our part.*

Becoming vulnerable about our fears and shame with others opens the door to real connection and healing. It is the same with our relationship with God. We need to encounter handing over our pain and then, learn to trust Him. We have to literally "lean into" His Presence. In exchange, He gives us healing, security, and an intimate relationship. This is a much better alternative than staying on the wall. It's lonely at the top. Maybe it is time to lean back into the Father's Presence.

DRINKING FROM THE WELL OF RELATIONSHIP

True security lies with Jesus. However, He often uses people to serve as His conduits. For me, Diane, it is not uncommon for people to have to learn to trust me before I can help them restore their trust in God. Once trust is gained, I am able to speak and they are able to hear. I am able to assure them of their value. I am able to emulate His love and they are able to develop their own relationship with the Father. They now are willing to encounter God's truth.

Remember Julie, the friend who struggled with trusting men and who fell into an addiction? We discovered early on that her journey of growing in trust towards God was going to take patience. What's more, Julie's healing had to take place within a supportive community. God did not create us to be independent or self-sufficient. Our brokenness can be used to provoke us into a healthy relationship with our Heavenly Father, the body of believers, and our family. She found tools to help her stay accountable to living a godly lifestyle as well as experiences that immersed her in the Holy Spirit's Presence. Thankfully over several months of inner healing prayer and intentional time spent with the Father in prayer and the Word, Julie began to release her old identity of shame and fear. She moved from a person who would not naturally look you in the eye to a woman whose primary ambition was to love others well.

As any parent knows, our children take on many of our traits, both good and bad. You end up looking like those with whom you spend time. Julie began to look like Jesus. Safe and secure in her Maker's love, she is now happily married to a great man. She also serves as a greeter and prayer minister at her church. She tells us it is her mission to love others into the Kingdom of God!

There is an unspoken agenda in many church settings that hints at the idea that God is only faithful when we're good enough, that He can only use people who are totally whole. This is why there are so many people who are afraid to be honest at church. We all want to show up Sunday mornings with our act together.

"Me, struggling with depression? Have you ever seen someone smile more than me?"

"My marriage is great. We never argue. *Ever.*"

"My children are pretty much perfect. My daughter doesn't struggle with drugs. No way."

The truth is, this comes from a lack of understanding God's faithfulness in our lives. God is faithful when we are at our worst. This is the glory of His covenant; He will never forsake us, and He will never leave us.[250] He wants you in a healthy community, to be unafraid to speak words of blessing and words of restoration. He wants us doing real life with those around us, just like Julie.

COUNTERFEIT PROMISED LAND

The Promised Land provides us a picture of how God's government works. God made the initial promise to Abraham for the land long before it became a reality. Then with Moses, He took his people on a journey to prepare them to trust Him and Him alone. His goal was not just to get His chosen people to the Promised Land. It was to prepare them to rule and reign over the enemies they would encounter in the land, enemies in the natural and in the spirit. This merging of the spiritual and physical realms continues to illustrate how God intends to mature His Church today. We are to naturally flow with redemption and restoration for a world bound by deception and chaos. The world will notice. However, unless we have the courage to cross the Jordan, we too, like the Israelites, will spend our years on earth wandering around in no-man's land.

If we are not seeing fruitfulness in our Christian lives, we need to ask the hard questions about where we have taken up residence. If we are not living on the right side of the Jordan, *it is time to move.* Don't strive to paint your wilderness green. And if we are living in the wilderness, it is time to ask the harder question: *Why?*

250: Deuteronomy 31:6

For one thing, the idea that life is to be endured on earth until we arrive in Heaven blinds us from God's full restoration power. We see the world's problems and we hope for a quick escape. This is a cop-out and a cheap substitute for the abundant life Jesus promises us.[251]

Many Christians view the world as their enemy, or they may fear the power they carry is really not sufficient to overcome today's evil.

Many of us have not experienced real power in action. We may not have seen people healed or delivered. Sure, we've read about it, but unless we experience it, uncertainty will linger. And so, doubting His ability to work miracles today, we allow ourselves to live a life of indifference and complacency when it comes to the heart of the Gospel.

What's more, we intuitively know deep down that giving up control creates a place of reliance on someone else. This causes us great fear, and in turn we keep people at a safe distance, including our heavenly Father.

WALKING THE WALK

Religion without power gives us an illusion of who God is. Experience proves that it is difficult to have full confidence in something that only lives in a lifeless ritual. Devoid of power, is it any wonder that the Church has marginal influence over society? Perhaps the real reason is that much of the Church is not engaged, or at least not using the real power, wisdom, and love He intended us to use on earth.

How do we help bridge the gap and walk with the same conviction, compassion, and boldness as our Lord?

First, we must become aware of those things that hold us back; things that may not seem harmful on the surface, yet keep us from pressing deeper into the genuine Good News. Jesus came to not only save us, He came to free us.

251: John 10:10

It is important to look at evil through a spiritual lens. We must see it clearly as a spiritual condition in need of a spiritual solution. The Church has a mandate to rise to her position of authority, to carry more than our own human power in the natural. We do this by walking in intimacy with the Father, not by spending any more time and energy disagreeing with fellow Christians. Or, worse yet, by remaining passive, confused, or ignorant.

One of the ways we often get stuck in the wilderness is isolation and self-sufficiency, feeling we have to *earn* our way into the Kingdom of God, *earn* His Promises, and *earn* our eternal salvation. This stronghold spirit urges us to operate on our own strength and wisdom instead of God's power, grace, and wisdom. This is a counterfeit version of our faith. It tricks some into thinking they've got it "made in the Kingdom shade." However, counterfeits are not capable of producing lasting fruit in His economy. Be careful of the counterfeit of resting in your own understanding or experience Lean on His.[252] Jesus died so we could live in Him, not so we could continue in our own works of the flesh.

The religious spirit is a particularly dangerous counterfeit because it also keeps us isolated. When we measure our merit by our own might, we will always come up short, leaving us feeling unworthy and ashamed. In this place, it is easy to choose distance over vulnerability. Paul says, "Now if we died with Christ, we believe that we will also live with Him."[253] When we live with Christ, we cannot keep expecting to earn our way to the Father's heart. Quite the contrary; we are already there!

We must also embrace meekness. The Bible tells us, "But the meek will inherit the land and enjoy peace and prosperity."[254] In our culture, we view the meek as pushovers. How could they possibly impact society?

The proper translation of *meek* is "acting in humility," like Moses. Yet, he walked in great leadership. True meekness is not trusting in our own strength, but learning to rely on the Father. As our trust and understanding

---

252: Proverbs 3:5
253: Romans 6:8
254: Psalms 37:11

of our Father becomes larger, we begin to function closer to the victorious life available in Him. Our hearts become joined with Him and we look more like Him. We "take heart," not in our own victories, but in His.

Finally, we must realize that our Promises in Christ are fully established only in community. While it might be easier for me to operate without living in close connection with others, it is the plan He uses to advance His Kingdom. Furthermore, it is God's desire that we be joined with one another in covenant to truly carry the fullness of the Gospel, "This mystery is that through the gospel the Gentiles are heirs together with Israel, members together of one body, and sharers together in the Promise in Christ Jesus."[255]

NO MORE COUNTERFEITS

If living out of your flesh is a counterfeit kingdom, then our reliance on our performance turns out to be a *counterfeit god*. This issue is essentially a question of authority. We have to learn to trust in God, and "God is Spirit and his worshipers must worship in the Spirit and in truth."[256] If you want to be a God-worshiper, you have to be a Spirit-and-truth worshiper.

In Dutch Sheets' fabulous article, *Partnering in Authority: Who is Ruling Your World?*, he writes:

> *Even now, your outer world fights to have authority over you on a daily basis. It might be your job, or your family, your finances, or something completely different altogether. Whatever the case, living in bondage to your external world was never God's intention for you.* **You have been called to live under the rule of Christ, and consequently, to rule and reign over the earth in partnership with Him.**[257]

255: Ephesians 3:6

256: John 4:24

257: Sheets, D. "Partnering in Authority: Who is Ruling Your World?" *The Elijah List*. Albany: Elijah List Publications. April 27, 2017. Emphasis mine.

We cannot serve two kingdoms, as "Such a person is double-minded and unstable in all they do."[258] Adam and Eve were brought down in the Garden because they joined the wrong kingdom. If we aren't careful to clarify which kingdom we want to reside in, we too run the risk of separation due to sin and shame.

We can all end up serving idols created in ordinary things that we may not consider to be a problematic. They are our modern day equivalents to the Biblical "high places" where people worshiped in the Old Testament. We may not have stopped to think about how our careers, workouts, diets, kids, self-images, or bank accounts have kept us from being vulnerable with our Father. Anything or anyone that gives you more security than God is a wrong altar, an idol.

We know that we may be worshipping at the wrong temple when our consciences tell us something is off. Our *conscience* is our spirit warning us something is wrong.

As you are reading this, you may be thinking of obvious sins like immorality or hatred. But, the same can be said of going through the motions by going to church rather than living out the genuine Gospel in power. Or even serving others out of obligation rather than stepping into the assignment given to us by God Himself. Paul teaches us that those who live "having a form of godliness but denying its power...have nothing to do with such people."[259]

SETTING OUR WILL

When we set our will to do God's will, we find strength and purpose. Jesus said, "My food is to do the will of Him who sent Me and to finish His work."[260]

258: James 1:8
259: 2 Timothy 3:5
260: John 4:34

Self-will is a noun. It is defined as being stubborn or having an obstinate willfulness, as in pursuing one's own wishes and aims.[261] When we set our aims above God's, He cannot nourish us. It is as though we have clenched our jaws shut from receiving His blessing.

Our wills are continually before the face of God. He always knows whether our hearts are submitted to His plans and purposes, or whether we are set on having it our own way. Derek Prince teaches that our will, like the grain offering on the altar of the Temple, must be ground down to a fine flour. Our Father wants us as a pure substance, ready to be made into a pliable dough without resistance or opposition to His stretching and molding.[262]

We have the ability to choose to submit our will to His will. And when this choice is made, a world of healing is opened to us. It is His desire that we take on His name of love and leave our past names of shame and sin behind. The obstinate self-will holds on to negative labels and difficult life experiences. The soft, pliable, submitted will humbly believes they are who God says they are: loved, accepted, and important.

Our renewal is not built by our works *but by our full surrender.* When our desire is to allow Him to do what He desires, we are transformed. The more we allow ourselves to be led by the Holy Spirit, the more the resurrection power of Christ will reside in our mind, our wills, and our emotions. We will enter the Promised Land.

WALKING IN TRANSPARENCY

The enemy of our soul seeks to create agreements with habits or people who weigh us down and keep us from our ultimate freedom, essentially keeping us from our God-given destiny. Our hearts may desperately want to walk in transparency and freedom with the Father, but our insecurities hold us back.

261: "self-will." *www.dictionary.com. Unabridged.* Random House, Inc. 9 June. 2017.
262: Prince, D. *Entering the Presence of God: Moving Beyond Praise and Thanksgiving To True Worship.* New Kensington: Whitaker House, 2007.

Truth and transparency with the Father, and with each other, is the only path to freedom from the counterfeit. Hiddenness causes us to despair and conceal ourselves from those who are called to love us into wholeness.

When I, Neal, was walking on the wrong side of the Jordan and "serving my flesh" in my personal life, I was humbled by the love of a group of men from my previous Bible study. They approached Diane and asked how they could help with our reconciliation process. She simply explained to them she didn't need anything, but I did. She told them she believed my spirit was in jeopardy. The best thing they could do was to get on their knees and intercede on my behalf.

God is always faithful to have a "remnant" contending for breakthrough here on earth.[263] He is doing it right now in your life.

These brave men met at a local church at 6:00 a.m. once a week to petition for my healing. They took up the cause to battle for me when I wasn't able to hold my own sword. They are the heroes of the faith that held me up before the Lord. How they honored our family didn't bring them fame before man, it did not make them rich. It was an ugly war they waged on my behalf.

We must be willing to get in the mud with our brothers and sisters to help them back on track. Our churches should be a little more chaotic and messy. *It is the nature of healthy, real, covenant relationships.* This is true ministry. This is what it means to lay down your life for your friends.[264]

Hurting people don't need more doctrine and judgment. However, messy people are complicated. It is all too easy to judge and walk away, and it's certainly much easier than plunging into their untidy restoration process. We must be led by the Holy Spirit to uncover the deep needs of wounded hearts so they can draw near to the Father and receive healing. He directs us with discernment and love.

263: Romans 11:5
264: John 15:13

Our cooperation with God in the rebuilding process matters. We must choose to want connection. Dutch Sheets continues,

The degree to which you allow Christ into your inner world is the degree to which you will have authority over your outer world...In the same way, your life will be a clear indicator of the depth of relationship you carry with Christ. Do you walk in peace and joy, or are you as stressed out as unbelievers around you? Is your family thriving? Are you living a lifestyle of prayer, or do you simply speak of its power from a distance?[265]

If we believe the subtle lie that a fake reality is safer than the real thing, or we value certainty and tradition over increased fruit and health, our lives are on dangerous ground. A truly loving community, dedicated to transparency and vulnerability, will not allow a "plastic reality" to replace the genuine repair and mending needed in people's lives. It moves us to look past ourselves and be truly concerned for others, challenging us to work in unity and covenant.

In doing so, the Church becomes a true representative of the Father, moving in His power, pouring out His love, reaping a harvest of freedom and healing. Together, we bear one another's burdens, face the enemy, and cross over the Jordan, leaving the wilderness behind.

Let us pray for you,

"Father, I know as our readers draw near to You, You are drawing near to them. As they lay down their fears and hurts, You will fill them with Your love and freedom.[266] Pour out so much love on them that it spills over onto those around them! Amen."

265: Sheets, D. "Partnering in Authority."
266: James 4:8

CHAPTER ELEVEN
Something's Gotta Go

"You have taken off your old self with its practices and have put on the new self, which is being renewed in knowledge in the image of its Creator."[267]

IN THE FIRE

"The yellow flower," she told me, Neal, as she released a deep breath. "I know what it is…"

Maria dug deep into the recesses of her early childhood memories as a street urchin in Bogota, Columbia, as she attempted to answer my question in a ministry session.

My parents adopted Maria when she was around five years old. There were no birth records, so it was the doctors' best guess. As a toddler, Maria's birth parents could not afford to feed her. So, they chose to put her out on the streets of Bogotá. For over a year, Maria survived as a member of a group of toddlers who begged for food.

267: Colossians 3:9-10

Once my parents brought her home, it was years before she felt safe enough to go to bed without a little money for food hidden under her pillow. And that was the tip of the iceberg. It is almost inconceivable for most of us to suffer the kind of abandonment Maria had. The pain and fear she endured at such a young age are hard to fathom.

Maria was about to embark on a new career and had come to Diane and me for prayer and direction. During the prayer session, Diane turned to Maria and asked, "What does a yellow flower mean to you?"

Maria shook her head and said she didn't know.

Prompted by the Holy Spirit, Diane kept going, "I think it has something to do with your childhood."

Maria waited a moment. A memory was sparked.

"I remember something from that time. There was a voice that would speak down into the hole." As a child in Bogota, she had hidden under some floor boards where she could peek out. After her parents abandoned her, she found refuge in the dirt under this structure.

But a voice? Maria had told me about this distant childhood memory before. However, she had never told me about this voice.

"Whoever it was loved me," she remembered. "They brought me food."

"Who was it?" we asked.

Maria told us, "I don't remember a face."

We prayed with Maria and asked her if she would be willing to explore that a bit further. She was clearly nervous but also curious of the memory. Together we asked Jesus to reveal to her the face behind the voice.

Maria sat stunned in the moment as a flood of shock hit her consciousness, "I think it was God! He was keeping me alive! He knew me and protected me!"

God supernaturally took care of the food Maria needed to keep her alive. However, as the realization of what God had done sunk in, *Maria began to panic.*

You see, Maria categorizes herself as an avoidant relating style. As a result, her go-to response to *any* feelings or emotional need was to shut it down. She often chose to seclude and separate herself from vulnerable relationships. She had been doing this since she was a toddler, literally in order to survive.

But at this moment in time, there was nowhere for Mary to go. "Neal, I don't know if I can take this. I don't know if I can do this." She stood up and began to head towards to the door. Diane stepped in, "Do what Maria? What is happening right now?" Maria stopped, and in that moment made a hard decision. She decided to face the giant in her life, *remembering.*

"The yellow flower," she said as she released a deep breath. "I know what it is."

Shaking so hard she had to sit down, she told us, "It's where I came from."

"I'm remembering…"

"A flower farm."

"I…I was born there…on a flower farm."

Pieces all started to fall into place as she allowed herself to feel the memory of her earliest days in Columbia. God's prompt to Diane suddenly all made sense.

Amazingly, for her whole life, Maria always associated the color yellow with love. Sunflowers always filled Maria with joy. In this session, God used the image of a yellow flower to remind her that He had been watching over her from the moment she was born. Maria was never alone. Not for one moment.

This story is an example of how Holy Spirit can access the inaccessible parts of our brains where trauma has occurred. Through His directing our prayer, and Maria's submission to His work, she received breakthrough, but it was all through the power of the Holy Spirit!

THE FRUIT OF FACING THE GIANTS

Not long after that conversation, Maria called us to tell us it was time for her to stop running from her past. She told us that she had felt God's love for the first time in her life. Not just in speaking about His love but *experientially feeling* it. In the session of the yellow flower memory, God's Presence touched Maria and changed her forever. The overwhelming feeling of love was new and strange and had gone right to the place of abandonment in her life. Her own family may have left her, but her Father God fed her in the wilderness.

The natural outcome was that she began to seek out more of those feelings. She began to move a little closer to her relationships and allow herself to risk loving others. For the first time in her life, she was ready to work through the process of forgiving all the people who had hurt her so badly.

Today, she is moving closer towards the community of believers in her Church family. She is slowly letting people into the parts of her life that feel so shameful, so vulnerable.

Ultimately, she has chosen to let go of her old nature and hurts and turn to embrace who God had created her to be. She has stepped into her identity as a beloved child of God. Safe in the Father's love, Maria is no longer content to survive in the wilderness. She is ready to move into her Promise Land.

The question at hand is, are you ready?

Refusing to let go of your old nature means that you don't get to cross over to the Promised Land of an abundant life. Rather, you remain in the wilderness of self-will. We can choose to protect our egos and outward appearances, but it comes at a steep cost. When we don't admit our fears or our struggles, when we settle for a distant relationship with our Father God, we continue to wander in the wilderness of life. When we choose to obey our flesh over His Lordship, we trade our birthright for a bowl of stew.[268]

CIRCUMCISION

Alive in Christ, we are destined to live life on earth in a radically different way.[269] He promised we would receive healing, restoration, expansion, provision, fullness, and abundant life![270] However, odds are, at some point, there has been a *giant* standing between you and the promise.

A life lived below the purposes of God creates pain, disillusionment, and ultimately death in your spirit and destiny. Vulnerability is the key that allows God to access our heart, removing the enemy's ability to use shame or fear to enslave us in our failures or perceived inadequacies. Insecurity in matters of your health, finances, mindset, or relationships must be submitted to God so He can slay the giant.

Paul says, "A person is not a Jew who is one only outwardly, nor is circumcision merely outward and physical. No, a person is a Jew who is one inwardly; and circumcision is circumcision of the heart, by the Spirit, not by the written code. Such a person's praise is not from other people, but from God."[271]

He also teaches, "Whoever sows to please their flesh, from the flesh will reap destruction; whoever sows to please the Spirit, from the Spirit will reap eternal life."[272] Our flesh is not neutral. It wars against the Spirit of God. It has to go.

268: Genesis 25
269: Romans 6:11
270: John 10:10
271: Romans 2:28-29
272: Galatians 6:8

The only way to deal with the flesh is *circumcision*. It is a required action before entering the Promised Land of a fulfilled life in Christ. Let me be clear, I am talking about the circumcision of the heart.

Circumcision in the natural symbolizes the covenant relationship established between God and His people. It's beginning is with Abraham and is repeated at every *brit milah*, or circumcision ceremony, to this day among Jews.[273]

We all raise our hands if someone offers transformation, restoration, or healing. Who wouldn't want those things? But circumcision? Losing something? A painful surgical procedure? Not so much. However, the truth is unless we submit to the process, we risk only sowing seeds of our unrestored flesh and reaping the same rewards. Circumcision of your heart ensures that your promise of an abundant life in Christ will be fulfilled completely in partnership with God. We must choose. He will not force us to chose Him. We must recognize it is possible to forfeit our inheritance. How horrible it would be to discover it was made available here on earth and we never realized it.

ADONAI IS SEMPER FI TO SANCTIFY

For us, the process of circumcision took six months of marriage counseling with a few different therapists. Within both of us, some things needed to die and others had to be brought to life. As we risked trusting each other again, we started to become more honest about our emotional needs and desires. The healing power of Jesus began to work on our hearts and in our lives. Our covenant with Him and with each other was reclaimed and renewed.

For anyone who has felt the sting of betrayal, you know that the hardest thing that I, Diane, had to do was to learn how to forgive Neal. I can honestly say that my greatest progress was made in time spent in the Presence of the Lord. Through the Word, prayer, and praise, the Holy Spirit

---

273: Genesis 17:7, Leviticus 12:2

ministered to me and spoke to me about His love and safety in my life. In my raw vulnerability, I began to trust both Father God and Neal once again. My personal journey to security had hit a huge bump in the road. But the destruction the enemy planned took a sharp detour when I chose to *lean into* Jesus. Regardless of what happened inside Neal's heart, regardless of what happened to our relationship, I had to forgive him fully.

On the other hand, for me, Neal, the hardest thing I had to do was *forgive myself*. I needed to recognize that God's love for me was not based on my performance. I had always been proud of my family heritage of hard work and integrity. I feared I had lost the very things I held most dear: my reputation and my family. In the wilderness of my bad decisions, I found myself unemployed and not sure who I was anymore. I was constantly appalled by the choices I had made, and the hurt and embarrassment I had caused my family.

In addition to all the family repair and healing, a geographical move was necessary for our fresh start. In the process, we lost our support groups and gained the stress of starting over in a new city. On a positive note, the move forced us to rely on each other as friends in a way we had not done in years. I often found myself on the floor in front of my Father God, pouring out my heart in repentance. Floods of grace and peace overwhelmed me during those times. I discovered how He continued to love, accept, and value me even when I couldn't do that for myself. Unfortunately, I learned dependence on Him as a last resort.

As our flesh was removed, the Lord allowed us to see more clearly the hideous destructive potential caused when we don't follow God's purposes for covenant and connection. He gave us eyes to see the garbage in our lives as well as the hurt it had caused. We moved from a place of judgment and hiding the truth, to a new place of freedom, where we exposed our failures and insecurities.

LIVING IT OUT

"Whoever can be trusted with very little can also be trusted with much, and whoever is dishonest with very little will also be dishonest with much. So if you have not been trustworthy in handling worldly wealth, who will trust you with true riches? And if you have not been trustworthy with someone else's property, who will give you property of your own?" [274]

Living a circumcised lifestyle means that you are no longer your own. You belong to Jesus. Everything you have is His. And everything He has is yours. He is the only righteous king with your best in mind. Anything you hold back from him is still under a different kingship.

All of that sounds good and true until you really ask yourself if all of your life is surrendered.

When you worship, do you worship with an abundant heart, or do you preserve your dignity? We are to be like Mary; our worship is perfume at His feet! The aroma will fill the room. Worship is warfare over your life and your family's destiny. It might annoy others at how much it costs us to worship the way we do, but when we are in love with Jesus, we won't notice the naysayers.

What about your money? Have you traded your inheritance for a bowl of stew like Esau? How are you feeding your appetites? With critical or judgemental thoughts? With easy entertainment? Are there things you engage in that might appear harmless? Perhaps your time is more precious than that particular activity or habit? Maybe it is something as simple as the Lord asking you to not click on a certain link, or not to engage in a particular conversation, but you ignore Him.

The counterfeit world is the lion crouching at your door, because "No one can serve two masters. Either you will hate the one and love the other, or you will be devoted to the one and despise the other. You cannot serve

---

274: Luke 16:10-12

both God and money."[275] The counterfeit always leads to destruction and death. It is a lie to think otherwise.

SELF-AWARE

We all have areas that need a fresh baptism. We all have areas that need pruning, a fresh circumcision. On the other hand, maybe you are already whole and living in the Promised Land! However, your old habits and patterns deceive you into thinking you are still living in the wilderness. Though the Lord has set an abundant feast before you, you are still living like you are a desert nomad. To put it another way, even though the Lord has healed you, you keep looking for something to be wrong with you. Or, worse yet you keep falling back into old unhealthy patterns.

As an example, consider Beth and her mother.

Beth told me that she was never really close to her mother growing up. It seemed that her mother saved all the frustrations of her day to let them loose on Beth each evening. Beth's mother would complain about how worthless and lazy she was, and how she never was going to find a man who would love her with all her faults.

Unfortunately for Beth, she grew up believing the same things about herself. After several relationships that ended in abandonment and betrayal, she was hopeless about her future and turned to the Lord.

It didn't happen overnight, but Beth slowly became immersed in her true identity as the apple of her Father's eye.[276] She began to deeply realize her worth and understand her destiny and place in the Kingdom.

During her journey of restoration, Beth came to know that insecure people may think thoughts and act out of their own hurt. Beth rejoiced in the fact that her mother's words no longer had the ability to enter into her

---

275: Matthew 6:24
276: Psalm 17:8

estimation of her personal value or stability. She knew her heavenly Father and trusted His wisdom and words above those of her family. She had crossed over.

THE TEST

Not long ago, Beth found the opportunity to go home for a holiday visit. During one of their discussions, her mother delivered an offhanded comment about Beth's physical features.

Beth said when she heard those words of critical judgement they didn't bring the usual pain and hurt. In fact, she told us, at that moment, she felt empathy for her mom. The moment caught Beth by surprise. It was a small but tangible evidence of how much God had done in her heart. Instead of plummeting emotionally for a week, she felt steady. She *felt* confident because she *was* confident. She knew who she was. Her mother's words were hurtful but did not pack the same power. She waited for that familiar feeling of shame and embarrassment to crop up, but it never did. Sure, she could have "gone there." However, Beth chose not to repeat the old cycle. Why would she deny what God had done? Why would she re-enter the wilderness?

GIANTS IN THE LAND

"They gave Moses this account: 'We went into the land to which you sent us, and it does flow with milk and honey! Here is its fruit. But the people who live there are powerful...they are stronger than we are.'" [277]

In many ways, we can easily make friends with our pain more than our promises. Like the ten spies, in the passage above, we see the giants in the land much more clearly than we see God's Promises for our lives.

277: Numbers 13:27

Earlier in Numbers 13, God told Moses to appoint chiefs from each family and send them into the land to inspect the land He was giving them.[278] After forty days, the men returned with a testimony of the fertile beautiful land, accompanied with terrifying tales of large fortified cities filled with giants. As the description of the giants grew and grew, the monsters quickly overshadowed the blessings of the land and God's promised inheritance. Consequently, they ended up living in the desert for another few decades.

God knows we must travel through the desert. He will maintain us with manna, quail, and shoes that will not wear out.[279] However, He does not want us to stay there. How long the trip takes is up to us. Ultimately, maintenance in the desert is choosing to stay in the place of struggle instead of claiming our Promised Land.

Maintenance is not reformation or winning the victory; it is maintaining the status quo. "Holding on till Heaven" is not revival, healing, or faith. It is not the fulfillment of His Promises for your life. It is just sleepwalking through a ritual or attendance on Sunday, hoping the sermon will not last too long so you can get back to *your* plans.

In order to claim what is ours, we must cross the Jordan from living in the flesh to living in the Spirit. We must surrender our thoughts to take on His wisdom. Then, we must learn to trust God enough to drive out the giants occupying the land.

ACTIVATE YOUR DESTINY

We've spied out the land. We've seen the promised blessings. However, we've also seen something there that scared us right back to the wilderness: *giants*.

What are your giants? Have you taken time to inventory them? We don't always see them well by ourselves. They like to hide from us. Pride, gossip, bitterness, or possibly an addiction. The list of giants is endless.

278: Numbers 13:1-16
279: Exodus 16:4, 13, Deuteronomy 29:5

What the Israelites missed was the fact that God would be with them. Of course on their own, they would never gain victory. But with God? Nothing is impossible; in fact, the victory is already complete in Him.

You are only responsible for exposing the giants holding you back. *Honesty births freedom.* We have to name the giants. We must stop running from them, hiding from them, and living with them. When we transfer our trust to God and partner with His sanctifying work, the giants will be driven out. But it takes partnering with the Holy Spirit.

Why doesn't God remove the giants for us? Let's go back to Numbers 14:9: "Only do not rebel against the LORD. And do not be afraid of the people of the land, *for they are our bread.* Their protection is gone, but the LORD is with us. Do not be afraid of them."

This verse tells us our struggle is also our bread or our sustenance. In fact, our struggle is what causes us to understand our victory is achieved only by fully relying on him. If we study this closely we find an incredible picture in the Hebrew words: *lechem* means bread[280], and *milchamah* means war[281], both of which share the same root word. We can draw from this play-on-words that battle and bread are intrinsically linked. God has more in mind during your battle than survival. Feasting and victory go hand in hand. Essentially, God says, "In your struggle, you will succeed because you'll have learned to fully trust Me. You will now occupy and govern the land with Me, and not just take a vacation there."

However, our natural response is often like that of the ten spies. It seems if we are going to occupy the Promised Land, and if *God is good,* He should just get them out of the way so that we can live in peace. However, that's not how it works. God knows that struggle is the door to bring us into occupying our Promises. While we can get tunnel vision regarding whatever giant we face, He always sees the bigger picture.

280: "H3899 - lechem - Strong's Hebrew Lexicon (NIV)." *Blue Letter Bible.* Web. 13 June, 2017.

281: Deuteronomy 29:7; "H4421 - milchamah - Strong's Hebrew Lexicon (WLC)." *Blue Letter Bible.* Web. 13 June, 2017.

On the other hand, if we see struggles as something within our power to overcome, we'll try. Hence, by leaving giants in the land, He offers us the chance to partner with Him to fully occupy His Promises.

God may or may not remove the struggle in your life. He alone has the ability to fully deal with whatever your issues might be.[282] His thoughts are bigger and better than ours.

Despite that, when things do not turn out the way we want, our natural tendency is to stop trusting God. When we do not understand what has happened, we sometimes reject our Father or question His goodness. Striving to make God understandable, we actually set ourselves above Him. This is shaky, dangerous ground, but not uncommon, especially in Western culture.

Trust God to see you through to completion. Trust Him to make you into the image of Christ. Trust Him to bring His Promises to pass. Surrender all that holds you back, nothing hidden. Shield none of your old man, your mind, your will, or your emotions. Let them all be transformed into a Spirit-led life. Demonstrate your trust by letting Him lead you.

No matter what, do not remain content to just survive wandering around in the wilderness. God has so much more for you than shoes that last a few decades. He has a Kingdom waiting for you. The Lord has already prepared a place for you inside the Promised Land. The city is built. It is beautiful and constantly growing. The fields are ready for harvest. The fruit is larger than you could ever have imagined.

Let's pray,

> *"Heavenly Father, we thank You for Your provision for us to live an abundant life on earth, even before we are in Heaven! I ask for wisdom as You lead me along the journey of surrender. Help me to fully trust You, to lean not unto my own understanding. May I seek You in all things no matter how small or insignificant they may seem. You can guide me to the peace and security that rests only in You. Amen."*

282: 2 Corinthians 12:7

163

CHAPTER TWELVE
Yes and Amen

"For no matter how many promises God has made,
they are 'Yes' in Christ. And so through Him the 'Amen'
is spoken by us to the glory of God."[283]

THE GOOD LIFE

We all have received promises from God. For the Israelites, it was the Promised Land. For some of us, it is a future relationship or business opportunity. Maybe your family will be reclaimed, your finances will have no lack, your body will be healed, or your heart will be restored.

Inside the Promised Land, there is always a bountiful harvest. His Kingdom is made to naturally multiply. Inside the Promised Land, we attain rest and joy; striving and struggle do not exist in the land of blessing. He also provides specific, individual promises for each one of His children. These are yours.

God promises that those who believe in Jesus and are baptized for the forgiveness of sins will be saved.[284]

283: 2 Corinthians 1:20
284: Mark 16:16, Acts 2:38

God promises to supply our every need as Paul assures us, "And my God will meet all your needs according to the riches of his glory in Christ Jesus."[285] God obligated Himself only to the extent of our *actual* needs. That includes food, clothing, shelter, companionship, love, and salvation (not necessarily a Ferrari!) through Jesus Christ.

God promises us victory over death.[286] He promises that we will never be separated from His love.[287] His grace is sufficient for us; His children will not be overtaken with temptation, "To Him who is able to keep you from stumbling and to present you before His glorious Presence without fault and with great joy."[288]

God promises that all things work together for good to those who love and serve Him faithfully.[289]

He promises rest: "Come to me, all you who are weary and burdened, and I will give you rest."[290]

He promises a good future: "'For I know the plans I have for you,' declares the Lord, 'plans to prosper you and not to harm you, plans to give you hope and a future.'"[291]

He promises power and strength, peace and confidence.[292]

His promises go on and on. But the most important thing to remember is not how many there are, but the fact that He keeps every single one. The only thing holding us back from accessing these promises is insecurity.

285: Philippians 4:19

286: 1 Corinthians 15:3-4, 57

287: Romans 8:37-39

288: 2 Corinthians 12:9, Jude 1:24

289: Romans 8:28

290: Matthew 11:28

291: Jeremiah 29:11

292: Isaiah 40:29-31, John 14:27

His promises are for everyone residing in "the city on the hill." If you are not moving in the power of the Spirit, laying hold of what He died for you to possess, odds are you are living on the wrong side of the Jordan.

Jesus purchased all authority on the Cross. He desires to share it with us, and the time to share the power He deposited in us is *here* and *now*. He will complete you if you let Him.

COACHING

"Really, coach?!" His eyes just about bugged out of his head. Jeremy obviously thought this was a bad plan.

Jeremy was a player of mine when I coached fifth grade basketball years ago. He sat at the end of the bench. He had a lot of strengths, just not in the area of athletics. As every good grade-school coach knows, fifth-grade sports teams have a normal bell-curve of talent. Jeremy was part of the bunch on the low slope.

However, our problem ran in a different direction. Your see, Jeremy struggled with his inside more than his outside. He tried to just blend in, but he obviously felt uncomfortable. His security level was low, and I desperately wanted to see him become a part of the peak of the curve in his emotional stability.

We were down to the last practice before the second to last game of the year. One of these boys, specifically Jeremy, *needed* to score. So, I had an idea.

"Guys," I said, turning to two of my best players during practice before the game, "every time you get the opportunity, I want you to pass it to Jeremy."

Later on, I told Jeremy, "Every time you touch the ball, I want you to throw it at the basket. I don't care how you throw it. You're shooting *every time* you get the ball."

His uncertain and shocked expression demanded reassurance.

"Yeah!" I said.

"Really?"

"I just want you to score," I encouraged. My goal was for all the team members to feel some measure of success on the court. I *wish* I could say it was my coaching philosophy, but it was not nearly that well thought out. As a father of three boys, I simply knew that a measure of success as a fifth grader can carry you a long way.

At the outset of my plan, things looked bad. The first couple of times Jeremy threw the ball all the way over the backboard.

Thankfully, he finally, he made one—swoosh!

Miraculously, the next time down the floor, he made another!

To the crowd, it might as well have been a slam dunk. The gym went wild, erupting into cheers.

Jeremy had the most surprised and satisfied look on his face as he took off running around the gym.

The next day rolled around, which happened to be our last game. I was quite surprised when I got a special visit from Jeremy's mom and dad, which as a coach is usually not a great thing.

"Can we talk to you?"

I braced myself internally as I racked my brain trying to remember if there would have been any reason throughout the season to cause them to be offended, especially after last night.

"We wanted you to know something. Our son slept in his jersey last night."

Their words sank deep into my heart as I imagined the young timid boy now filled with hope, *and hope for his future.*

In the supportive environment of a coach and teammates who were determined to see him succeed even in a small victory, Jeremy began to see himself as valuable.

In just one moment, his parents had a new kid on their hands. Jeremy no longer thought of himself as the uncoordinated kid on the bench. No, Jeremy now saw himself as the team player. He started to think of himself as a real athlete, and he had, in fact, become one. A few years down the line, he ended up playing on the high school team.

I still get choked up telling this story. Little did I know that one practice would birth a significant part of Jeremy's future.

We often do not know what God has in store for the people around us. Are we willing to believe in God's divine purpose when our eyes see human frailty or failure?

HEAVEN ON EARTH

Jeremy latched onto his true identity in a way few of us ever do. Most of us fear we are not good enough, that if others truly knew us, they would reject us. We fear that, if given the chance, we might fail, not just ourselves, but everyone connected to us. Our fears compel us to seek approval from the wrong sources or try to overcompensate for our "lack." Or worse, we refuse to try the very things God created us to do.

However, what happens when we receive our inheritance and actually use it? We become the city on the hill. We become like Jeremy and take over the game. We begin to cooperate with God's plans and purposes rather than remain enslaved to fear or hurt. You lead your team, your family, and your neighbors to achieve victory over the powers of darkness and bring Heaven to earth.

When we do this as the Church, we will determine the crime rate, our security, the health and wellness of our families, our economy, our city, our nation, and ultimately, the world. He has given us authority and dominion over evil; not in the future, but today! Not in Heaven, but here, on earth! After all, "The reason the Son of God appeared was to destroy the devil's work."[293]

The evil schemes of the enemy are not things we can ignore or hide from. The Church was not created to be a gated community, protected from the world. There is a game going on outside the walls of the church. The Lord wants us to play to win, transforming the world through the power and love living in us. His love is more powerful than any wickedness we encounter. *Greater is the power in you.*

The deceiver, wily fox that he is, tries to keep us from believing that we actually have what Christ says we have. Don't let fear keep you on the bench. Your perfect and forever encouraging Father wants you on the court. He wants you to score. In Him your success is assured; He is not limited by your stutter or lack of confidence. But you have to trust Him. If He says go for it, go for it.

THE MAKINGS OF A WINNER

What will it take to score a victory? It will take *our transformation,* to see with His eyes, to love with His love. It will take us fully joining with His plans, His power, and purposes. If we are going to meet the test of this hour, we must be fully engaged in the game. By spending time in His Presence, no matter the circumstance, we will gain His strength and perspective. We will be able to recognize the voice of the enemy and fight back with His truth.

Jesus was led by God into the wilderness to be tempted by Satan. He spent forty days fasting and praying.[294] At this point, Jesus was emotionally and physically exhausted. He was easy prey. Satan is a devouring lion and saw the state Jesus was in and thought he had hit the jackpot. He had found another Adam to deceive.[295] Jesus was isolated, tired, probably a little fuzzy

---

293: 1 John 8:8
294: Matthew 4:2
295: 1 Peter 5:8

brained, because while fasting is spiritually filling, it is also physically and emotionally exhausting.

It didn't matter, Jesus was prepared. He knew what was coming. He spent time with His Father and He knew His voice. His spirit could recognize the lies of the enemy. He fought back with the sword of the Word. He fought back again and again with, "It is written," and then repeated Scriptures' promised truths.[296]

It is easy to visualize our lack or the things that we think are keeping us from stepping into His Promises. We must choose to see His reality above our own; we must choose the superior Kingdom and lay hold of His Promises, arming ourselves with the truth of His Word.

PAUL'S STORY

Neal's co-worker, Paul, like many of us, desired love and tended to settle for finding it wherever he could. He told us that he was drawn to the attention and even the inappropriate affection of his new childhood stepfather. Unfortunately, the nature of this relationship left Paul even more wounded. He admitted the abuse and subsequent legal action had caused him confusion about himself and his worth. Paul's thoughts and emotions were definitely ruling his behavior at home and at work. He was desperately seeking a sense of peace.

Paul was the definition of a highly fearful attachment style. Paul feared both abandonment and intimacy in his relationships when he actually worked up enough courage to attempt to include someone in his life. His testimony included horrible stories of abandonment by his father and the physical abuse by his stepfather. Before he married Cindy, Paul spent most of his weekends in local bars and would often end up hungover in a stranger's bed. Similar destructive patterns followed him into marriage. The ensuing hopelessness and feelings of worthlessness were debilitating. Paul needed

---

296: Matthew 4:4

help for his crumbling marriage and career. His fear of vulnerability and lack of trust were slowly killing him.

How could one person have experienced so much harm by the people who should have kept him safe? How could Paul, currently so hopeless, move to a place of victory in his identity?

All the training in the world cannot heal a broken spirit. Yes, it can help curb unhealthy behavior, but at this level, true healing only comes from God. His need was so great, and we felt terribly inadequate to help our friend.

We cried out to the Lord for Paul's restoration, to reclaim what the devil had stolen from him: his childhood.

One morning, I, Diane, woke up and heard the whisper of the Holy Spirit, "Do you want to know how to fix Paul's deep-seated identity problems?"

Of course I did!

He continued, "You need to start below the surface, the places you may not immediately see. You need a balance of truth and love. If the first thing you do is address the consequences of his pain or sin, then he won't hear you. In fact, he will rebel from your attempt at correction."

That made sense.

"Start at the beginning of his hurts."

I nodded in understanding, He wanted to go after Paul's attachment wounds.

Even though Paul had experienced horrible abuse, he had also suffered ongoing abandonment in his early childhood. This left him in constant pursuit of finding the love of a father, someone who would speak life into his innermost being and identity.

Neal and I set up a meeting with Paul and we worked together on a reparative plan that included immersing him in the perfect security of God's Presence. We understood the power of allowing Paul to experience Father God's joy and pleasure over his life. Paul also agreed on some significant time spent in a mentoring relationship that provided safe "family" interaction. All of these connections created security and accountability in his life, paving the way for healing.

Relational healing is often a process where we can allow the deeper layers of our own experiences to slowly unravel. It is in this space of vulnerability that we can make sense of them, one by one.

There were many hours spent pouring life and love into Paul's broken and hurting world. We had a front row seat to his metamorphosis as God showed him his true Kingdom value and significance.

In the Presence of God's love and grace, Paul found forgiveness, restoration and peace birthed out of a desire to look like his heavenly Father. Paul began to walk out the destiny of who he was created to be. His name was changed from bondage to freedom and life. His career began to stabilize. Paul and his wife repaired their relationship and found healing for their battle-worn family. He crossed the Jordan, he faced and allowed God to slay the giants, and he took up residence in His Promises.

He was so thankful for his new freedom and peace that he decided to find a way to help others struggling with this type of betrayal in their lives. The last time we spoke, he was in the process of starting a support group for men that were victims of abuse. This is quite the harvest! And an enormous victory for the Kingdom.

TAKING OUR PLACE

"Although I am less than the least of all the Lord's people, this grace was given me: to preach to the Gentiles the boundless riches of Christ, and to make plain to everyone the administration of this mystery, which for ages past was kept hidden in God, who created all things. His intent was that now, through the church, the manifold wisdom of God should be made known to the rulers and authorities in the heavenly realms, according to his eternal purpose that he accomplished in Christ Jesus our Lord."[297]

If all we do is look at our "needs," we don't get back on our feet and take our place as victors. We often stay in our pain *and* fall apart in the process.

When Neal and I began the journey of starting over and reclaiming our marriage, it seemed insurmountable. We thought we were benched for good. Our whole family was desperate for healing and stability. In a new city, we fought to forge a new relationship with one another, we fought to start new careers, and we fought to find a new community and church. The entire crossing had born a toll on our bodies, souls, and emotions.

So, what did it take to be victors?

Our job was to keep our eyes on Him and not the size of the difficulties. We made it a priority to carve out time for the Word, prayer, and worship. In addition, we often quoted our prophetic Promises back to the Father. We made it a habit to faithfully remind each other of God's love for each other. We filled our lives with the life-giving Presence of Father God. Then, we inhaled and took a leap of faith. We got back in the game. We grabbed hold of our security in our heavenly Father, and not in ourselves.

You are not disqualified because of what you have gone through. Our Father God does not expect perfection, and we all fall short.[298] However, that does not change the Lord's willingness and power to do everything

---

297: Ephesians 3:8-9
298: Romans 3:23

He says He will do. Including His promise to deliver us safely to the Promised Land.

And what a land it is. Inside the Promised Land there is no scarcity; His Kingdom knows no lack. Inside the Promised Land, we are filled with the power to "Heal the sick, raise the dead, cleanse those who have leprosy, drive out demons."[299] Inside the Promised Land, His love supernaturally fills us and overflows out onto the world. Our own compassion is insufficient. Life becomes more abundant beyond what we can ask or think.

I'm ready to lay hold of my Promised Land. Are you?

Let's pray,

> *"Father, I thank You that You have abundant plans and purposes for my life. I ask for wisdom and discernment. Show me how You want me to serve others. I ask for help to live in Your Kingdom Promises. Amen."*

299: Matthew 10:8

CHAPTER THIRTEEN

Discovering the Abundance of God:
What's in Your Checkbook?

"I remain confident of this: I will see the goodness
of the Lord in the land of the living."[300]

"I am coming to You now, but I say these things while I
am still in the world, so that they may have the full measure
of My joy within them."[301]

ABUNDANT LIFE

You have a checkbook with an enormous amount of resources in it just for you from your heavenly Father. If you are willing to invest your suffering and loss into God's great plan, adversity can be your springboard for healing and multiplication.

Most people have no idea what's in their checkbook. The enemy does not want us to cash in on what is ours because when we do it represents his defeat. It is all too easy to believe that our inheritance, the goodness of God, is only available once we reach Heaven. This lie is birthed out of a re-

---

300: Psalm 27:13
301: John 17:13

ligious spirit and a poverty mindset. We are deceived into believing that we are "just barely making it through" or "enduring till the sweet by and by."

Understandably, this can make us feel anxious, hopeless, and insecure. We live each day wondering if we have been good enough or done enough to please God. Is it any wonder that the joy, peace, rest, and grace that God promises us always seems just out of our grasp? Our local pastors once said, "What most Christians have, the world does not want, or more importantly, desire to follow."

The reality is that "very few people want what Christians have." This stands in stark contrast to the prophet Haggai's proclamation that, "What is desired by all nations *[which we believe is the inheritance the Father has given us made manifest in Christ himself]* will come, and I will fill this house with glory." (Haggai 2:7).

Until we step into our full identity as God's children, including stewarding our inheritance here and now, all creation continues to suffer the effects of the fall. The world is desperate to discover the key to overcoming depression, sickness, and deficiency. They are waiting for a Church to show the world His glory. It is imperative that followers of Christ be mature in faith and display His victory, conquering defeat. This means letting go of our insecurities and carrying what He put in our checkbook into a hurting world.

YOUR TALENT

After hearing the spies' report about the giants occupying the Promised Land, many voted to go back to Egypt.[302] They didn't understand the weight of their inheritance and felt they would rather live in the certainty and stability of slavery rather than the freedom and prosperity of the Promise. Why? Because all they knew was slavery. They had never tasted freedom. However, even though they still trusted slavery more than freedom, it did not change the reality that freedom existed.

302: Numbers 14:1-4

Sadly, their refusal to receive their inheritance stemmed from a wrong picture of who God is and who He made them to be. Let me explain: they didn't know what to do with the provision that God had given them to steward their talents.

In the parable of the talents, a master entrusts his property, or finances, to his servants before leaving on a trip. He doled out various amounts for each one of them to take care of. One got five bags of gold, another two, and the last, one.[303]

The first two servants invested the money and doubled it! But the third, afraid to risk losing the single bag, buried it.

When the master returned home, he rewarded the servants who grew his wealth. These two had earned more responsibility. However, the third was punished, and his single talent was taken away and given to the servant who had the greatest return on his investment!

It was fear that kept him from stewarding the master's talents. Don't bury what God has given you. We may not even know we have buried our treasure because we are unwilling to have God show us what our treasure is. We sometimes think if we don't acknowledge these talents, God might not hold us accountable for growing them.

Remember, simple obedience to God is an act of worship. When obedience stems from trust, we learn the art of stewardship. In that place, we even learn how to steward loss and suffering.

Admittedly, suffering and loss may be bags of gold we are all tempted to bury. However, in the Kingdom, pain does not represent loss and failure; it represents breakthrough and new realms of dominion. Think about these extreme Promises of God and what he exchanges for our suffering when we are in Christ.

303: Matthew 25:14-30

"And the God of all grace, who called you to his eternal glory in Christ, after you have suffered a little while, will Himself restore you and make you strong, firm and steadfast. To Him be the power for ever and ever. Amen."[304]

"Not only so, but we also glory in our sufferings, because we know that suffering produces perseverance."[305]

"These have come so that the proven genuineness of your faith—of greater worth than gold, which perishes even though refined by fire—may result in praise, glory and honor when Jesus Christ is revealed."[306]

"You intended to harm me, but God intended it for good to accomplish what is now being done, the saving of many lives."[307]

Joseph was sold into Egyptian slavery by his own brothers.[308] As a slave, he earned his master's trust and rose to a level of prominence over the other household slaves.[309] Not long after, the deception and accusations of his master's wife landed Joseph unjustly in prison.[310]

Behind bars, God granted Joseph the ability to interpret dreams, and one day he interpreted a dream which could have been his way out of jail. Sadly for Joseph, the man who should have spoken for his freedom forgot about him *for two more years.*[311]

Through a fascinating plot twist, when Joseph was finally released from prison, it was to take an elevated position in the government.[312] Through the Holy Spirit, Joseph knew the region would go through a devastating

---

304: 1 Peter 5:10-11
305: Romans 5:3
306: 1 Peter 1:7
307: Genesis 50:20
308: Genesis 37:28
309: Genesis 39:4-5
310: Genesis 39:20
311: Genesis 40-41
312: Genesis 41:40

famine.[313] His efforts to prepare the region for survival were so successful that in the end, he rescued his own brothers who sold him into bondage in the first place.[314]

During his trials, Joseph trusted in the Promises of God. He knew that God had a plan for his life. He endured the difficulties because of his faith in God's Word and stepped back to watch God work. He refused to retreat into depression, anger, or unforgiveness. Ultimately, what we view as devastating loss and rejection in Joseph's life, God used as the vehicle to save millions of lives.

There is always a bigger picture than what we can see from our perspective.

DEALING WITH CRISIS

The man pointed in my, Neal's, direction and spoke, "Someone on this side of the church is very ill and God wants you to know that he is going to heal you." At about that time, God's Presence overtook me. My body heated up as if on fire and stayed that way for the rest of the service.

Not long before, I had gone in for a routine exam and was barely awake when the doctor started talking to Diane and me. "You have a large mass, it doesn't look good, I am pretty sure it is cancer. We need to schedule surgery as soon as possible."

I remember the fear on his face more clearly than his words. It was Stage 3 cancer. I was only thirty-eight years old.

The following two days were frantic. I remember praying with our pastor before they wheeled me into surgery. Everyone was trying so hard to be brave, but I could feel their fear and hopelessness.

313: Genesis 41:27
314: Genesis 42:3

Thankfully, the surgery was a success and they got the whole tumor, several inches of my colon, and several areas of my lymphatic system.

The bad news: I had a 40% chance of surviving another two years.

What did that even mean? The words didn't make sense. We had just had our third son. I still had to coach their teams. I needed to see them graduate, to get married, and to start their own families!

My answer to that diagnosis was strange even coming out of my own mouth.

"I've risked deals on lower odds than that. We will beat this."

Yet, after a year of treatments including chemotherapy, radiation, and a radical change in diet to protect my immune system, it didn't seem like we were winning the battle.

No matter how weak I was, I found great peace in being with the Lord and the people of faith. My healing did not happen overnight. My numbers didn't drastically change in an instant, although for some this has happened.

What was different? *I knew* that God was fighting for me and I was safe in His plan for my life. *Whether I lived or died, in that moment it became clear that God would be faithful to me and my family.*

The faith He deposited in me in those precious minutes strengthened me to face my illness and carried me through future life struggles. My more avoidant relating style was still learning to trust the Lord to fight for me. However, I discovered God is faithful and He *will* recover all things, even when *we don't know how* he will do it.

UNDER PRESSURE

Every Christian must reach the place where they know beyond a shadow of a doubt that there is no peace or safety apart from God, that the fullness of life is found only in Him.

This fullness is beyond what we understand. We must look beyond the pain and struggle to trust for our breakthrough. Our feelings of pressure and suffering produce godly character if we let it!

Over and over again in the Bible, we watch how the Jews react under pressure. For instance, the more pressure Pharaoh exerted on the Jews in Egypt, the more God raised their stature and blessed them. This persisted to the point where, not only did God deliver the Israelites from slavery with great drama and fanfare, but He made sure they left loaded down with their former master's gold, jewels, and livestock.[315]

Human perspective says the Israelite's pain, suffering and slavery, would only produce exhaustion and failure. God's perspective said it would produce a new identity, vast wealth and freedom.

For me, the process to freedom took time. Now, I am living a full life and I am cancer-free. Facing a serious illness, with a young family, pleading for my life from a hospital bed, was not one of my many life plans. We learned that our lifespan is not within our control. We also realized we could not take the little things in life for granted. Moments with the children or special events became much more precious to both Diane and me. My children's laughter and their tears took on more significance. I would never give up how we were transformed during those years.

God is working the events of our life with the hands of a skilled craftsman. It's a mistake to believe God is not there with us during our trials. We must let Him have His way. We have to trust Him to see us through until the end. No matter what talent He gives you, invest it wisely. It will yield a priceless return!

315: Exodus 3:22

SABBATH: THE REST OF THE STORY

"And without faith it is impossible to please God, because anyone who comes to Him must believe that He exists and that He rewards those who earnestly seek Him."[316]

Not long ago, I, Diane, was complaining to God because of my workload.

"Why do the busy people get asked to do more?" I prayed.

It certainly felt unfair!

My family taught me to be a hard worker and have high expectations for myself. These values were good, in and of themselves. However, I was getting tired and the load was *heavy*.

I told Him, "I love You, God, and I feel privileged that You want to use me. But, maybe we could spread the workload out a bit? I have some thoughts about this if You would like my help."

I very quickly heard the Lord whisper; "I trusted you with three talents and you did well, so I have given you more!"

This reality is a key principle in His Kingdom. His natural law of multiplication!

He continued to instruct me, "It's not that you're just a hard worker. It's that you have learned how to multiply this seed well. You have earned the ability to have more."

He paused.

"But...you need to work out of a place of rest."

The Sabbath rest of the New Testament is defined as shifting from the natural kingdom into a Kingdom where *He* drives out the giants, *He* creates

---

316: Hebrews 11:6

the victory, *He* establishes us as *His* reigning representatives in the earth. We are often guilty of trusting Him for our salvation but not much else in our lives. The truth is that through Him, all the families of the earth are to be blessed by us. *It is His effort, not ours.*

Hebrews 4:9-11 tells us:

> *By faith [Abraham] made his home in the Promised Land like a stranger in a foreign country; he lived in tents, as did Isaac and Jacob, who were heirs with him of the same promise. For he was looking forward to the city with foundations, whose architect and builder is God. And by faith even Sarah, who was past childbearing age, was enabled to bear children because she considered him faithful who had made the promise.*

Our Sabbath is no longer to stop working one day out of seven, though that is healthy. Rather, as believers, we are to *continually* rest in the Person of Jesus Christ and His finished work on the Cross. We allow His Spirit to rule over our soul, and through faith, our "work" becomes obsolete. Growing in the security of His love removes the need to strive in anything we do. Our rest is found only in Jesus who accomplished all of God's work in our place.

But, do not confuse "works" with fruitfulness. We are given a clue of what fruitfulness looks like in Genesis 28. In this chapter, Jacob dreams of a ladder proceeding into Heaven with angels *ascending* and *descending*.[317] In Christ, the Sabbath rest means to "come up higher," hence the ladder. But when we are fearful or do not see success the way God does, we become stuck in an endless cycle. It is as if we are sprinting, but on a treadmill going nowhere, becoming exhausted in the process. But God offers us a different choice to ascend to the place where victory is assured. A position where we do not have to struggle or scheme anymore. It is already complete. Jesus is inviting us to come up higher with him.

317: Genesis 28:12

THE FRUIT OF REST

"Enlarge the place of your tent, stretch your tent curtains wide, do not hold back; lengthen your cords, strengthen your stakes. For you will spread out to the right and to the left; your descendants will dispossess nations and settle in their desolate cities."[318]

God always asks us to be producers, not just consumers, in the Kingdom. In business, I teach a principle to my teams and call it the parable of the "Haves and Have-Nots."

"Have-nots" operate differently than "Haves." Have-nots complain about their losses. They get stuck when they hit a wall and never seem to find their way out of the ditch. They are unwilling to re-examine or to make changes in their approach. They keep better track of what they don't have rather than seeking diligently to grow the seed they already have into more.

Insecurity causes the Have-nots to reject feedback and constructive criticism as threatening arrows to be discarded quickly. They are quick to blame others for their lack of success and keep score. When they see others who are moving on or moving ahead, they say, "Oh, isn't this awful. I'm stuck." All of this behavior shuts down any chance of multiplication in their lives.

On the other hand, the Haves, who are those who walk in security, don't think about the blocks and barriers any longer than necessary. They keep their eye on the prize. They celebrate the victories in their own lives and in the lives of others. Failure is a challenge to succeed, not a ticket to defeat. That's how we chose to look at our battle with cancer.

Haves are secure and unafraid of reevaluating their approach. They know that constructive feedback provides useful fuel for the next attempt.

Many people in places of leadership or power are there because they were, at one point, responsible with small things. The parable of the talents is a

---

318: Isaiah 54: 2-3

natural law. The Haves in the story end up with something. The Have-not's end up with nothing. Don't bury what you have been given.

All of us can stand a little examination and constructive feedback. We have so little time and we don't want to waste what we have been given.

The fruit isn't always readily apparent. For example, during the Azusa Street Revival, there was an unknown evangelist whose heart was set on fire. The evangelist traveled to a specific town in Germany on assignment from the Holy Spirit. However, the German church leaders refused to allow him to hold a revival meeting in their village. Dejected, the evangelist returned to his car where the Holy Spirit prompted him to turn around and go back to the church leaders. I am sure he felt excited about the possibility of getting rejected twice. He was told to ask if there was anyone in the village who needed prayer for healing.

Only one man, apparently, needed prayer for healing. The evangelist prayed for the man, he was healed, and he was saved. *The one man was worth it.*

Multiplication is God's natural Kingdom principle. From the very beginning, multiplication was front and center in God's plan. Genesis 1:28 reads, "God blessed them and said to them, 'Be fruitful and increase in number; fill the earth and subdue it. Rule over the fish in the sea and the birds in the sky and over every living creature that moves on the ground.'"

He created and released this nature into plants and animals. These multiply without being taught. *It is Creation's natural order to be fruitful and multiply.* Like Isaiah's prophecy in 54:2-3, in proper alignment, God's Kingdom has an ever-expanding flow. The ladder is always moving upwards. It is unnatural for Christians not to multiply. To not produce fruit is a violation of how our *natural state* works. However, this does not always mean that you will see the fruit of your labor.

Sometimes the return on your investments will come back much later or in a different vein than you expect.

The man who was healed and saved in the story above had a grandson. His name happened to be Reinhard Bonnke, who went on to see over 75 million salvations on the continent of Africa and continues his ministry today.

We must never judge the fruit of our lives. We do not know what our investments will yield for future generations.

Let us bless you,

> *"Father God, we thank You for the plans and purposes You have stored up for each of us. God, I ask You now to move mightily on behalf of whoever is reading this, and that today will mark a powerful shift in their life where they begin to taste and see Your fruit in their lives. We bless them with fruitfulness and increase in their finances, their relationships, their futures, and their health. We say 'be healed' in Jesus' name, and expect that a change has already happened! We ask You to fill them up with power as You are pouring out Your Spirit on them. Amen, and Amen!"*

CHAPTER FOURTEEN

God's Economy: Where True Wealth is Multiplied

"But seek first His Kingdom and His righteousness, and all
these things will be given to you as well."[319]

HOPE FOR CHANGE

God's economy, unlike ours, does not start in the natural world. It is established in the heavenlies. If you are in the middle of a waiting season, God is not absent. Rather, He is working behind the scenes to mold you into a better son or daughter to carry out your Kingdom assignment once you step into the Promise. However, God's definition of His Promise and riches may be different than yours.

At some point in all of our lives, we grow weary of waiting for our breakthrough or for our circumstances to change. The problems we see with our children, our marriages, our finances, our church or health often seem more real than the truth of God.

We hear stories of those who are restored and blessed. However, when it comes down to living with our losses, it can appear as if there is no light

---

319: Matthew 6:33

at the end of the tunnel. We give up hope and begin to doubt His word. We question ourselves. Maybe we were wrong? Maybe God didn't say that? Maybe I didn't hear Him right?

Before you spiral out of control in your thoughts, let's look at the facts. The reality is our thoughts are worth doubting, but *God's Word is not.* Instead of asking yourself if God is faithful, ask yourself if your perspective is aligned with His unchanging truth.

TRUE RICHES

True riches include eternal security, peace with our souls, and thankfulness in the midst of trials. God is always after lasting beauty and the molding of our character. As it says in Matthew 6:33, we are to seek God's Kingdom before anything else. This is the principle of beginning *at the source of truth.* His perfect truth is unchanging. Rather than fight His timing and purpose, we must learn to allow Him to refine us and mold us into rulers focused on His good and perfect will.

This is not a soft or pleasant truth. However, received with a yielded heart, it will make the waiting period much more bearable and valuable. You will look back and exclaim with wonder at how you have been transformed, shocked that you ever doubted His word.

I remember when Neal and I were in the middle of our transition. It felt like *everything* was going wrong. Internally, I was still trying to heal. I had received a blow to my self-worth and security.

Neal and I had come through the worst of the crisis, but rebuilding our marriage and starting new careers were demanding.

In addition, we needed to sell our house, but it wasn't moving. As unpaid bills mounted up, so did our stress. We were pressed on every side. All the uncertainty felt paralyzing.

Whenever I came before the Lord, I heard Him say, "Double for your trouble, beauty for ashes."

In that same season, we attended a revival conference in Fort Mill, South Carolina. During the ministry time, Bonnie Chavda prophesied over Neal that he would see "three years of planting, three years of sowing, and three years of harvesting."

We clung to those life-giving words during the next several years. Whenever we felt pressured or trapped we would pray, "Lord, it feels like a long time, but we choose to trust you."

And so we waited. And we waited.

Sometimes, Neal and I would stare at the pile of unanswered questions and ask, "So, God…it sure would be nice to see that double!"

I half expected that one day I would walk outside and there would be a new car in my driveway. Or, maybe a buyer at my front door offering more for my house than the listed price. I guess, in my limited wisdom, that is how I expected God to reward me. However, my Kingdom knowledge was too narrow. God's economy works differently.

One day, in the middle of a worship session, God flashed a picture of our three boys in my mind. Our boys were, and are, our pride and joy. In my opinion, we had persevered, grown very close and suffered together through the family restoration. We had moved to a completely new region and survived Neal's cancer scare. We were thankful that they seemed to have escaped the difficult seasons pretty much emotionally unscathed.

They had not been perfect by any measure. But, as the Lord showed me each of their lives, I can honestly say through both high school and college, they worked to be examples for the Kingdom. They were scholars, athletes and most importantly, lovers of God. They had run worship teams, Bible studies, and campus ministries. Each greatly surpassed the examples set by their parents.

The Lord told me, "They all love me and they all are serving me."

I began crying and laughing. Of course!

That is God's economy. My boys were my spiritual inheritance. My beauty for ashes. Even through all the heartache and pain, it was an absolutely worthy exchange.

Most of us have lived so long in the wilderness we don't even expect His riches. We have made friends with loss or compromise. Living under the curse, we believe the lie that "this is it" and whatever we have is "good enough."

Yes, we are called to be content in any circumstance![320] However, *we are not called to partner with mediocrity, maintain a survival mentality, or leave gaping emotional wounds.* When we do, we risk losing the life God has called us to. And when we choose to be directed by our mind, will, and emotions rather than our spirits, we live to please ourselves and take care of our own needs, instead of working to further the Kingdom of God.

God may call you to hard things. But, take heart, you can do it all through the strength of Jesus. *That,* according to Paul, is the secret to being content![321]

Like Paul, you may have seasons of great suffering in this life. Yet what riches Paul received! Many of us today are reaping the harvest of his labor roughly two thousand years ago. Can you imagine having that sort of impact? Can you imagine your life having that sort of multiplication?

KERNELS

When you are adopted into God's Kingdom, you receive a new spiritual DNA. This DNA includes what I, Neal, call the *Principle of Multiplication.* This principle takes a single seed of corn and turns it into two or three ears

---

320: Philippians 4:12
321: Philippians 4:13

192

on a single stock. One seed turns into approximately sixteen rows, with fifty kernels on each ear of corn per row.

His world of multiplication is eight hundred for one. You and I did not teach the corn to reproduce like this. This is His design for all His creation. He is the author of abundance.

His Kingdom is the land flowing with milk and honey.

Ours is the land of famine, drought, discord, and sickness.

His Kingdom brings freedom.

Ours carries striving, slavery, and abuse.

His Kingdom is joy, peace, and thankfulness.

Our kingdom is depressed, anxious, hurting and never satisfied.

Exposure to His Kingdom increases our understanding of what has real and lasting value. In His Kingdom, riches are multiplied endlessly. His Kingdom is more than sufficiency. It is an increasing *abundance* for us to bless others as well. When we yield our souls and our plans to Him, we become territorial kings in His Kingdom.

Like Abraham and Sarah, we are to father and mother entire nations.[322] We are to produce territories in the natural with renewed hearts and lives. In doing this we transfer the domain from our decaying human kingdom to one which is ever expanding and multiplying in both life and glory. We trade earthly kingdoms under the curse for those brimming with the blessing and abundance of God's mercy and wisdom.

Having an attitude that is expectant of multiplication will shift our perspectives from hiding to activating. We stop being a group of people who stow away behind the walls of their fort lobbing grenades into the darkness.

322: Genesis 17:5

Instead, we will proclaim, "We are God's people, He's called us to rule and reign and create a new Kingdom culture, and this is His city. We will not stop until we see it prosper!" This victorious group of overcomers will become "the desire of the nations."[323]

If we seek the Kingdom of God first and His righteousness, we are assured that "all these things will be given…as well."[324] We can fully trust Him to reward us, and His rewards are everlasting. Galatians 6:9 encourages, "Let us not become weary in doing good, for at the proper time we will reap a harvest if we do not give up. We will reap what we sow in due season if we do not quit!"

And how do we not give up when the going gets tough?

According to Philippians, we cultivate a thankful heart and exchange our anxiety with prayer, supplication, and thanksgiving.[325] When we are in a waiting season, we are not to doubt, lose sleep, or have panic attacks. We are to pray without ceasing and boldly praise and thank Him for all that He has done and all that He will do. We are to count the victory before it arrives because we know the author of our victory.

The result?

The peace that passes all understanding will wash over our souls. We will have traded our will for His. His will that promises to always work out things for our good.[326] In the Father's perfect will we will be able to handle any circumstance with grace and poise.

Waiting on God is both passive and active. There are things we should do and things we should not do while we wait. Paul encourages us to be passive about anxiety and to actively pray and maintain a thankful heart. Thankfulness reminds us that we are important and have a purpose in the

---

323: Haggai 2:7
324: Matthew 6:33
325: Philippians 4:6-7
326: Romans 8:28

Kingdom. If you are feeling low, try it out and take a few moments to reflect on God's goodness and how He has helped you establish new realities in your life.

THE THANKFUL LAB

We can scientifically support that an increase in thankfulness improves sleep and reduces anxiety.[327] Research tells us when we consciously choose to be thankful, we receive feelings of well-being as well as physical and emotional peace.[328]

A recent group of experimenters studied blood flow in various brain regions. They asked those under observation to think about feelings related to gratefulness. An MRI scan revealed that people who showed more gratitude had higher levels of activity in the hypothalamus, which controls many bodily functions, including rest and anxiety.[329]

Science tells us that activation in this area of the brain causes improved sleeping patterns and reduced stress levels.[330]

Thankfulness does, in fact, produce peace!

In addition, neuroscience researcher Alex Korb, PhD., explains that feelings of gratitude activate the regions in the brain that are associated with the increase of dopamine and serotonin.[331]

327: Digdon, N., Koble, A., "Effects of Constructive Worry, Imagery Distraction, and Gratitude Interventions on Sleep Quality: A Pilot Trial." *Applied Psychology: Health and Well-Being*, 3, 2011. 193–206.

328: Serani, Deborah. *Living With Depression: Why Biology and Biography Matter Along the Path To Hope and Healing.* Lanham: Rowman & Littlefield, 2012.

329: Zahn, R. et al. "The Neural Basis of Human Social Values: Evidence from Functional MRI." *Cerebral Cortex, 19 (2)*, 2009: 276–283.

330: Digdon, N., Koble, A., "Effects of Constructive Worry, Imagery Distraction, and Gratitude Interventions on Sleep Quality: A Pilot Trial." *Applied Psychology: Health and Well-Being*, 3, 2011. 193–206.

331: Korb, A. *The Upward Spiral: Using Neuroscience To Reverse The Course of Depression, One Small Change At A Time.* Oakland: New Harbinger Publications, 2015.

Alesio, G. "Gratitude and Happiness: The Link Based on Neuroscience." *www.versiondaily.com.* September 23, 2015.

Dopamine is what *motivates* us to take action toward our goals. It also gives us a surge of pleasure when we accomplish them. On the other hand, feelings of low value, self-doubt, and a lack of enthusiasm are linked with low levels of dopamine.[332]

Serotonin is associated with the regulation of mood, appetite, and sleep. Loneliness and depression are natural results when serotonin levels are low. High serotonin levels result in improved mood as well as helping to create a sense of well-being. Serotonin flows when you feel loved and valued.[333]

What Wood's research team revealed is that staying in a place of gratitude leads to higher levels of perceived social support (connection and relationship), and lower levels of stress and depression.[334]

However, the benefits of thankfulness don't stop there. Gratitude has another powerful impact on your life because it also engages your brain in a cycle of empathy. In this pattern; an increase in thankfulness leads to more empathy, which leads to more thankfulness and then even more empathy. The result? Gratitude also causes us to better understand and have greater care for the feelings of others.

On top of all of that, your brain loves to fall for what the science community calls the "confirmation bias." This is where gratitude actually causes our brains to start looking for more and more things to be thankful for. Examples of this would be reflecting on past successes or sharing our testimonies with others. These types of activities allow the brain to re-live the positive experiences. Since our brain has trouble telling the difference between what is real and what is imagined, it produces more serotonin in both cases![335] Heightened levels of serotonin not only allows us to have increased feelings of worth but it is a recipe to forming new healthy habits.

332: Korb, A. *The Upward Spiral*; Alesio, G. "Gratitude and Happiness."

333: Korb, A. *The Upward Spiral*; Alesio, G. "Gratitude and Happiness."

334: Wood, A., et al. "The Role of Gratitude In The Development of Social Support, Stress, and Depression: Two Longitudinal Studies." *Journal of Research in Personality, 42 (4)*, 2008.

335: Fox, G.R., et al. "Neural Correlates of Gratitude." *Frontiers in Psychology, 6*. 2015. 1491.

WORTH IT

When the knowledge of who we are moves from our minds into our spirits, we begin to do His works out of our identity. Through this, the Body of Christ is activated to bring positive change and redemption to families, cities, and nations. This is the purpose of the Church. This is what Christ died for. We must believe God intends for us to be kings who bring reformation to our cities.

However, God may take you on a journey to learn to manage your inheritance. There is always a process of learning how to prepare a family, a business, a city, or a nation that propels us to carry God's favor. This is so that it brings Him glory and does not destroy us in the process.

For example, if you had a $50 million dollar business with hundreds of employees, would you turn the whole operation over to your twenty-year-old child? Would you hand him his inheritance "lock, stock, and barrel," with no training and no management experience?

I wouldn't! Not only would your business fall apart, but your child would likely crash and burn, too. The right way to do things would be to spend years preparing the successor to take over. If we want our children to be secure and successful leaders, we must train them. Their coaching is not just for their sake, but for the sake of the business and the welfare of all the employees.

God is working with you to take over the land in the same fashion. It might feel too slow or too fast, depending on where you are at spiritually, emotionally, or physically. If you are in the training process, He will bring "mothers and fathers" to work with you and to speak wisdom into your life. One thing that you *can* absolutely trust in this process is your Father. He is giving you the family business and territory at the speed you can manage. He is not withholding anything from you. He knows what you can handle. Trust Him.

What you see impacts how God will fulfill His promise to you. Remember, not all the spies saw the Promise, some only saw the giants. This is why Caleb and Jacob were the sole participants allowed to enter the land. Their perspective changed their lives, their futures, and the destiny of their descendants.

On the other hand, the fearful spies died in the wilderness. Their spiritual blindness and refusal to trust in God's word cost them dearly. This can seem harsh, but God allows us to choose. And if we make a bad decision, He is ready to redeem when we turn to Him.

Joseph helped a nation overcome famine because of what he learned during the waiting period.[336] He not only saw the future, but God gave him a strategy to deal with it. He saved many more than just himself or his immediate family. However, his process of learning how to handle the power God entrusted him with was painful and long. Looking back through history's perspective, we would all agree that even though Joseph suffered rejection, slavery, wrongful termination, and imprisonment, it was all *worth it.*

God wants us to be wise rulers, not ones who are corrupt or self-centered.

Most of us do not see ourselves as rulers. The truth is, this story may not make sense in our current situation or season. Caleb and Joshua got to actually see their inheritance. They knew the Promise was real. If you feel like you are still in Egypt or the wilderness, don't be alarmed. Your Promised Land may show up in *seed form.* We all know that it takes time for seeds to grow into full-fledged oak trees. Be faithful to nurture the seed He's given you, and it will grow beyond what you can ask or think.[337] And, He will also ask you to prove yourself competent to steward the details and the people in the organization before He hands the family business over to you.

Thankfully, He has not left us alone to muddle through. On the contrary, God has been making us ready all along the way. He has been preparing us to use what He's given us for the purposes He intends. His great com-

---

336: Genesis 41:54
337: Ephesians 3:20

mission was to go and establish His Kingdom and create freedom for the captives. His economy will create lasting fruit.

While we wait, all He asks of us is to *maintain a thankful heart* and exchange our fear and worry for His peace.

Let's pray,

"Jesus, I seek You first in my life. I am thankful that You are forming me into the kind of leader You need me to be in every area of my life. I hold nothing back. I believe in You and Your ability to prepare me for the Promises You have in store for me. Give me patience while I wait. Help me to trust You through every circumstance. Cultivate a thankful heart within me, and teach me to rest in Your Presence. Thank You in advance for the expansion, and thank You for this moment too! Amen!"

CHAPTER FIFTEEN
Occupying the Land: Your Place of Destiny

"'Well done, my good servant!' his master replied.
'Because you have been trustworthy in a very small matter,
take charge of ten cities.' The second came and said, 'Sir,
your mina has earned five more.' His master answered,
'You take charge of five cities.'"[338]

"Give, and it will be given to you. A good measure, pressed down,
shaken together and running over, will be poured into your lap.
For with the measure you use, it will be measured to you."[339]

Jesus' power only comes to us through the deepest levels of intimacy. He offers one provision for ruling alongside him: becoming one with Him. Jesus said that we must eat His flesh and drink His blood. In this place of oneness, we become free.

Free people pursue their destiny with abandonment, like little children. God loves to set people free. Nothing brings Him more glory than His grace and liberty on display among the body of Christ. It's His mercy to

---

338: Luke 19:17-18
339: Luke 6:38

set people free and see them gain victory, to follow His voice instead of the lies of the enemy.

We believe that one of the reasons we've not completely understood His Kingdom is that we keep trying to get there on our own. Our efforts are based on things like Biblical principles, methods, theology, and our own understanding or experience. This is not big enough for our God. His ways are different than ours. His Kingdom is on display at a different level.

ROGER'S STORY

Roger is a good friend of our family, and he is currently answering his calling as a priest in another part of the world. He would call us now and then for ministry prayer. A few years ago he stopped by to say hello. Roger was always pleasant but continually maintained an exceptionally quiet and reserved demeanor.

As his story started to unravel, it seems he had been hurt again and again by those under his leadership. Because of this, he said he had started to display some real signs of depression and had barricaded himself in his house, isolating himself from the world, refusing to reach out for help.

Our sons had recently returned from the Bethel Supernatural School of Ministry and were leading a ministry session for our local leadership group. Since Roger was in town, we invited him to join us. During worship, the Presence enveloped the room. One of our sons was filled with the joy of the Lord and was gregariously laughing. We could see Roger watching the interaction carefully with more than a hint of suspicion.

As Roger continued listening and watching, I sat down beside him and asked if I could pray with him. He nodded yes, and I prayed a simple prayer over what I felt the Lord had shown me. By that time, the joy had begun to sweep the room as our sons prayed and gave words of encouragement to the group. At one point, I caught their eye and said, "If it is okay with him, I need you to spread a little happiness to Roger."

Our son's joy from the Holy Spirit was contagious. I watched as one of them smiled in Roger's direction, walked over and then enveloped Roger in an enormous hug, laughter spilling out. Roger acquiesced and cautiously took the hug. Then, he started to smile and laugh. To our surprise, Roger couldn't stop laughing. He sat right down where we were standing and kept going!

We didn't know it at the time, but Roger had actually come to town to talk with us about his serious feelings of burnout in the ministry. He was just about ready to call it a day. He had been bitten by one too many sheep, as the saying goes.

On the living room floor that day, Roger had a major encounter with the love and the Presence of the Father. Nothing we could have said or done would have compared to the quick, complete work of the Holy Spirit in his life at that moment. As we said goodbye the next day, he radiated the love of the Father and could not stop smiling. He left us renewed and restored to carry the fullness of the real Gospel of redemption.

The last we talked, Roger had gone home and started a prayer team at his local parish. Not only that, but he tells us he has gained the reputation of being a "hugger."

If we had known what our priest friend was struggling with, we may have tried to handle his situation in a different way that day. And yet, in our ignorance, God instantly touched Roger and replaced his hurt with acceptance and his hopelessness with joy.

At some point, Roger became desperate enough to seek community and the Lord's peace. He decided to meet with the Father on His terms. He was radically transformed into a more secure and healthy member of the ministering body. The Holy Spirit is the best counselor. *Roger chose to release his hurt and receive God's healing.*

Today, Roger's new security allows him to learn and execute healthy community with fresh relational tools. He happily resides in the Promised Land attending to his sheep with an increased capacity to love.

THE EVER-EXPANDING KINGDOM

God's Covenant Promises are built into the world around us, often in ways we don't realize. I, Neal, actually believe that the business world is more closely aligned with how the Kingdom of God should function than many modern churches.

Why? The whole point of business is to produce fruit and to multiply. If you build a business with an unhealthy ecosystem, it dies. While these deciding factors are more readily understood and applied in the workplace, these truths are universal for all organizations. The time is *now* for the local church and family to face the realities of the laws of sowing and reaping.

I have worked with dozens of large scale corporations over the course of my career as a consultant. Working with billion dollar companies has taught me firsthand the principles that create, or destroy, an ecosystem for sustainable, healthy growth.

I have also worked with many church organizations. In both situations, I have seen the repercussions of a small scale autocracy. In business, when one person is in charge, making all the decisions, typically the leader will end his career defeated. This is not the result of competing organizations, but rather, by the uprising of the organization's employees and their demands. Like a coup d'etats, the leader will quickly be discarded and replaced.

The same principle holds true with the compounding of investment returns. This is a fundamental business premise where everyone involved in the enterprise, from the owner to the employee to the supplier to the customer, deserves a healthy return on their investment. It requires that everyone keep improving to expand the harvest each year.

No organization can survive long without keeping this mutually beneficial relationship in balance. Customers can go elsewhere, employees can take jobs at better businesses, and the shareholders, if they don't earn a reasonable profit, can move their investment. It requires honest and consistent interaction between all the parties. If one is taken advantage of, the system will become unstable and collapse over time. Reality presses in. Business autocracies have short expiration dates in the "real" world.

Interestingly enough, I have witnessed a different pattern altogether in the Church.

In the case of an over controlling church leader, the congregation is never given permission, much less encouraged, to use their gifts to grow in maturity. As a result, the church ends up functioning in a "fake reality."

This plastic face disregards the need for true community, sharing burdens, and vulnerability in weakness. *There is no real fruit.* No real friendships. Just some nice songs, a nice sermon, and pews filled with people that you never really get to know.

So, how *do* we create sustainable healthy ecosystems that produce good fruit? How do we occupy the Promised Land and continually expand its territory?

CREATING LASTING KINGDOM

First and foremost, we must look to God and His creation. His rules are enduring and pervasive. If He created it, He knows how it works. Remember the Principle of the Corn.

Kings build kingdoms by occupying the land. Kings *establish* the customs of the Kingdom they represent. Kings *take responsibility* for cities and regions, and they care about the welfare and the prosperity of every member of their territory. If I'm a CEO of a company, governor of a state, or head of a ministry, I don't just care about my job alone. It is my job to care about the well-being of the organization and all the organizations connected to it.

In order to be an effective leader, *one must care for the whole territory.* I only succeed if everyone succeeds. That's just good business.

I believe these principles can be easily applied with the use of three simple keys. When these tenants become pervasive it becomes possible to create healthy, sustainable organizations. To see this sort of Kingdom growth, I recommend:

1. Honoring those who have gone before you.

2. Living in covenant with those He has called you to live in covenant with.

3. Blessing those who cannot bless you back.

When you honor the people who have gone before you, you get to partake in their inheritance. We are all living where we are today because of the breakthroughs of those who went ahead of us. We are all "swimming in waters" that they stewarded first.

Second, we are all called to be in covenant relationships with specific people and the Body of Christ.

Our spiritual inheritance is linked to God's covenants directly when God says, "Honor your father and your mother, so that you may live long in the land the LORD your God is giving you."[340] By honoring our parents, we are aligning ourselves with the Promises God made to our spiritual and physical forefathers. It all matters to the Lord. Generations carry blessings in the measure that they walk in honor.

Psalms 133:1-3 tells us that it is good and pleasant when we live together in unity. The word unity, *yachad*, means "united together," like a covenant relationship.[341] To the Lord, this sort of unity among His children is essential. Don't we want to live in a place where God commands His blessings toward us? That is where I want to be!

Finally, there are those we are called to bless who cannot pay us back. God wants us to be in relationships where we continue to give with no strings attached, for the simple reason that we are accountable to Him. He is

---

340: Exodus 20:12

341: "H3162 - yachad - Strong's Hebrew Lexicon." Bible Hub. June 13, 2017.

the source of our resources. We are to model His heart to the widows and orphans, to those who do not have a voice, and to those who have suffered oppression.

Our middle son Zach has been a continuous, walking example of this type of unconditional honor and love. During his high school years, he was always the person asked to serve and would without regard to own his schedule or needs. He patiently reminded us that it was ministry.

I remember one of these situations where he was asked to tutor a young boy, David, with his math. The tutoring group had told him that David loved computers, just like Zach. They hoped that Zach might have some headway with David where they had hit a wall.

Though on the surface it seemed a good idea, the truth was that Zach was already overextended! He was involved in advanced classes, football, Church high school ministry, a small business, and worship leading, in addition to the usual pressures of just being an upperclassman. He was the definition of *busy*. Nevertheless, Zach started meeting with David before football practices, and under his encouragement, David flourished.

It was a great sacrifice for Zach's time and energy. Neal and I were humbled in his choice to love David without expecting anything in return.

One day, many months later, an envelope appeared in the mail with Zach's name on it. It seems that David had done so well that his parents decided to bless Zach with a beautiful and heartfelt gift. Zach asked for nothing, but our Father who sees everything provided an opportunity for him to experience Kingdom principles in action.

If you are continually active in honoring those who have gone before you, working with covenant partners, and giving to those who cannot pay you back, you will see supernatural multiplication. You *will* see fruit that has an ever-increasing impact.

LOOK TO JESUS

If we really want to understand how to occupy the Promised Land, we must look to Jesus. He is our Promised Land, the One who can complete us.

Jesus was known for His miracles. Consider the time He fed the five thousand. With signs and wonders like that, it makes perfect sense that so many followed Him. They were drawn to Him. However, it is not enough just to follow signs and wonders. The Israelites followed the cloud by day and the fire by night.[342] They also ate the miraculous manna for forty years, and yet that alone was not enough to enter into the Promised Land.[343]

Following signs and enjoying God's provision is not enough to qualify you to enter the Promised Land and live as rulers.

What hinders us from entering fully into this Kingdom? Relying on ourselves, giving into fear, or believing we can earn the Promised Land by striving for it.

In Genesis, Jacob thought he was his own source of security and success. He lived in fear of what might happen to him next, continually scheming for ways to prosper.

In Luke, Martha strove to prove her devotion, and she thought everyone else ought to do the same. Others would not play by her rules and this made her bitter.

Jacob had to endure a wrestling match to understand God's Promises are established in Him alone, not us. When he tried to excel on his own, it left him exhausted and nervous over what might go wrong next. But when he truly encountered God's full restoration, he became Israel. Only in this did he find the rest his soul longed for.

342: Exodus 13:21
343: Exodus 16:35

Martha had to come to the end of herself to see that rest is the only way to intimacy. Only at His feet would she find the acceptance and affirmation she desperately needed.

The Promised Land is entered through the gate of surrender, not striving. As appealing as it might be to try to drive out the giants on our own, we cannot. It's impossible to fix ourselves, trust me. Self-help approaches are useful to a point. But, even the best tools can never release freedom or life. The giants might quiet down for a bit, but they won't be dead. We need a supernatural approach that releases God's Presence to give us permanent victory.

We need the voice of the Holy Spirit to bring us into our Father's Kingdom so we can dream with him. If we are walking in rebellion we need the gentle correction of a patient spiritual parent. If we are struggling with our identities and destinies, we need His security and safety.

We must walk toward our Land of Promises and we must occupy; it is His free perfect gift.

The Kingdom is *already* ours if we "do not despise these small beginnings."[344] Your breakthrough has already been purchased. It is completed in Him; He is fully able to make it come to pass. What's more, if we prove ourselves faithful stewards, He will increase our responsibility and take us from glory to glory.

Sadly, many find the level of intimacy that this requires frightening. Consequently, they never release full control of their lives to the Jesus. It was one thing to enjoy the fish and loaves on the beach or the manna and quail in the desert.[345] It is quite another to eat Jesus' flesh and drink His blood and to live before Him with nothing hidden.[346]

344: Zechariah 4:10
345: Luke 9, Exodus 16:35
346: John 6:56

But, by consuming Him as the Bread of Life, our lives make the statement that He is our consuming desire. We will not feed off of any other substitute or counterfeit. The statement opens the door for us to take our place by His side in the Kingdom. Here, we rule and reign with Him in the Promised Land, becoming the desire of nations in the process.

Let us pray in the words of Isaiah 60:1-5,

"Arise, shine, for your light has come, and the glory of the Lord rises upon you. See, darkness covers the earth and thick darkness is over the peoples, but the Lord rises upon you and His glory appears over you. Nations will come to your light, and kings to the brightness of your dawn. Lift up your eyes and look about you: All assemble and come to you; your sons come from afar, and your daughters are carried on the hip. Then you will look and be radiant, your heart will throb and swell with joy; the wealth on the seas will be brought to you, to you the riches of the nations will come. Amen."

CHAPTER SIXTEEN

Milk and Honey: Fruitfulness in Christ

"The trees will yield their fruit and the ground will yield its crops;
the people will be secure in their land. They will know that I am
the LORD, when I break the bars of their yoke and rescue
them from the hands of those who enslaved them."[347]

"If the Lord is pleased with us, He will lead us into that land, a
land flowing with milk and honey, and will give it to us."[348]

Living in the Promised Land looks and feels radically different than living
in the wilderness on the banks of the Jordan. We remember when our
oldest son, Matt, made the decision to step into the favor of God into his
Promised Land of abundant life in Christ. Matt has always been highly
intelligent. He would honestly tell you that his grades came easy and he
never had to study very hard. As far as his education was concerned, Matt
was pretty self-sufficient. However, when he entered law school, he needed
to trust God with his schoolwork in a unique way. He would often call us
before big assignments, asking us to pray with him for discernment and
favor, which we gladly did.

347: Ezekiel 34:27
348: Numbers 14:8

As he continued to put his confidence in God with the outcome of his education, God faithfully opened new doors of opportunity. Many of these he never knew about or could have opened on his own. Matt is occupying new territory because God is blessing him to do so. Favor makes us more aware of the goodness of our Father. It truly is beyond what we can ask or think.

It is important to note there is a by-product of differentiating the fruit of your hard work and the fruit of God's favor. You can always judge your own work; you are the one who did it, right?

This mindset pushes you to the edge of the comparison cliff, and from there, it is only a short shove till you fall into Martha Syndrome, "Why do I have to do the hard work, while my sister is over there enjoying life?"[349] Alternatively, you go the other direction and become puffed up with pride, believing your hard work earned you the favor you have.

To occupy the Promised Land, we actually have to get to a level where we are secure in God. Comfortable enough that, when things don't go our way, we don't reach for the steering wheel.

Instead, we say, "Lord, keep me focused on You and Your desire through me. Keep my heart pure, continue to refine me for Your purposes. What are your plans for me today?"

Along the same vein, when we are mistreated, we need to be able to say, "Lord, help me see the person who hurt me on the terms that you see them." Or even as Stephen prayed in Acts 7:60, "Lord, do not hold this sin against them," as he was stoned to death by the religious leaders.

If you can honestly pray those prayers when you are in the middle of the fire, you are living in peace, at rest in the Promised Land.

Don't compare your fruit to the fruit of others. Live knowing you are each called to a specific identity and assignment. Other believers have their own

---

349: Luke 10:40

identities and destinies, and that's a good thing! Taken together we all have important roles to play for the full display of His Kingdom here on earth. How could you possibly be jealous or compare?

Security means you are comfortable to let Him drive. You know He is taking you to a place you could not imagine. You no longer need to know everything to follow Him. Trust allows you to obey without seeing.

FULL EXPOSURE

God's desire for the Jews was not just for them to follow a set of rules and remember a bunch of stories. He planned and accomplished the salvation of mankind by sending Jesus to deliver us from evil. However, we must realize that Jesus also came to save and deliver us from ourselves. We miss the mark when we turn His covenant into a set of rules or practices. *He aims to be in us and with us.* We are to walk so close to God that in every circumstance we hear His voice and speak it.

This does not mean that biblical principles are wrong. Far from it! It simply means that a biblical principle cannot be all we have in Him. He desires to bring us into a living, breathing relationship with Himself. Remember, Jesus said, "He can do only what He sees His Father doing."[350] They had a face-to-face relationship.

There are twenty-four examples of Jesus healing people in the New Testament. Each one is different. Why were they not the same? The obvious answer is so we don't turn the healing into a formula. For example, "Jesus prayed that way to heal that disease. So, healing for that disease can only happen when we pray that exact phrase and use that specific action." This mentality removes the need to be dependent on God.

But, there is actually more to it than that. Every healing Jesus demonstrated was an encounter with a principality or a power. When we function without the protection and wisdom of our Savior and the Holy Spirit, we can be led

---

350: John 5:19

into deception and the snare of the evil one. We may unwittingly partner with falsehoods or strongholds which blind us from our true destiny and exalt themselves above the one true God.

A stronghold is *a habitual pattern of thought,* built into one's thought life. The mind is the citadel of the soul, and he who controls the mind controls a very strategic place! Satan and his minions want to capture our minds. Romans 8:5-6 teaches, "Those who live according to the flesh have their minds set on what the flesh desires; but those who live in accordance with the Spirit have their minds set on what the Spirit desires. The mind governed by the flesh is death, but the mind governed by the Spirit is life and peace."

Often, we will only see the *outward* effects of strongholds; blatant idolatry, erratic behavior, immoral conduct, etc. This is why God instructed His kings to utterly destroy all the high places in the Old Testament. This is also why Jesus first dealt with eliminating strongholds before dealing with physical healing. (In Matthew 17, Jesus healed the little boy of seizures by first casting out the demon afflicting his body. Jesus healed the child because He walked in the knowledge God provided about the stronghold.)

We may be living in God's Promise and favor, but at the same time, believing the lie of the enemy concerning our identities. Relying on God principles alone will keep us powerless and frustrated in the real healing work God must do in many circumstances. We must rely on God's direction for each healing situation rather than just follow our "go-to" prayer with the hope that maybe God will show up.

The good news is that God sees beyond our limitations. He still has our destinies intact and ready to go. All we need to do is step into His Presence, into the Promise. God knows how to battle strongholds, He knows how to tear them down, *if we're willing to expose them.* He is our Protector and Provider.

HIS TIMING

God seeks to bless the entire earth through you. He not only wants your freedom and destiny to come to pass; He also wants the freedom of your family, your city, your nation…your whole world.

In Revelation 22:2 we read, "the leaves of the tree are for the healing of the nations." Compare that to John 15:5 where we are taught that Jesus "is the vine" and "we are the branches." These verses give us the full picture of our inheritance and our calling. He is showing us a restored olive tree with all believers, Jewish and Gentile begin to demonstrate the fullness of the kingdom and his heart of restoration. We are in covenant with the Son, wrapped in the complete love of the Father as brothers and sisters. This is the true picture of the Father's heart.

The *leaves* of this tree becoming the healing for the nations is the fulfillment of God's plan. This is a visible manifestation of the proper flow of the nourishment of His Presence to the world. United as the restored olive tree, His power is free to flow through the body and into the world. Together, in covenant relationship, God's desire becomes complete.

It is our deepest hope that you become aware that your identity can be transformed to be fully secure in covenant with Him. This relationship is not found through any measure of self-help or the lies we might chase.

Once we realize that the source of our security is *only* in Him, we each need to make a choice to follow Him in obedience regardless of our understanding. This requires new eyes and ears. It requires tuning into eternity. Thankfully, this journey is not to be done alone; He will guide us, even when we fail. It might not always go the way we think it will. We will make mistakes. But if we stay connected to Him, He restores, rebuilds and creates glory, even where we see loss.

Hopefully, our story encourages you to take heart and to step into greater power, pressing through whatever battles you may be facing. We want to see hope restored in your heart. It is our great desire for you to believe that God can and does change circumstances, and more importantly, *people*.

All it takes is for you to be open, honest, and vulnerable with your Heavenly Father. He is waiting for you in the place of intimacy. He is ready to meet you even if you are in a place of desperation. He is prepared to heal all the brokenness and is able to take your insecurity and transform it into real security in Him. God wants to wipe away all the shame and the effects of bondage in your life. He is the longing your heart truly desires.

We would consider it an honor to bless you,

> *"Dear Father, We know that You are near, closer than our very breath. We know that You want the best for us and You long for us to step into our destiny, to leave the desert for the land You have promised us.*

> *"Father, we ask that You would reveal the hidden things that cause us fear and condemnation, and shed light on the darkness that is the enemy of our souls. Lord, we know that You have a good future for us, that we are called by You no matter what we have seen, what we have done, or what has been done to us.*

> *"We want to step into our inheritance, Father, and we want everything for which You suffered and died on the Cross. Show us who we are in Your Son, that we might understand how to receive and steward the great gift you purchased for us on the cross.*

> *"Lord, may we impact those You call us to lead into freedom and their destiny. May we be faithful covenant mothers and fathers of those who need hope. This is what we were created to do. Thank You, Father God, for Your Holy Spirit leading us into all truth. Thank You for guiding and leading us where we need to go. In Jesus' Name, Amen."*

May you enjoy the journey and encourage others along the way, and in so doing, build the body and the city you are called to impact. We pray God's blessings and favor on you and your journey.

Tell us your story at *www.everincreasingimpact.org,* we would love to connect with you.

Much Love,
Neal and Diane

APPENDIX

More Information on Healing from
Traumatic Emotional Experiences

We as a family have had some wonderful breakthrough in our hearts and emotions through what is commonly referenced as inner healing and refers to the experiences described in this book.

Simply put, inner healing is part of your salvation as a follower of Jesus. His death and resurrection purchased your freedom for eternity and today.

Below we've recommended some of our favorite ministries that offer great tools if you feel like God is pulling you to dig deeper into this subject. Check out some of these transformational resources as the Holy Spirit leads you.

- Clark, R. (2016). *The healing breakthrough: creating an atmosphere of faith for healing.* Minneapolis, MN: Chosen, a division of Baker Publishing Group.

- Christian Healing Ministries with Judith and Francis McNutt. Healing Events and Healing Ministries located at *www.christianhealingmin.org*

- Restoring the Foundations Ministries. Klystra, C., & Klystra, B. (2001). *Restoring the foundations: an integrated approach to healing ministry.* Santa Rosa Beach, FL: Proclaiming His Word Publications.

- SOZO Healing Ministry. Silva, D. D., & Liebscher, T. (2016). *Sozo: saved, healed, delivered: a journey into freedom with the Father, Son, and Holy Spirit / Dawna De Silva; Teresa Liebscher; foreword by Danny Silk.* Shippensburg, PA: Destiny Image.

- To learn more about your attachment style, take the free assessment online: *Online attachment styles and close relationships quiz:* www.web-research-design.net/cgi-bin/crq/crq.pl

WORKS CITED

Ainsworth, M. "Attachment Across The Lifespan." *Bulletin of New York Academy of Medicine, 61.* 1985. 792-812.

Ainsworth, M. *Attachment & Human Development, 1 (2),* 1999. 217-228.

Alesio, G. "Gratitude and Happiness: The Link Based on Neuroscience." *www.versiondaily.com.* September 23, 2015.

Bowlby, J. *Attachment and Loss, Vol. 1. Attachment.* New York: Basic Books, 1969.

Bowlby, J. *A Secure Base.* New York: Basic Books, 1988.

Boyd, J. *Bible Dictionary.* Ottenheimer Publishers, 1958.

Bradshaw, J. *Healing The Shame That Binds You.* Deerfield Beach: Health Communications, 2005.

Brewin, C., Andrews, B., Valentine, J. "Meta-Analysis of Risk Factors for Posttraumatic Stress Disorder in Trauma-Exposed Adults." *Journal of Consulting and Clinical Psychology, 68,* 2000. 748-766.

Brookes, J.D., PhD. *The Neurobiology of Spiritual Warfare.* [Scholarly project], n.d.

Brown, Brené. "Listening to Shame." TED. March 2012. Lecture.

Cassidy, J., Shaver, P.R. *Handbook of Attachment: Theory, Research, and Clinical Applications.* New York: Guilford Press, 2008.

Clinton, T., Straub, J. God Attachment: *Why You Believe, Act, and Feel the Way You Do About God.* New York: Howard Books, 2014.

Clinton, T., Sibcy, G. *Why You Do the Things You Do: The Secret to Healthy Relationships.* Nashville: Integrity, 2006.

Cozolino, L. *The Neuroscience of Psychotherapy: Building and Rebuilding the Human Brain*. New York: W.W. Norton & Co., 2002.

DePrince, A. et. al. "Motivated Forgetting and Misremembering: Perspectives from Betrayal Trauma Theory." Belli, R.F., *True and False Recovered Memories: Toward a Reconciliation of the Debate (Nebraska Symposium on Motivation 58)*, New York: Springer, 2012. 193-243.

Digdon, N., Koble, A., "Effects of Constructive Worry, Imagery Distraction, and Gratitude Interventions on Sleep Quality: A Pilot Trial." *Applied Psychology: Health and Well-Being, 3*, 2011. 193–206.

Easton, M., M.A., D.D., *Illustrated Bible Dictionary, Third Edition*. Public domain: Thomas Nelson, 1897.

Easton, M. "Entry for Covenant." "Easton's Bible Dictionary." Web. June 19, 2017.

"Ephesians 1 (KJV) - Paul an apostle of Jesus." *Blue Letter Bible*. Web. 8 June, 2017.

Fox, G.R., et al. "Neural Correlates of Gratitude." *Frontiers in Psychology, 6.* 2015. 1491.

Frost, J. *Experiencing the Father's Embrace*. Lake Mary: Charisma House, 2002.

"G2192 - echō - Strong's Greek Lexicon (ESV)." *Blue Letter Bible*. Web. 25 May, 2017.

"G3339 - metamorphoō - Strong's Greek Lexicon (NIV)." *Blue Letter Bible*. Web. 2 June, 2017.

"G3340 - metanoeō - Strong's Greek Lexicon (NLT)." *Blue Letter Bible*. Web. 8 June, 2017.

"G342 - anakainōsis - Strong's Greek Lexicon (NIV)." *Blue Letter Bible*. Web. 13 June, 2017.

Gray, J. *What You Feel, You Can Heal: A Guide For Enriching Relationships*. Mill Valley, CA: Heart Pub., 1994.

Guastello et al. *Chaos and Complexity In Psychology: The Theory of Nonlinear Dynamical Systems.* Cambridge: Cambridge University Press, 2009.

"H3162 - yachad - Strong's Hebrew Lexicon." Bible Hub. June 13, 2017.

"H3899 - lechem - Strong's Hebrew Lexicon (NIV)." *Blue Letter Bible.* Web. 13 June, 2017.

"H4421 - milchamah - Strong's Hebrew Lexicon (WLC)." *Blue Letter Bible.* Web. 13 June, 2017.

"H7965 - shalowm - Strong's Hebrew Lexicon (NLT)." *Blue Letter Bible.* Web. 8 June, 2017.

Hazan, C., Shaver, P. "Attachment As An Organizational Framework for Research on Close Relationships." *Psychological Inquiry, 5,* 1994. 1–22.

Hazan, C., Shaver, P. "Conceptualizing Romantic Love as an Attachment Process." *Journal of Personality and Social Psychology, 52,* 1987. 511-524.

Howe, D. *Attachment Across the Lifecourse: A Brief Introduction.* London: Palgrave, 2011.

Jennings, T.R. *The God-Shaped Brain: How Changing Your View of God Transforms Your Life.* Downers Grove: InterVarsity Press, 2017.

Johnson, S. *The Practice of Emotionally Focused Couple Therapy: Creating Connection.* New York: Brunner-Routledge, 2004.

Johnson, S., Williams-Keeler, L. "Creating Healing Relationships For Couples Dealing With Trauma: The Use of Emotionally Focused Marital Therapy." *Journal of Marital and Family Therapy, 24,* 1998. 25-40.

Kirkpatrick, L., Hazan, C. "Attachment Styles and Close Relationships: A Four Year Prospective Study." *Personal Relationships, 1,* 1994. 123–142.

Korb, A. *The Upward Spiral: Using Neuroscience To Reverse The Course of Depression, One Small Change At A Time.* Oakland: New Harbinger Publications, 2015.

McMinn, M., Phillips, T. *Care For The Soul: Exploring the Intersection of Psychology & Theology.* Downers Grove: InterVarsity Press, 2001.

National Center for Fathering. Osborne, C., McLanahan, S. "Partnership Instability and Child Well-Being." *Journal of Marriage and Family, 69,* 2007. 1065-1083. 2012. Retrieved March 21, 2017. http://www.fathers.com/statistics-and-research/the-consequences-of-fatherlessness.

Prince, D. *Blessing Or Curse: You Can Choose.* Grand Rapids: Chosen Books, 2006.

Prince, D. *Entering the Presence of God: Moving Beyond Praise and Thanksgiving To True Worship.* New Kensington: Whitaker House, 2007.

Rau, A. *Fathers & Faith: New Poll on Struggles with Dads and God.* Bible Gateway, 2015. www.biblegateway.com/blog/2015/02/fathers-faith-new-poll-on-struggles-with-dads-and-god/.

Roisman et al. "Earned-Secure Attachment Status in Retrospect and Prospect." *Child Development, 73 (4),* 2002. 1204-1219.

Schore, A.N. "Attachment and Regulation Of The Right Brain." *Attachment and Human Development, 2(1),* 2000. 23-47.

"self-will." *www.dictionary.com. Unabridged.* Random House, Inc. 9 June. 2017.

Serani, Deborah. *Living With Depression: Why Biology and Biography Matter Along the Path To Hope and Healing.* Lanham: Rowman & Littlefield, 2012.

Sheets, D. "Partnering in Authority: Who is Ruling Your World?" *The Elijah List.* Albany: Elijah List Publications. April 27, 2017.

Siegel, D.J. "Attachment and Self-Understanding: Parenting With The Brain In Mind." *Journal of Prenatal and Perinatal Psychology and Health, 18 (4),* 2004. 273-285.

Siegel, D.J. *The Developing Mind: How Relationships and the Brain Interact to Shape Who We Are.* New York: Guilford Press, 2015.

Siegel, D.J. *The Mindful Therapist: A Clinician's Guide to Mind Sight and Neural Integration.* New York: Norton, 2010.

Siegel, D.J. *Mindsight: The New Science of Personal Transformation.* New York: Bantam/Random House, 2010.

Simmons, B. *The Passion Translation*. BroadStreet Publishing Group LLC, 2015.

Simpson, A. *Troubled Minds: Mental Illness and the Church's Mission*. Downers Grove: InterVarsity Press, 2013.

Singer, I., Adler, C. *The Jewish Encyclopedia*. London: Funk & Wagnalls, 1902.

Thomas, C.B., Dudzynski, K. "Closeness to Parents and the Family Constellation in a Prospective Study of Five Disease States: Suicide, Mental Illness, Malignant Tumor, Hypertension, and Coronary Heart Disease," *Johns Hopkins Medical Journal, 134 (5)*, 1974. 251-270.

Tronick, E. "Emotions and Emotional Communication In Infants." *American Psychologist, 44 (2)*, 1989. 112–9.

U.S. Census Bureau, Current Population Survey. *Living Arrangements of Children under 18 Years/1 and Marital Status of Parents by Age, Sex, Race, and Hispanic Origin/2 and Selected Characteristics of the Child for all Children 2010*, 2010.

Van Der Kolk, B. *The Body Keeps the Score: Mind, Brain and Body In The Transformation of Trauma*. London: Penguin Books, 2015.

Vine, W. "Transfigure - Vine's Expository Dictionary of New Testament Words." *Blue Letter Bible*. 24 June, 1996. Web. 2 June, 2017.

Waters, E., Weinfield, N., Hamilton, C. "The Stability of Attachment Styles From Infancy to Adolescence and Early Adulthood: General Discussion." *Child Development, 71*, 2000. 703–706.

Wood, A., et al. "The Role of Gratitude In The Development of Social Support, Stress, and Depression: Two Longitudinal Studies." *Journal of Research in Personality, 42 (4)*, 2008.

www.jewishvirtuallibrary.org/edom

Zahn, R. et al. "The Neural Basis of Human Social Values: Evidence from Functional MRI." *Cerebral Cortex, 19 (2)*, 2009: 276–283.

ABOUT THE AUTHORS

Neal and Diane Arnold are the proud parents of three amazing young men and mentors to many future revivalists. Their passion is to help people experience God's heart and His healing presence in their lives. They are focused on bringing restoration to hurting leaders and families.

Neal has spent thirty-four years in financial service leadership positions in both large public and private organizations as CFO, Treasurer, and consultant. He has led the ABA's banking schools at the University of Colorado and spoken at numerous industry events. Neal is focused on recruiting and mentoring leadership teams in the midst of rapid growth and difficult turnaround situations. Diane is a licensed professional therapist with specialties in family and marriage counseling. She is also the co-founder of 'The Grace Center,' a healing and prayer center located in South Carolina.

Neal and Diane feel fortunate to have participated in revival and missions for the past thirty years. They continue to travel and speak on the importance of family and leader restoration so that we can all better demonstrate God's love, wisdom, and power to those in need.

Made in the USA
Monee, IL
08 February 2020

Studies in
Physiological Optics

Studies in
Physiological Optics

By

MELVIN L. RUBIN, M.S., M.D.

Assistant Professor of Ophthalmology
University of Florida College of Medicine
Gainesville, Florida

and

GORDON L. WALLS, Sc.D.

Late Professor of Physiological Optics
University of California School of Optometry
Berkeley, California

With a Foreword by

Kenneth N. Ogle, Ph.D.

Mayo Clinic and
Mayo Graduate School of Medicine
Rochester, Minnesota

C H A R L E S   C   T H O M A S   ·   P U B L I S H E R
Springfield   ·   Illinois   ·   U.S.A.

OPTOMETRY

Published and Distributed Throughout the World by
CHARLES C THOMAS • PUBLISHER
BANNERSTONE HOUSE
301-327 East Lawrence Avenue, Springfield, Illinois, U.S.A.
NATCHEZ PLANTATION HOUSE
735 North Atlantic Boulevard, Fort Lauderdale, Florida, U.S.A.

© *1965, by* CHARLES C THOMAS • PUBLISHER
Library of Congress Catalog Card Number: 65-15810

*With THOMAS BOOKS careful attention is given to all details of
manufacturing and design. It is the Publisher's desire to present
books that are satisfactory as to their physical qualities and artistic
possibilities and appropriate for their particular use. THOMAS
BOOKS will be true to those laws of quality that assure a good name
and good will.*

Printed in the United States of America
N-1

To

Paul Boeder
a master teacher, scholar and friend

In Memoriam

Of all my close friends, no one individual impressed and excited me more than Gordon Lynn Walls, Professor of Physiological Optics at the University of California School of Optometry. Fifteen years ago as a freshman student, I was first introduced to him and was visibly struck by the appearance of the man who was to reshape my future career. He did not fulfill the stereotype I had established for a prominent university professor.

He was a relatively slight man with sharp features; a pair of frameless, thick myopic spectacles crowded his face; a cigarette and cloud of smoke were omnipresent, coupled with a continual throat-clearing snort because of a persistent post-nasal drip. He wore a bright red open-necked sport shirt with an imposing shiny gloss from countless pressings. His loose trousers also shone with a mirror-like finish. From his belt hung an enormous ring of heavy keys which persistently tugged at his trousers, which he valiantly retugged. I had to be assured he was not the building custodian. Such was my initial impression of G. L. W. It was only later that I learned it was not unusual for him to appear garbed in his open-necked sport shirt and pendant ring of keys at a formal meeting.

I was steered to Gordon because of my interest in binocular

vision and my hobby of stereoscopic photography. He took me in hand, planted seeds of curiosity and watered them with a profound knowledge of factual, theoretical, and sometimes ethereal information which continually streamed from him. Always outwardly gruff, he was actually an "impatiently" patient individual. In spite of an ostensive hostility towards medicine, he did his utmost to direct me into medicine and ophthalmology—a masterful bit of maneuvering for which I remain everlastingly grateful.

Gordon was a mechanical engineer and a zoologist by training. He did his early post-doctoral work in comparative anatomy of the vertebrate visual system which culminated in his classic textbook, *The Vertebrate Eye*, published in 1942. His interest in vision was manifest in a long series of papers and monographs; early, along morphologic lines, later, in physiological optics, always with a yen for testing (sometimes wild) hypotheses in attempted correlation between anatomy and physiology. The exciting subject of color vision occupied his attention during his last years. He displayed a magnificent knowledge in this area, and was engaged in writing a text on color vision when he passed away.

Although he was known everywhere as a superb teacher, speaker and writer, he was not known for mild manners and sweetness. He was a blunt, outspoken critic of many scientific publications and his commentaries and reviews were biting and sarcastic, though always entertaining and beautifully expressed. He was an enviable man in many ways, a walking encyclopedic source of visual science information; however, his tragic personal life exacted its toll on his tremendous energy.

Walls died suddenly in mid-1962 and left a vacuum which is only partially filled by his many fine publications. His death deprived the world of a truly wonderful teacher and myself of a fine friend. All who came under his tutelage were extremely fortunate for the opportunity of knowing him, working with him, and even more importantly, learning from him. Most assuredly, he will be missed.

M. L. R.

Foreword

It is becoming increasingly important that
qualified personnel be attracted to the fields
of vision, visual science and visual health. Good eye care is being
increasingly sought after by the public, as sight conservation programs stress the economic and sociologic burden of blindness. To
all who are professionally concerned with each of these areas, and
to others, it is apparent that interest in vision must be stimulated.
Because the need for trained personnel is so great, it is necessary to
interest the student in this area early in his scientific training.

There is no question that there exists a large number of students of general physiology who would be receptive to a study of
visual physiology. However, there has been a lack of emphasis in
this area in the general courses of physiology. An ever-increasing
number of ophthalmologists also are coming to believe that
postgraduate residency training programs need strengthening in
optics and visual physiology. The American Committee of Optics
and Visual Physiology has been especially concerned, and has even
adopted the slogan, "Let's put Helmholtz back into Ophthalmology." The problem of how best to achieve this end is a difficult
one. More men and women professionally trained in optics and
visual physiology must be added to the medical school and residency training staffs. But, unfortunately, this is not always
possible.

Heretofore, there have been few suitable texts which would provide the student with an organized set of simple experiments that would introduce him to a study of vision and that would, hopefully, lure him to a further study of visual science. The following monograph by Dr. Rubin and the late Dr. Walls was written specifically for the student, and is admirably suited as an introduction to optics and visual physiology. The appeal of this presentation lies in its simplicity. The numerous observations and experiments suggested enhance the value of the book beyond that which could be obtained from just reading the text. The monograph is well suited as introductory material not only for the physiology student but for the resident in Ophthalmology as well. The style is breezy and at times "slangy," yet this seems to increase the ease of reading. The initial section of the book is devoted to simple, pertinent observations that might properly be classified as psychological optics, and leads the reader smoothly and naturally into the more important aspects of physiological optics.

We must be grateful to Dr. Rubin for making this book available, for it most definitely fills a need in all curricula where training in the physiology of vision is desired.

KENNETH N. OGLE, PH.D.
Mayo Clinic and Mayo Graduate
School of Medicine
University of Minnesota
Rochester, Minnesota

Preface

Vision has provoked more scientific interest and more intensive research for a longer period of time than any of the other special senses (or, for that matter, any other subject in the vast field of physiology). Yet, in the medical physiology curriculum, the oldest segment of that basic science has not received the emphasis it deserves in proportion to its contributions toward general physiologic knowledge.

About ten years ago Professor Gordon L. Walls of the University of California School of Optometry asked me (then, a medical student, but formerly, a physiological optics student of his) to help him organize a series of interesting yet simply performed experiments about the eye and vision. We discussed almost fifty separate subjects and methodically narrowed down our list, deleting those which required too much in the way of elaborate equipment. We finally "boiled down" the list to those subjects covered here and Professor Walls utilized these experiments for the laboratory portion of an elementary course in physiological optics until he died in 1962. A mimeographed laboratory syllabus entitled, *Simple Experiments on the Eye and Vision,* was initially duplicated and distributed to the students by the school; but because this task was laborious, in 1958 a local Berkeley bookstore, the California Book Company, was enlisted to perform this function.

There was no question in my mind that the material had a broad appeal and could aptly be used in general physiology courses, as well as in psychology, optometry or ophthalmology training programs. However, it was not until this year that I was given the opportunity to prove this impression. I was asked to organize a laboratory course in visual physiology for our medical student physiology classes at the University of Florida. I began by revising my and Professor Walls' original notes and constructed a laboratory manual for this course. Encouraged by student response, I felt that the material did offer to physiology a large amount of practical and theoretical information on the subject of vision and could, quite easily, be utilized by any department of general physiology interested in such a presentation. Thus, through the courtesy of Professor Arthur B. Otis, Chairman, Department of Physiology at the University of Florida and Professor Meredith Morgan, Dean, University of California School of Optometry, we are making the revised experiments available in published form.

Regretfully, I have found it necessary to leave unmentioned such basic optical phenomena as diffraction and interference and such interesting visual physiology stories as the Purkinje Shift, the course of dark adaptation, photopigment chemistry, analysis of the Haidinger Brushes and many, many others. These have been neglected not because of their intrinsic lack of importance, but because it was difficult for me to set up *simple* experiments to demonstrate them in a meaningful way in the short time alloted. Therefore, I would plead that the student and reader approach the following explorations into visual science with the realization that the collection of experiments presented is but an elementary introduction to the subject and in no way attempts to be exhaustive.

To give full, proper credit to each reference utilized in the construction of this manual would require many additional pages of print. Also, many of the experiments are based on phenomena which were observed in antiquity and the true "first description" could not be located by this author. Thus, with much soul searching, I have decided to list only a group of general references, and not a complete list, which a student might logically expect to find in a syllabus such as this.

Laboratory time may be insufficient to allow completion of all the experiments. The results of most, however, can be anticipated and fully comprehended even though one does not actually perform them; to obtain the full impact, of course, one should experience each one personally. Take, for example, Experiment No. 12 in which one demonstrates vividly that the retinal image is reversed—an elementary and obvious fact. It is remarkable how much of an impression is left when one demonstrates this simply and clearly to himself. One *feels* himself (via his kinesthetic sense) place a pin into view from one direction, and yet he *sees* it appear from the opposite side. To quote an overused expression, "It must be seen to be appreciated!"

Most of the following experiments require little or no unusual equipment and can easily be done by a student, alone or with a laboratory partner. Some are best performed by the instructor for small groups of students.

The use of the necessary common items of equipment is fully explained in the text. Those less common are pictured in various figures throughout the text.

Throughout the text and experimental instructions the reader will find notes to "observe the posted pictures, etc." Since this manual was designed to be used as a laboratory adjunct, those notes refer to diagrams and photographs which are to be "up on a wall" somewhere in the laboratory. Almost all of these pictures are duplicated in the body of the text.

Portions of the text which come to the left hand margin of the page contain the general pertinent information; the deeply indented paragraphs contain the special instructions for doing something observational or experimental. The experiments are organized into six groups of more or less related items. There is, however, no need for performing them exactly in order.

As a suggestion, I would emphasize that to glean as much as possible from the laboratory periods, the student would be wise to read over the details at least once, preferably twice, before performing the experimental observations. I am quite confident that the reader's intellectual curiosity will be piqued by much of the material to follow and so will be stimulated to do ancillary reading. This, of course, is as it should be.

I would like to express my sincere thanks to Mr. Maurice Sherrard, Instructor in Surgical Illustration at the University of Florida, for his fine sketches and diagrams, and to Mrs. Martha Musselwhite for her typing and proofreading of the many revisions of this manuscript.

Melvin L. Rubin

Contents

	Page
In Memoriam	vii
Foreword	ix
Preface	xi

Section I
Visual Perception and Spatial Localization

Experiment

1. Visual Perception 3
2. Perception–Figure-Ground Relationships 22
3. Perceptual Constancy 29
4. Visual Direction 34
5. Visual Distance ("Depth") 37
6. Stereoscopy 45
7. Fusion and Some Alternatives 54
8. Visual Solidness 57

Section II
Basic Visual Optics

9. Accommodation 60
10. Refractive Errors 62
11. Light Sources and Eye Opacities 66

Experiment   *Page*

12. Inversion of the Retinal Image 69

13. Pupillary Size and Pupillary Reflexes 70

Section III
Visual Field and Eye Movements

14. Objective and Subjective Light 74

15. The Visual Field 75

16. The Physiological Scotoma 78

17. Eye Movements 80

18. Protective Reflexes 84

Section IV
Adaptation and Brightness

19. Adaptation to Light Intensity 86

20. Local Retinal Adaptation 88

21. Equal Final Brightness from Unequal Intensities 89

22. Craik Blindness 91

23. Brightness Versus Intensity 92

Section V
Acuity and Sensation-Times

24. Intensity Discrimination 95

25. Visual Acuity 97

26. Visual Sensation-Time 101

27. Visual Persistence-Time 104

28. Visual Movement 110

Section VI
Color

29. Subjectivity of Color 114

30. Color Mixture 115

31. Blackness 119

32. Spatial Induction of Color 120

33. Color Blindness 121

   References 125

Studies in
Physiological Optics

Visual Perception and
Spatial Localization

1. Visual Perception

IMAGINE WHAT OUR WORLD WOULD BE LIKE WITH-
OUT VISION. SOUNDS, SMELLS, TOUCHES—THESE
would serve as our only contact with the environment, the representation of which is at best poor when compared with that given
us by our visual sense. How difficult it is for us to understand
exactly how a congenitally blind individual can have any appreciation at all of visual realities. Even if he has a set of the most highly
developed senses, he can never know exactly what he is missing.
He does not even have any visual imagery. Hallucination induced
in him (e.g., by hallucinogenic drugs) are *never* visual; even his
dreams are not "visual."

Being duly appreciative of our gifts, let us see what having
"vision" does for us. Let us examine how retinal image patterns
are interpreted into percepts which give us our clues as to space,
size and orientation in our environment.

As we look around, the retinal image of external space is
really a two-dimensional pattern of distribution, on the retina, of
high and low light intensities and spectral compositions. All of
the information about our surroundings that we obtain by way of
our eyes, we have to extract from this retinal "stimulus configuration" by "referring" parts of it and combinations of parts of it
"out there" into subjective external space. We do not see our

retinal *images* of things—we see the *things*. The kinds of information our eyes can give us are:

a) Visual sensations.
b) Visual percepts.
c) Visual knowledge of events.
d) Non-visual information conveyed by visual symbols such as words, mathematical signs, drawings, signals and codes.

The last two categories are self-explanatory and can be ignored here, particularly as there is certainly nothing physiological about them. We shall concentrate on the first two. A visual sensation ought to be a visual experience of the simplest possible kind, in a situation where we might find that we were sensing a particular brightness but nothing else (visual) whatever, or redness with no other visual accompaniment, or flicker all by itself, etc. But pure, simple visual (or other!) sensation is extremely rare and very hard to arrange for. Unless the entire visual field is occupied by the stimulus, the experience is bound to have a size and a shape, practically forcing us to localize it at some distance, and we find ourselves seeing a "thing" and placing some interpretation or other upon it, reading some meaning or other into it. In short, we find ourselves "perceiving" and not merely "sensing," no matter how simple we try to make the stimulus-configuration.

A bisected ping-pong ball is about the simplest apparatus with which we can give ourselves a visual experience simple enough to deserve to be called a sensation. Get two half-balls from the supply table and, if bright sky is available, go to the window — otherwise, sit facing a bright light-bulb or slide projector, so that your face is bathed with illumination. Install the plastic shells over your eyes like monocles, lowering your eyebrows to hold them in place so that you can take your hands away. It will not much matter whether your lids are open or shut, but try to keep them open. The translucent plastic will diffuse the light and homogenize the illumination of your visual fields. It will be very hard for you to convince yourself that you are seeing any "things" or that the neutral brightness pervading your visual world connotes anything, signifies anything, represents anything. With luck, then, you will be experiencing a simple sensation of light.

The moment a visual stimulus makes us suppose that "out there" before us there is a this, a that, a such-and-such, a so-and-so, we have a percept and not just a sensation. Most visual experiences are percepts, and most of these are identifications, recognitions. Visual identification does not require that we be shown the very same stimulus under the very same conditions. A phenomenon called "stimulus equivalence" is forever coming to our aid. You have never seen a live horse that was only three inches high, but if you were shown one, you would call it a horse. A toddler with his right eye covered could be taught what a triangle is and would proceed to recognize the first triangle ever subsequently presented, even if only to that right eye.

Perception is the seeing of *things*. It is very hard *not* to see things; we are so organized, through developmental processes and early learning, that we inevitably "make something" (make some *thing*) out of every patch of the total retinal image that can possibly be conceived *as* a thing. It is this powerful propensity that ensures that the visual world shall seem real and filled with real things, with these all outside of ourselves and localized in stable fashion in real-seeming space. This is most fortunate for our sanity and our confidence in dealing with our environment, for the average person lives and dies without ever knowing that he has never seen or heard or touched a *real* object but has only seen *visual* objects whose properties were all in his own mind, and heard *auditory* objects, and handled *tactual* objects—each, a conglomeration of purely sensory attributes bearing only a psychophysical relationship, never an identity, with any real physical property of the real object.

No matter how simple the retinal stimulus-configuration may be, we usually succeed (and, without even trying) in attaching meaning, interpretation. This insistent process of combining interpretation-as-something with what would otherwise be simple sensations is carried out by ill-defined portions of the brain which we may call, collectively, our "perceptual apparatus." This has available to it the "filing-cabinets" of memory (another little-understood mechanism) and the streams of incoming information from other sense-organs. When we perceive an object bearing down upon us to be a locomotive, we are not entirely dependent on what is in the retinal image at the moment. We "associate" the hissing, the clanking, the trembling of the ground, the hot-oil smell, with the strictly visual impression. Of course, most of us have seen a locomotive before, and would recognize one in a picture—but we would know it was not real.

Visual percepts result from the operation of the perceptual apparatus, which to all intents and purposes is an unconscious process. The perceptual apparatus needs no help from our "reasoning" and acts so independently that we often continue to perceive the same thing in the same way even after reasoning has informed us that we are "in error." Sophistication can alter perception but often only after a prolonged struggle.

By definition, illusions are "false" perceptions. When we do experience an illusion, we experience certain things which fail to correspond with the situation as objectively measured. (There is, however, always a corresponding, clearly apparent, external stimulus present. This is in contrast to a hallucination which is an abnormal percept without an apparent objective stimulus.) Anyway, here is a small collection of the classical "optical illusions"— all merely demonstrations that you will perceive this way or that way depending upon circumstances:

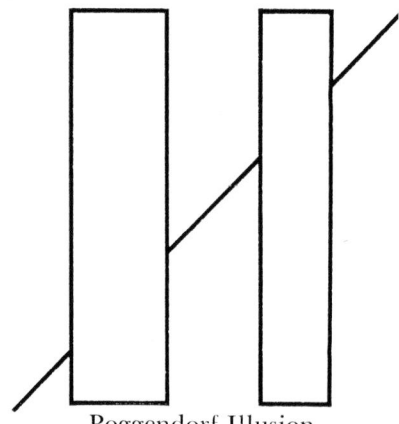

Poggendorf Illusion

The three diagonal lines do not appear to be parts of one straight line. Even after you put your eye close to the page and sight along the diagonals, and see that they are indeed aligned, you will still perceive them as misaligned when you view the page in the normal manner.

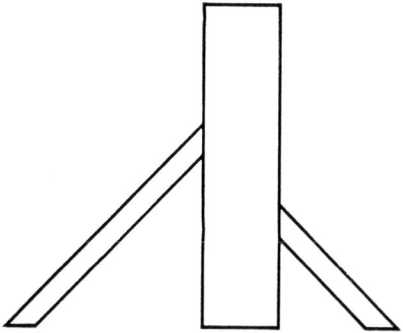

Helmholtz Illusion

The oblique lines on the right-hand side are really directed to the points where those on the left hand side meet the upright column, although this is contrary to the impression produced by the drawing.

Perception is insistent, even when thinking can point out its errors. In the following illusion the line which looks like a spiral is indeed composed of concentric circles. Trace out a path around the center from any point on the line and see. Yet it continues to look like a spiral.

The legs on the two gentlemen below are straight, if observed without reference to the checkerboard. Raise the book to eye level and observe.

Move the book slowly as though you were rinsing something in a pan and you will note dark sector radii moving about.

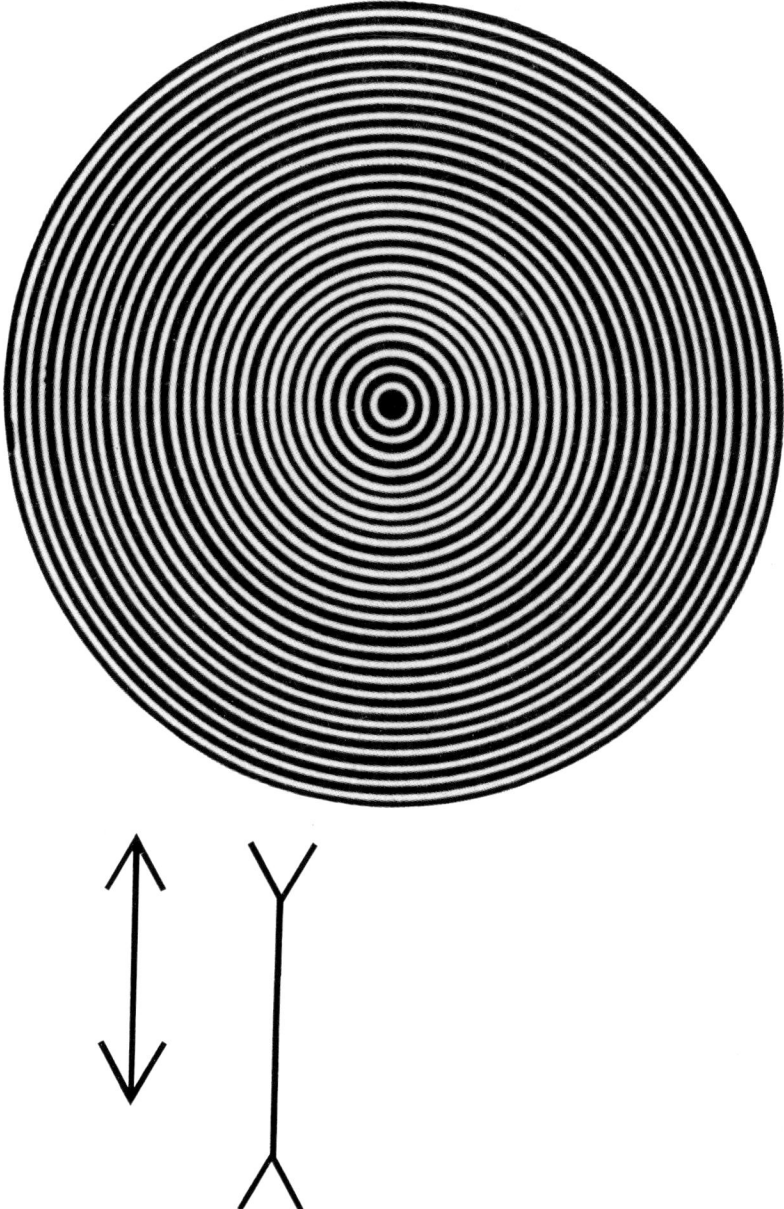

Muller-Lyer illusion — both vertical lines are the same length.

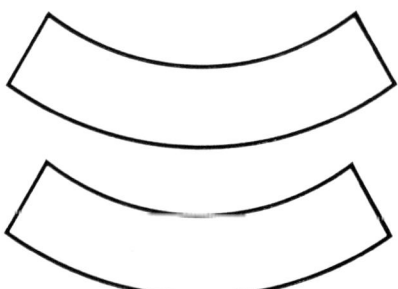

The figures are congruous.

The hat, though seemingly much
taller than the brim, is actually
of equal measurement.

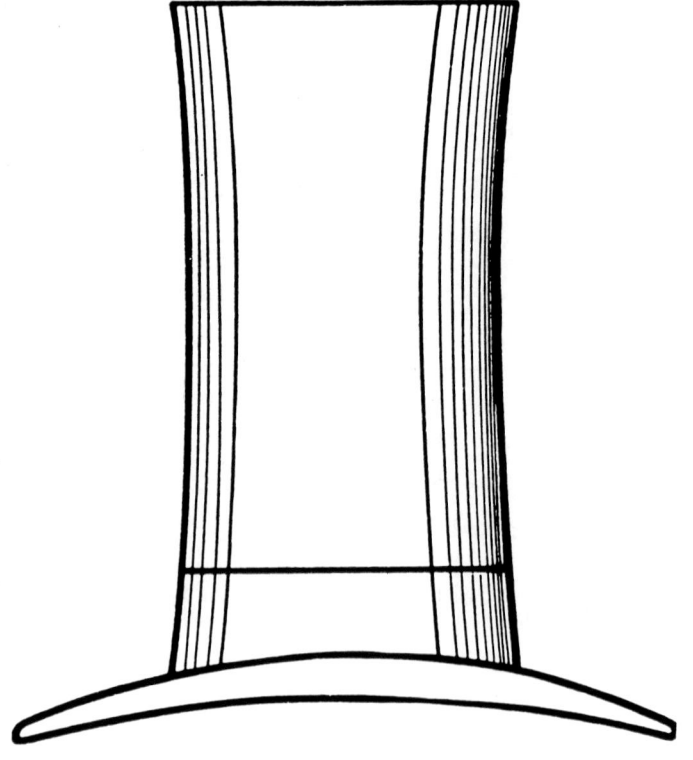

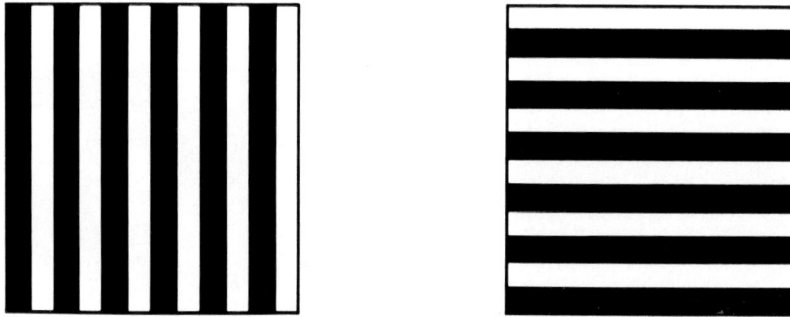

The square on the right seems oblong horizontally, while that on the left seems longer vertically.

Zollner illusion

Hering illusion

The long lines are parallel in each of these illusions.

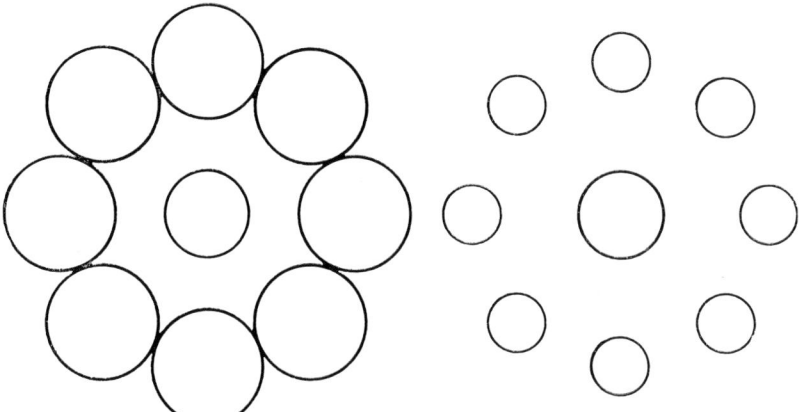

Titchener Illusion
The central spots are equal in size.

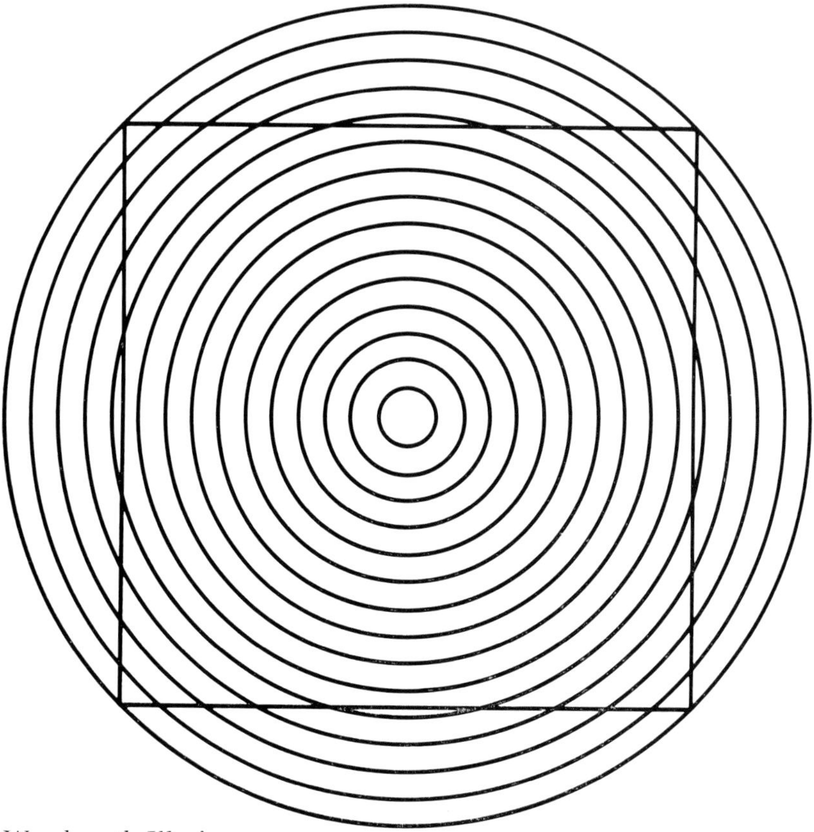

Woodworth Illusion
The square's sides are truly straight and not curved as they appear.

Past experience and sophistication help to determine which thing, out of various possibilities, we will perceive corresponding to a given chunk of the stimulus-configuration. The retinal image of a large white cylinder bearing a spiral red stripe arouses the percept of a gigantic peppermint stick in a little girl. Her father sees there a barbershop sign. An African pygmy who knows nothing of candy or barbers might see a section of elephant tusk with blood smeared neatly around it. However, any normal person whatever will see a red stripe on a white background, and in turn will see a white cylinder upon its background. The cylinder may have no meaning whatever for a given person, but this does not keep the cylinder from standing out as in integrated entity, as something distinct from its context and backdrop. The cylinder is a "figure," with respect to which everything around it is its "ground."

Our perceptual apparatus seems bound-and-determined to "organize" the stimulus-configuration into relationships of figures and grounds ("Gestalts"). As a further step in the elaboration of a finished percept, it adds related material from memory, and makes use of any impressions being concurrently received via other sensory systems. The usual end-result is that the figure is identified as a particular *thing*. If, however, nothing pertinent is available in the form of memories, and if the other senses are being left unstimulated, the perceptual apparatus will still elaborate a figure-ground relationship, and we will then have to say that the figure seems meaningless.

If we look at a simple black ink-blot on a white card, we perceive the black as constituting a figure, whereas the white is a ground. The ground has no shape—it is only the figure that has shape. The ground has no boundaries—the contour of the black belongs to the black alone, and not at the same time to the white. The ground is continuous—it seems perfectly natural to think of the spot as standing forward from the card, at least far enough to let the white ground be continuous, *unbroken* behind the spot.

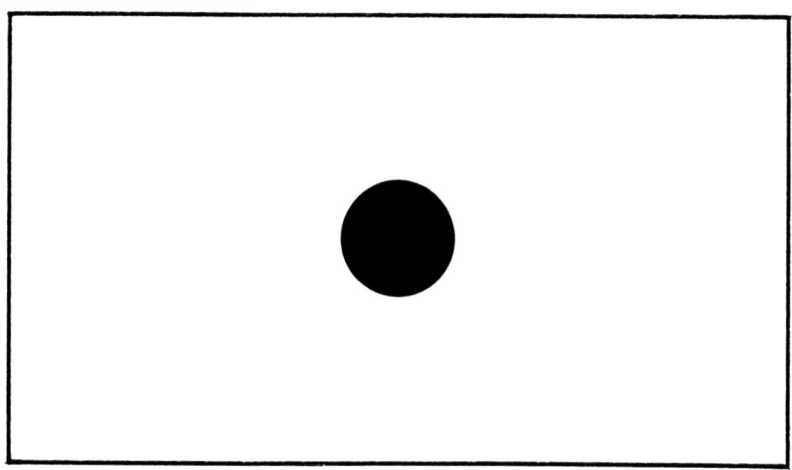

In the next experiment, No. 2, more about figure-ground relationships will be discussed.

Symmetry is a factor in figure-creation. Parts of a figure may be tied to each other to make one figure (instead of belonging to several other figures), in accordance with several laws of perception besides the law of symmetry.

Consider this situation:

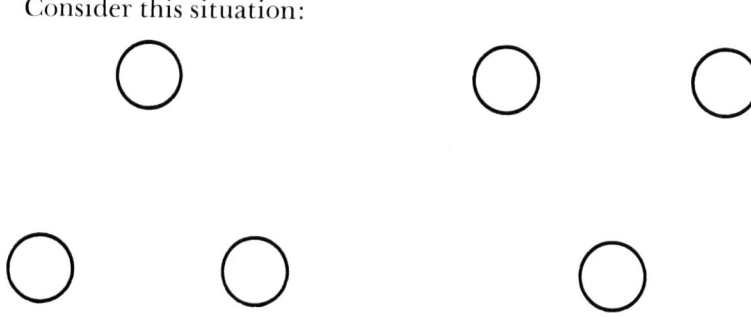

What do you see here? A group of six spots? No—two groups of three each. Why? It is the proximity of some spots to others that makes them form a group, the lack of proximity that keeps them from belonging instead with other spots in another group. Each *group* of *several* spots is a figure, *one* figure. We readily perceive *two triangles* here; and, we do not have to imagine hypothetical straight lines connecting up the spots in each group—we *perceive*

just such connections, as so-called "bridge lines," without having to picture lines in our mind's eye at all. The bridge lines would be there, tying the figures together, even if we had never seen a triangle in our lives.

Now consider this situation:

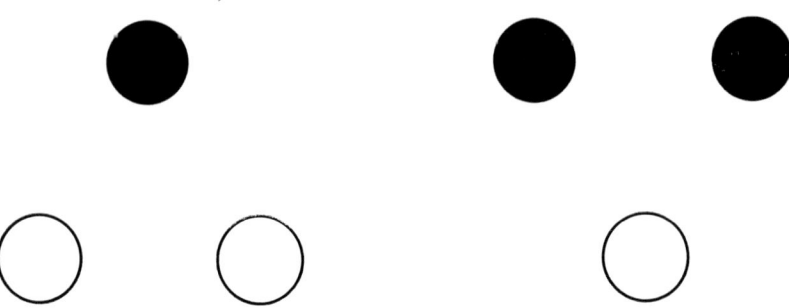

The proximity factor by itself would make the two dark spots at the right form a figure along with one of the clear spots. But, we do not perceive that clear spot as belonging with the dark spots. Instead, it and the two clear spots on the left form a group of their own, and the dark spots form a group that contains only dark spots. The group-making agency here is similarity, and this overrules proximity when the two are put into conflict.

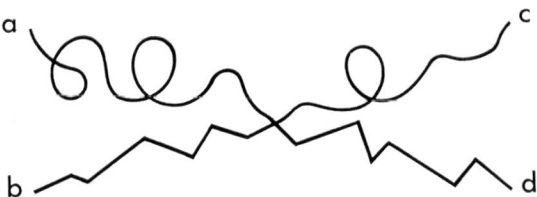

In the above configuration, we are in no doubt that a-c is one line and b-d is another. The similarity factor is enough to keep us from readily perceiving such a line as a-d, or b-c.

Continuousness with each other, alignment with each other, can reinforce similarity in making lines appear to comprise a single contour or the boundary of a single figure. *Closedness* gives to a contour a great boost toward constituting the outline of a figure.

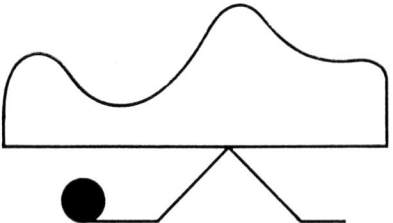

The preceding figure is readily perceived as being made up of:

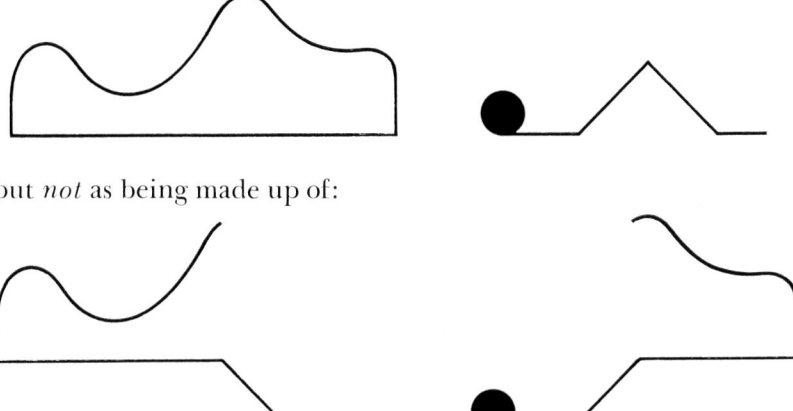

but *not* as being made up of:

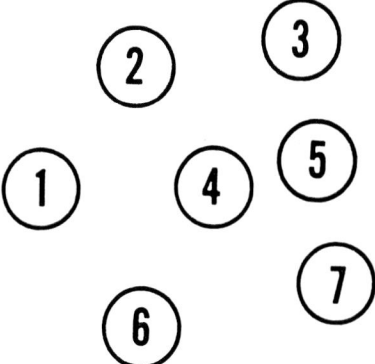

although these latter gadgets are just as much potential or latent in the retinal stimulus-configuration.

In the above cluster of numbered spots, none of the factors we have so far considered operates to make any three of the spots form a group, perceived as a discrete figure. Suppose, however, Nos. 1, 2 and 7 should suddenly start to drift to the left at the same velocity. Their *common movement* would instantly make those spots group into a figure. The four non-moving spots might or might not hang together and comprise a figure also—probably not, since they would still have nothing positive in common. It is common movement that keeps many a figure unified in spite of kaleidoscopic changes of the retinal stimulus-configuration. A man might have each sleeve and pantsleg and coat area in a different color and pattern, and he might be doing gymnastics, but he would be continuously perceived as a single entity by virtue of common movement of his parts.

The perceptual apparatus readily supplies "missing parts" and can "complete a figure" even when it is given very little immediate sensory raw material to work with. You have no trouble perceiving letters here:

even though, in retrospect, you find that not one part of any "letter" contrasts in the least with the paper. No contour is complete around any letter, and yet the whole of each block letter is "visible" and may even appear brighter than the ground. Some of the following demonstrations further illustrate the perceptual "completion of figures."

Seemingly random "spots" may be completed or filled in by a viewer provided the figural organization is already reasonably good. Some individuals have much stronger tendencies towards figural organization than others. Most people quickly supply the missing portions of the dog in the drawing above, but not everyone is able to complete the missing portions of the knight on his horse so promptly, and very few indeed ascertain that the third sketch is a kneeling man in an overcoat taking a photo through a Graflex view camera!

This same perceptual "filling in" is very common in reading; we jump to conclusions that certain words *are* what they seem, when we might not be able to distinguish single letters. This is what makes proofreading so difficult, since we recognize word *form* and tend to overlook spelling mistakes.

When the parts of a stimulus-configuration could just as well be organized into one figure as another, your perceptual apparatus will always present to you the "best possible" figure, if there is any choice at all as regards meaningfulness. You will be practically forced to perceive the "best" figure even when this one is asymmetrical, if the symmetrical figures which apparently you might just as well see "make less sense."

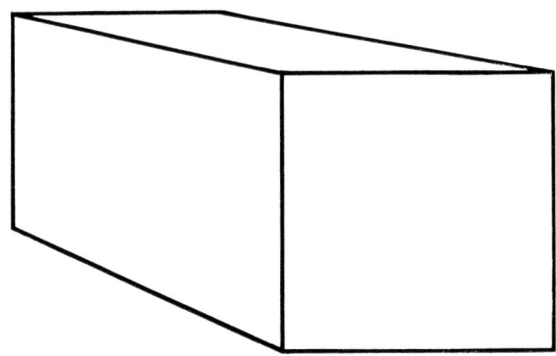

The above drawing illustrates the point. Perceived as a block in three dimensions it makes sense, it is a "good figure." Perceived as a group of continuous polygons all in one plane, it makes no sense. Only one of these polygons—the square—is in itself a "good figure." But the "block" employs all the lines of the square and all the other, otherwise useless, lines also, to constitute a larger figure. We perceive this larger figure that uses up all of the lines in the configuration, not the smaller figure (the plane square) which would give us an untidy clutter of unused elements "left over."

2. Perception—Figure-Ground Relationships

During everyday observation, all objects are perceived against some background; mountains stand out against a light sky, cherry blossoms against the leaves and branches of a tree, a group of jail-birds against a hard rock pile. In a painting, usually an obvious subject is presented against a background. In all these examples the "figure" is prominent, the "ground" is clearly defined. How-ever, when the ground and figure are not so clearly separated, shifts in perception may result, because of the lack of a reference. Wartime camouflage is the deliberate confusion of figure and ground. The protective coloration of certain animals is an instance of camouflage in nature. The figure and ground may be so closely linked perceptually that it may be difficult to decide which is which.

The following demonstration situations have been "rigged" so that the material perceived immediately as a figure is just as well able to constitute ground, provided the material first seen as ground can just as readily organize into figures. One of the best demonstrations of such a reversible figure and ground relationship is the "Rubin (no kin) vase," a reproduction of which follows. Also, look at the adjoining pictures of the sectored disc and of the hooks. In each of these drawings there is an instability of percep-tion, for their mutual contour is not mutual at all—it can belong only to one subject at a time.

> If you fixate the center of any part of any of the figures below, you will note how first one aspect stands out, then the other. At one moment, you see the black figures as though on a white background; the next moment you see the white figures as though on a black background. The frequency of such figure-ground fluctuations can be influenced by trying to hold one as long as possible. The figure *will* change, despite your effort to hold it, but it will very likely change less often.
>
> In the former drawings, both possible figures were "whole" and complete. An interesting relatively new illusion is the fol-lowing, which has its basis in the partial ambiguity introduced. Here *neither* figures seen is complete. If attention is directed to the right side of the model one figure is perceived; if, to the left, another. Both perceptions are mutually exclusive.

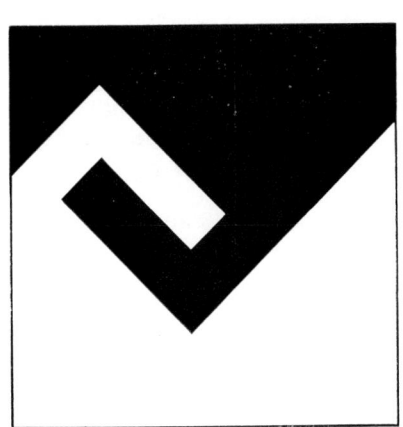

As in camouflage, context may serve to conceal a form. Complicated intricate patterns are not necessary to hide an object. For example, the form (A.) is present within each of the following figures although it gets more difficult to decide exactly where it is hidden in the last pattern.

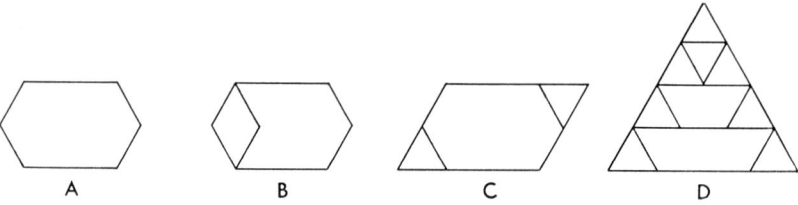

A   B   C   D

In the perception of certain drawings, such as the classical three shown below (The Schroeder Staircase, the "cubes," and the Necker Cube), the representation is seen as 3-dimensional (see experiment No. 5 on Depth Perception), but its depth spontaneously reverses from time to time, since the drawing is completely ambiguous—the object will be seen now sticking out of the page, now sticking into the page. By will—i.e., mental set—one may see the object for some time in one way; eventually it will reverse.

Following are three well-known ambiguous figures. At one instant the staircase will appear such, and the next will seem to be a piece of overhanging masonry. The cubes shift in or out and concomitantly change their number — count them! The third is a set of bi-dimensional drawings of the Necker rhomboids. The phenomenon visualized is described below.

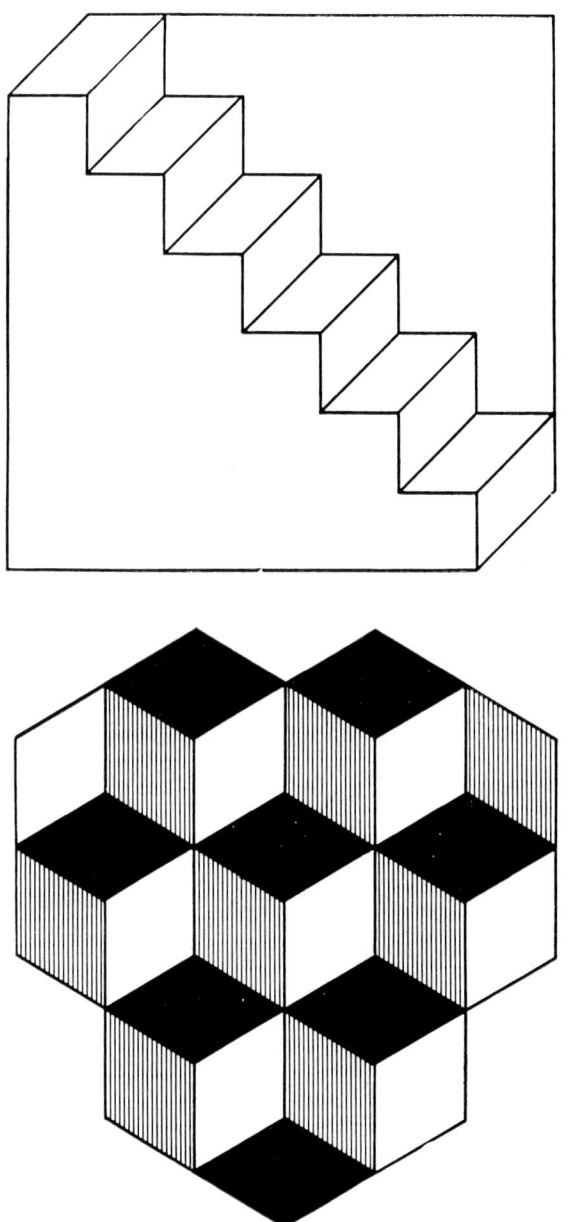

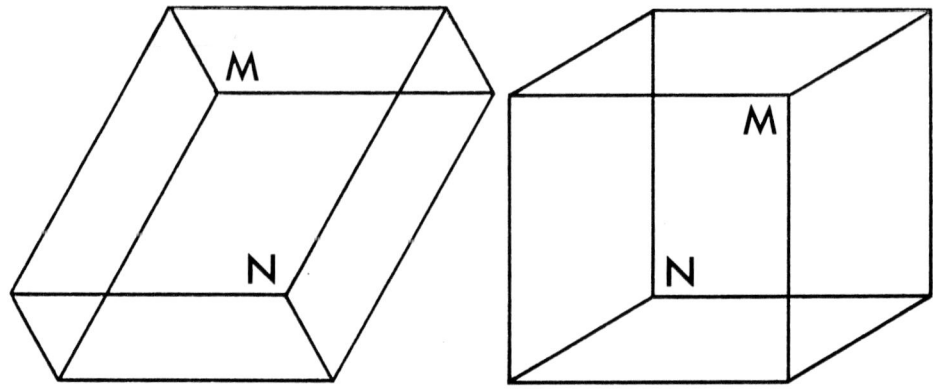

The rhomboid was Necker's original figure and is "reversed" more easily than the cube; this is probably because the rhomboid stands upon an edge and is not prejudiced in favor of one or the other perspective, whereas the cube is more readily perceived as resting flat on the ground (M near) than in the alternative peculiar uptilted position (N near). If either of the figures is drawn in true perspective (i.e., designed for monocular viewing from a specified distance) the ease with which they can be reversed is reduced, since the "reversed" figure will seem to have distorted sides (see Figure 1). Necker also noted that although the reversal of either of the figures may appear fortuitous, the change can be controlled by fixating M or N, for the corner fixated is generally seen as nearer to the observer and thus determines the object seen.

In this same way, one may perceive and reverse at will, a *real* cube (and not just a flat drawing of one) provided the cube is not opaque. The wire cube (called von Hornbostel's cube) is a favorable object.

> Hold the cube very still by its handle and close one eye. "Tell yourself" that the nearer face of the cube is really the farther, and vice versa. Shortly, the cube will "reverse." You will notice that the cube no longer seems to have right angles — it is not properly cubical, for its perspective now seems wrong (although you were not *conscious* of the perspective at all before the cube was reversed). Perspective, then, can sometimes be overcome merely by mental set.

Figure 1. Von Hornbostel's Cube—When viewed "unreversed," the cube appears in proper perspective; if viewed "reversed," the face and sides appear distorted (for a cube) and the cube looks like a truncated pyramid.

Slowly roll the handle of the "reversed" cube in your fingers. The cube's visual rotation will be in the opposite direction. The visual-spatial and tactual-spatial perceptions are in disagreement here, and the visual "wins" (as it usually does). Keeping the cube "reversed" monocularly, tilt it toward you or away — it will seem to be fastened to its handle not rigidly but by means of a hinge.

"Reverse" the cube and rotate it while a finger of the other hand rests on it or in it. Grasp the cube with this other hand, and rotate it with that hand instead of by means of the handle. Visual and tactual spatialities are in sharp conflict, but the visual "reversal" prevails and determines the apparent direction of the rotation of the cube. If necessary (i.e., if your mind forces it), the wires will seem to cut through the fingers.

"Reverse" the cube; hold it still. Cautiously open the other eye to bring retinal disparity and stereopsis (Experiment No. 5 on depth perception) into conflict with the mental set. Can you keep the cube reversed "inside-out," even if only for a few seconds? Can it be rotated a bit without it re-reversing, seeming "right-side-out"?

Last, try viewing the cube binocularly and "reversing it" without having reversed it in monocular vision first.

The block drawing at the end of the last experiment (No. 1 —Perception and Illusions) is a simple form, so that you are easily able to perceive the square as a square or a face of a cube, by just wanting to. But sometimes, in an ambiguous configuration, one of the two possible figures is *so* good, so complex, so entirely thing-like, that we see it first. Later, we may (or may not) notice the other figure. This sort of thing goes on all the time, as we suddenly find that we have been "mistaken" in the identification of a thing or a person, and promptly see something else or someone else there, without there having been the slightest change in the retinal image.

Much of the same set of one-track operation of the perceptual apparatus can be demonstrated by perceiving one of the two potential figures in a single configuration; it may be a strenuous mental exercise to discover the other figure at all, even though it is equally evident. Among the posted demonstrations (also pictured below), contemplate the reproduction of the classical "wife and mother-in-law" drawing, and the new one, "Indi-

an father or son." You may see only the wife or only the mother-in-law, or the old chief or the young one. Do not help your class-mates to see any figure they cannot see. If you are able to see both figures in each drawing, note that you cannot see both at the same time.

In all these reversible figures, the sensory stimulus remains the same, but perception changes with the meaning which the object has for the observer.

3. Perceptual Constancy

It has been emphasized that the visual impressions we have are of things outside of ourselves, at various distances in a sub-jective space which corresponds to real physical space, despite the fact that the real first step in vision is a photo-chemical disturb-ance in a thin layer of the retina. This "externalization" of visual impressions helps to convince the naive layman that his visual objects are the real objects, that the visual qualities and properties of an object are its real physical properties: the box *is* twice as tall as it is wide, its outside *is* red, its inside *is* dark, etc.

Besides externalization, there is another feature of visual per-ception that contributes powerfully to our deception (vitally necessary, but still a deception) about the realness of our visual world. This feature, "constancy," makes visual objects seem real by giving them an important kind of stability, a permanence-of-properties. Considering that the same real object, under differing circumstances, may be represented in the retinal image by patches of illumination that differ in size, shape, intensity, spectral dis-tribution, motion-over-the-retina, etc., it is essential that we be enabled to perceive it continuously as the same-object-all-the-time, and not see it apparently changing its size and shape, etc., when it is not really doing so. It is perceptual constancy that keeps the object's *apparent real intrinsic* properties (as distinguished, for instance, from the kind of light falling upon it) near enough to constant so that we are not perpetually confused by any seeming instability of objects.

Constancy is not one phenomenon but several, each perhaps with its own underlying mechanism. We can observe constancies of several different visual properties. Here, we can consider only the three most important: size-constancy, shape-constancy, and lightness-constancy.

Have your partner stand twenty feet from you. Estimate his height in feet and inches. Have him walk halfway toward you and stop. Again estimate his height. Do your two estimates differ materially? They are certainly not in two-to-one ratio, and yet your second retinal image of him was twice the height, four times the area, of the first.

You now understand what is meant by size constancy. It holds up very well, out to considerable distances. A six-foot man, fifty or even 100 feet away still looks like a six-foot man, not like a little doll. Of course automobiles seen from the top of the Empire State Building do look like toys; but perceptual size does not shrink much until the object is so far away that we cannot make out very much about it anyway, so that it does not matter if we are mistaken in our judgment of its size.

Shape constancy is even more important than size constancy, in keeping the object's identity and unity. The object is continuously "the same thing" despite enormous changes in the shape of its image on the retina. Its parts hang together to make a perceptually constant figure. Once you have approached an unfamiliar object from a couple of directions, seen it from a couple of angles, it could be rotated before you on a turnable and you would continuously perceive it as one-and-the-same thing, and as having a constant shape.

Pick up a large coin and slowly turn it over and over in your fingers. You see it continuously (even in monocular vision) as a perfectly circular object although your retinal image of the coin is circular only part of the time or perhaps none of the time. Recall circular dining-tables you have seen — you were in no doubt that they were circular; but, you never had a circular retinal image of a dining-table unless you happened to see the table standing on edge on moving day.

On the supply table, find the von Hornbostel wire cube (see Figure 1) with the handle. Use the light from a slide projector to form a small shadow of the cube on a screen. This shadow you know to be a meaningless jumble of intersecting lines, all in one plane. If you should rotate the cube, the shadow "ought" to go through an utterly confusing series of distortions, with its shape changing continuously and never meaningfully at any time. Now slowly rotate the cube. Do you perceive the shadow as a single integrated thing of constant shape, which is only changing its orientation — as the real cube is?

The shape-constancy mechanism of the perceptual apparatus can be tricked—making shape constancy break down—by the use of stimuli which organize a totally new kind of figure when seen from a new angle.

Following this paragraph is a drawing which may seem to represent some clubs lying on the ground. Hold this drawing almost horizontal, with the clubs pointing it towards one eye, and close the other eye. Upon bringing the drawing toward the eye you will find that at a particular distance the clubs rise up and become a group of "posts" perpendicular to the plane of the paper.

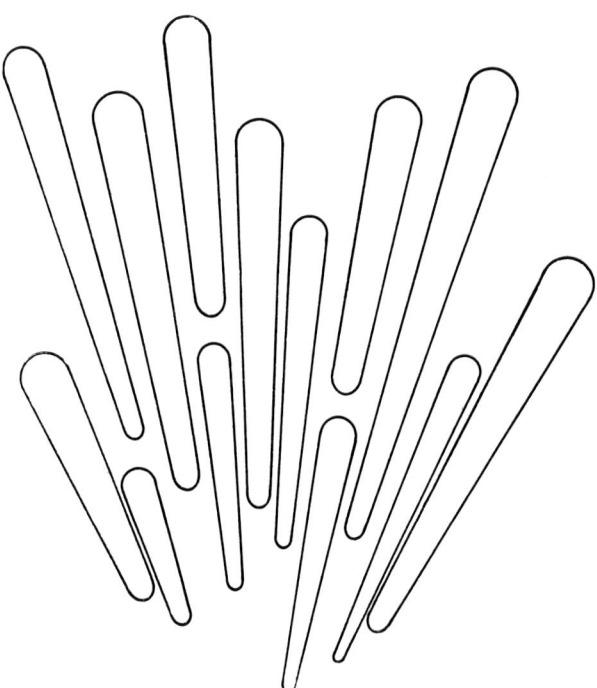

Lightness constancy (almost always called, mistakenly, "brightness" constancy) is of great importance in keeping changes of illumination from being misinterpreted to mean that properties of the object itself have mysteriously changed. A pile of snow is white in any intensity of illumination, and a pile of coal is black in any intensity of illumination. This is because what we respond to is not the *absolute* intensity of the snow itself or the coal itself, but the *relative* intensities of each substance and its surround. We directly perceive, as lightness, the reflectance or "albedo" of the material. Since reflectance is constant and independent of illumination, so is the perceived lightness.

Find in the room a small rectangular white block or box, or a cigarette package which is essentially white. Hold this near a window or other illuminant, and position it so that three sides meeting at one corner all receive different intensities of illumination. Do these sides appear to be gray surfaces of different shades—or do you find that you are unconsciously making allowance for the illuminations, and perceiving a "white-all-over" object?

Lightness constancy can also be tricked. Two examples follow: 1) A black cat sitting on a porch railing in the dark, illuminated by bright light from a window, may appear silver-gray or almost white to a person looking out through the window, even though it "should" appear black under any type of illumination. 2) Where the constancy of the lightness of a surface depends upon recognition that a "dark" area of the surface is really a shadow cast *on* the surface, this recognition in turn depends upon the fuzzy, "vignetted" margin which almost any shadow has. The following experiment was devised by Ewald Hering:

Put a piece of scratch paper under a fairly concentrated light source such as a small naked bulb, which will cast clean shadows with little penumbra (Figure 2). On the paper place any small object such as a coin on edge, a short piece of chalk, etc. Position paper and object so that the shadow of the object is at least as large as the object. Note that the patch of the paper on which the shadow falls is just as "white" as the rest, but perceived as being dimly illuminated by reason of the shadow. Now, with a pencil, carefully draw a heavy black outline around the shadow, thus concealing the vignetted edge of the shadow and substituting a sharp contour for it. Sit back and contemplate the shadow with a "fresh eye." Does it now appear to be a piece of dark substance lying on the paper, like an inkstain? Gently move paper or light until the pencil line no longer fits

Figure 2. An auto headlamp and a six-volt transformer yield a bright "point source" of light, which casts a sharp shadow.

the shadow and the latter's own edge becomes visible. Does the shadowed area of the paper once more become white-paper-dimly-illuminated?

4. Visual Direction

An absolutely empty visual field would have no dimensions. Subjective visual space is perceived at all only if, and because, it is occupied. Visual objects, their separations from each other, and their separations from one's self, fill up and make up visual space. Space is a sum-total of localities; and the locality of each and every visual object is compounded of two elements: the *direction* of the object and the *distance* of the object.

The visual direction of an object is laid off from one's self as a landmark, an anchor: it is an *egocentric* direction; for, one's the center of one's world. The visual self, however, the visual ego, does not have the size and the shape of the whole body. One sees the world as if from somewhere inside the head, as if one's visual self were a tiny man in there, looking out through a picture window. The egocentric directions of everything "out there" are adjudged as if from a single point in the head. This is only logical, for the visual ego could not very well be in two or more places at once.

In monocular vision the location of the ego—the point to which the directions of things are referred—is determined by the visual receptors of one eyeball. It is always the same eye, even when the other eye is the only one seeing. And, in binocular vision you still rely upon one of the eyes whenever you designate or determine the direction of anything from yourself.

If you stretch your arm out toward an object across the room and point steadily at the object, you will find upon closing first one eye and then the other that you are probably pointing (sighting) with one particular eye. If so, that eye is your "dominant" or master eye (the other being the "servant eye"). Most persons have a dominant eye and in most cases it is the right eye (but the fact that most people are right-handed is purely coincidental). Try not to forget that the dominant eye plays its special role in binocular vision, and that the phenomenon of dominance has significance only in connection with binocular vision—it is just because we have two eyes that one or the other of them has to be allowed to be the boss when both are in use. When we do have to do something with one eye only, such as sighting a rifle or using a telescope or peering through a keyhole, it feels most natural and comfortable to use the dominant eye. The eye that is dominant in binocular vision thus becomes the "preferred eye" in monocular vision. This preference does not constitute the dominance nor create it—it only identifies the dominance as being on the right or left side. One prefers his dominant eye for monocular tasks because one is more confident of the egocentric directions of things, and one's own orientation, via that eye.

Identify your own dominant eye by the following method, which excludes any bias from your handedness: Tear a hole about an inch in diameter in the middle of a piece of scratch paper the size of this page. Select some small object across the room to fixate. Hold the sheet of paper in both hands by its short sides at arm's length and with both eyes open, look at the chosen object through the hole. Keeping the paper still, close one eye and then the other. You could not be viewing the object with both eyes through such a small hole. With which eye are you actually seeing it? *That* eye is your dominant one.

The visual direction of a point in space is not wholly determined by the location of its image on the retina; for, the eye itself is free to move in the orbit. The retinal location of the image of an object can establish only the direction of the object relative to the direction of the visual axis (i.e., the direction of the fixation point). This is an *oculocentric* direction. Some other factor is required to convert it into an *egocentric* direction.

Have your partner move his finger slowly across your visual field while you: a) fixate his face steadily but take note of the *changing direction* (i.e., visual movement) of the finger; b) keep your head still but keep your fixation on the moving finger by turning your eyes to follow it.

In the above experiment, in "a," you saw an object (the face) whose image was stationary on your retina; you thus perceived it as being stationary, *i.e.*, in a constant egocentric direction. You also saw the moving object (the finger) whose image was sweeping across your retina and thus perceived it as moving, *i.e.*, in a succession of egocentric directions. In "b" when you fixated the moving finger, its image was stationary on your retina (on your macula) and yet you perceived it in a constantly changing direction; and although your partner's face was perceived as being stationary (did not appear to move in egocentric space) consider that its image was indeed moving over your retina.

Does this not seem paradoxical? Why in "a" was a moving retinal image (the finger) perceived as a moving object, and in "b" a moving retinal image (the face) was not perceived as moving? Clearly it is the presence or absence of *eye movement* that makes the difference as to whether the movement of a retinal image will cause perception of a changing egocentric direction of the object or not.

It must be eye movement *per se* that swings oculocentric directions about in subjective space and converts them to egocentric directions. If an object moves ten degrees across the visual field with the eye still, its image moves ten degrees on the retina, its oculocentric direction changes ten degrees, and its egocentric direction changes ten degrees. But if the object is motionless and the eye rotates ten degrees, this exactly compensates for the resulting ten-degree shift of the retinal image; so, although the oculocentric direction of the object again changes ten degrees, its egocentric direction does not change at all: the object "stays put." One's first inclination is to say that the object appears motionless *in spite of* the eye movement. Actually, it appears motionless *because of* the eye movement.

Now, what is it about the eye movement that combines with retinal-image location to determine egocentric direction? Will just any kind of eye movement suffice?

> Sit with your face within a couple of feet of an exposed light-bulb. Cover one eye and fixate the light steadily for fifteen to twenty seconds. With both eyes closed and turned toward a dim corner, you should see an after-image which should last some seconds. If it tends to fade, blink a few times to "revive it." Turn your eyes about, behind the closed lids; does the after-image move too, being seen wherever the eye is looking"? Now look again at the light as before, to renew the after-image. Close

the eyes and turn away; but this time, put a fingertip against the lower lid of the stimulated eye and push that eye-ball up and down. Does this make the after-image move, or not?

Obviously, a passive movement of the eyeball cannot alter the egocentric direction of anything which has a fixed location on the retina. There are known to be proprioceptors in the eye muscles, but no kinaesthetic information from *them* "gets into the act" of determining direction—else their stimulation during passive eye movement would have "moved" the after-image. No—it is the contraction of eye muscles, for active movements, that is required for directionalization. The activity may be either reflex* or voluntary. The "motor factor" in egocentric direction consists of the maintenance, within the visual system (as if by a stenographer) of a continuous record of all orders sent to the eye muscles. The "stenographer" thus knows the posture of the eyeball in the orbit at all times. The perceptual apparatus consults the "record of innervation" and combines these data with retinal-image-location to cause you to perceive the object in a particular egocentric direction.

Apparently, in an individual who has a strongly dominant eye, what *makes* that eye the dominant one is the fact that a "record of innervation" is kept only for the muscles of that eye alone.

5. Visual Distance ("Depth")

We shall not be concerned here with seen distances from left to right or up and down in the visual field, but with distances "in the third dimension," in the direction toward-and-away-from the observer—*i.e.*, with "depth-perception."

You *perceive* the distance of an object from yourself, just as much as you perceive the object itself. A prime factor in your

---

Exception: Labyrinthine reflex eye movement does not alter egocentric directions, for the visual system "assumes" that such a movement will always be accompanied by the head-movement it is designed to compensate for. So, during nystagmus induced by rotation in a Barany chair, or calorically (by induction of convection currents in the semicircular canals through instillation of warm or cold water in the outer ear canal), the whole visual field swims since the eyes' movements are going "unrecorded" and the changing oculocentric directions of objects connote movement of the *objects*.

estimation, your judgment, of the distance is the size of your retinal image of the object. This so-called "phenomenal size" of the
object is, however, entirely ambiguous. Two retinal images can
be identical, where one is of a small object nearby and the other is
of a large object far away. An infant has to learn to tell a low-
flying bird from a high-flying transport plane, has to learn to stop
reaching for the moon. In the perceptional interpretation of a
given size of retinal image, object size and object distance are
completely "interchangeable." From just the retinal-image size
(appreciated as the amount of visual field taken up by the object),
we do not know the distance of the object unless we know its size
and, we do not know the size of an unfamiliar object unless we
know its distance. If we are wrong in one of these respects, we will
be wrong in the other—an object misjudged as to size will be misjudged as to distance.

If the situation is one in which we could not know, could not
be expected to know, one of these dimensions, our perception of
the other will be profoundly affected. Consider this fact: either a
microscope or a telescope accomplishes the same end—it enlarges
our retinal image of the thing we are looking at. The things we
look at through a terrestrial telescope are mostly familiar; we
know their sizes fairly accurately, and we know those sizes to be
fixed. So, the things we see do not seem enlarged but instead are
"brought closer" by the telescope. We have no real conception of
the true (naked-eye) sizes of the things we view through a microscope, however. There, the size-constancy phenomenon cannot
operate, and the enlargement of the retinal image causes us to
perceive the objects as being "enlarged," not as being "brought
closer"—the apparent distance of an amoeba on a slide is about
the distance of the slide itself.

An object whose retinal image is made smaller or larger by an
optical trick will seem to have changed size only if it is something
we know could come in various sizes, such as a cloud or a balloon.
If it is something we know cannot change size (a dime, for
example), we will perceive it as having changed its distance
instead.

The retinal-image width of a thing is its "subtense at the eye,"
subtense meaning *the angle subtended* (see Experiment No. 25—

Visual Acuity). Lines drawn from the eye to the left and right edges of the object include between them an angle, a subtense, which fixes the size of the retinal image. Above, we have considered the "subtense cue" in the perception of distance, and its unreliability for objects of unknown or misjudged size.

A sort of extension of the subtense cue creates *geometrical perspective*. This is the apparent tapering, in the "away" direction, of objects which actually have constant height (and/or width) along their length. If one stands between railroad tracks, they appear to converge and to meet at a "vanishing point" on the horizon. Beyond early childhood, this no longer deceives us, and we learn that unless the subtense of an object does decrease away from us, the boundaries of the object are *not* parallel. So, the continuous change of subtense that we call perspective becomes an enormously valuable cue for the perception of relative distance and the orientation of objects in the third dimension.

In a picture, if the subtenses of all objects are not appropriate to their true sizes and true distances, then either their sizes or their distances will be falsified. One of the posted pictures is a classical demonstration of this — the one showing three figures of equal subtense, but in a perspective setting so that the "farthest" looks gigantic.

The same principle is demonstrated by the following sketch, where the observer automatically takes into account the distance-size relationship. The object farther back seems larger, although it is identical in size to the nearer one.

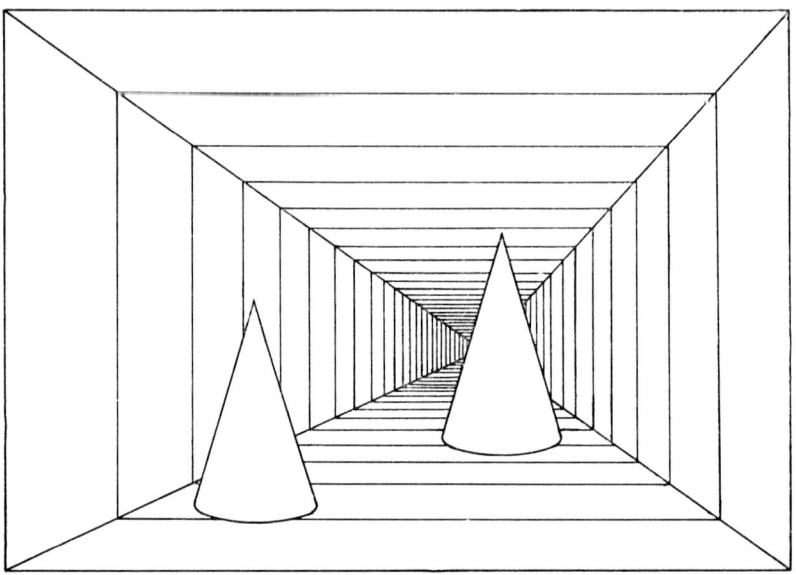

Another aid to the estimation of the distance of a single object is *aerial perspective*. This is the slight blurring and slight bluing of things seen through long atmospheric pathways. Distant mountains, for example, have hazy contours and look bluish. If we have learned to use this cue, then in an unfamiliar climate with exceptionally clear air we may badly misjudge distances, and set out for a short hike to some point actually more than a day's journey away. Conversely, we may nearly collide with something seen through mist, because we judged it to be much farther than it was and are taken by surprise when it comes closer.

Still another cue to "absolute" distance is *elevation*. The farther an object is, the more we must raise our gaze to view it, with the horizon usually setting the limit to this.

It is important to know what *supposed* cues to absolute distance are actually worthless, although they are widely taught as having great value: The extent to which the eye is accommodating to focus the retinal image sharply tells the visual system nothing about the distance of the object—Mother Nature might have arranged for this, but she did not. And, the extent to which the two eyes converge, to see an object singly, does not influence our perception of distances greater than four or five feet.

Turning now to *relative* distance—the perception of which two objects (or parts of one object) is the nearer and which the farther: There are three important cues which, like all the above cues to absolute distance, are just as useful in monocular vision as in binocular. These cues are *overlap, illumination perspective,* and *motion parallax.*

Overlap is the partial concealment of one object by another. The object wholly visible must be the nearer of the two; the object it partly hides must be farther away.

Illumination perspective is the whole complex of highlights and shadows cast by objects upon other objects. Taken in by the perceptual apparatus, this information tells us much about the shapes of the surfaces of things (the presence of humps and hollows) and the positions of things relative to each other in space. Accurate employment of this cue requires knowledge of the direction from which the illumination is falling on the scene. If we are deceived about *that,* spatial perceptions are falsified. Everyone assumes from his own experience that light "always" comes from above or from the side, never from below, thus, a concavity illuminated from below upward may be seen as a protruding convexity, because the shadow in it is now exactly where the shadow under a convexity would be if the illumination were normal (*i.e.,* downward from above).

In the pictures below the importance of illumination perspective becomes apparent. Stare at the photograph of the meteor crater. Appreciate the nuances of height and depth created by the shadows. Note the road to the rim of the crater, If you now turn the page upside down, *Voila!* The dips and hollows have become bumps and the crater itself, a mountain, with the road now extending to its base — all because the illumination causing the shadows is erroneously assumed to come from above.

In the second picture a ball appears as a flat disc in diffuse, even illumination; however, with sharp lighting and vivid shadows, the ball immediately looks spherical.

 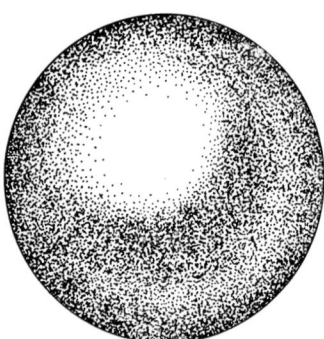

Motion parallax is by all odds the most potent of all cues to the relative distances of things.

Sit still and take a good look at the three-dimensional scene before you. Close one eye. Now move your head a few inches to the left. Do you note that foreground objects appear to shift to the right, and that the nearer they are, the faster and farther they shift? Background objects, on the other hand, either stay put or may appear to shift to the left.

These opposite shiftings of various speeds and extents, of nearer and farther objects relative to each other, make up the phenomenon of motion parallax. As a source of direct perceptual information about space and its contents, it is just as valuable to a one-eyed person as to a two-eyed one. It is the excellent judgment of distances afforded by motion parallax that makes a one-eyed driver of a car just as safe as anyone else. As long as he is in motion, he has motion parallax to rely on—and, it is only when he is in motion that he *could* cause an accident.

It cannot be over-emphasized that every one of the above cues to absolute or relative distance is available in monocular vision. It is often taught, but is simply not true, that most or all of our depth perception depends upon special binocular cues. For spatial vision, two eyes are better than one, but only a *little* better, as we shall be learning shortly.

Throughout the history of art until the most recent decades, artists who wanted to be at all realistic have made use of all the static cues discussed above, by incorporating them in drawings and paintings in order to produce "an illusion of depth." It was none other than Leonardo da Vinci who compiled the list of depth-cues available to artists. He pointed out that of all the "monocular" cues, motion parallax is the only one the artist cannot employ—but of course Leonardo never saw one of Disney's animated cartoons.

Go to the posted pictures and stand squarely before the colored magazine advertisement. (Figure 3 is a black and white copy of this ad.) —*Cover one eye,* keep your head absolutely still, and just stare at the picture. Within a few seconds, it will slowly "deepen" more and more, until you will be able to "kid yourself" that you are looking through a window at a real three-dimensional scene. You will even become able to estimate the distances from one object to the next one behind it, in feet and inches. Do not attempt this observation in a spirit of skepticism — *expect* the picture to develop considerable depthiness, and it will do so if you give it the necessary few seconds' time. Which

of the "monocular" cues can you identify? Now open the previously covered eye and you will find that the depthy effect is
markedly weakened, or even eliminated, since your binocular
impression tells you the picture *is* flat. You thus have a good
demonstration of how one's binocular certainty of flatness can
spoil what would otherwise be striking depth impressions.

Figure 3. This photograph demonstrates many of the depth cues. How many
do you note?

There are other ways of viewing appropriate pictures in order
to perceive them "depthily." Most methods involve monocular
vision, and all methods have one thing in common: The elimina-
tion of the certainty of the flatness of the picture. This certainty
stems from the absence of motion parallax and the absence of the
one cue to relative distance that is peculiar to binocular vision,
"retinal disparity" (to be explained in Experiment No. 6). In

normal binocular viewing of a picture, the fact that it is a representation on a plane surface is so inescapable that the depth-producing efforts of the artist or the photographer make their appeal more to reason than to perception. But let this "binocular certainty of flatness" be destroyed, and the perceptual apparatus leaps at the chance to show us all the latent depthiness that is there.

We are now ready to consider the special contribution that binocularity does make to depth-perception.

6. Stereoscopy

This word literally means "solid seeing," *i.e.,* seeing three-dimensionally. It has come, however, to have a narrow application. We do not speak of *all* depthy vision nor of all aspects of depthy vision as being "stereoscopic." This term is reserved for the kind of depthiness which one can perceive *only* in binocular vision

> To try to isolate the peculiarly binocular, stereoscopic depthiness from visual depthiness-as-a-whole, sit where you can view a scene containing many things at various distances. Take note of these relative distances and also take note of the three-dimensionality of each bulky object. Now close or cover one eye and keep your head as still as possible (it is best to prop your chin or cheek against something firm). To what extent does the scene "flatten" upon closure of one eye? Do some objects now appear to be at equal distances, which you know to be at unequal distances? Do some solid objects now appear the same as if they were painted representations of a flat surface? When the monocular appearance of the scene has stabilized and has been thoroughly digested, reopen the closed eye (still without letting your head move!). Do objects suddenly become separated in the toward-and-away direction, which had seemed to be in the some plane at a single distance from you? Do objects suddenly become unmistakably three-dimensional, which had been appearing like paintings or photographs of themselves?

These kinds and amounts of depthiness instantly injected into the scene, by the change from monocular to binocular viewing, constitute "stereoscopic depth." This perceptual phenomenon has its entire basis in a single simple fact: the left-eyed and right-eyed retinal images of a visual object are never identical unless the object is a flat surface viewed perpendicularly, or else is such a thing as a smooth ball in diffuse illumination.

Hold motionless, and vertical, before your face, your own thumb or a six-sided pencil or other small irregular object. Close first one eye and then the other, and note that their two views of the object differ — the left eye sees farther around to the left side of the object, the right eye farther around on the right. With a more distant object, even one much wider than the distance between your two eyes, you will still find that your left- and right-eyed views of it are different.

Think now of the two retinal images as being flat pictures. The "raw material" in them, from which the perceptual apparatus constructs stereoscopic depth, consists of a difference between the images. Not the entirety of *all* difference between them, but one particular kind of difference — the difference in the widths, the *horizontal* dimensions, of comparable or homologous parts of the two images. For example, if each retina bears an image of a block, thus:

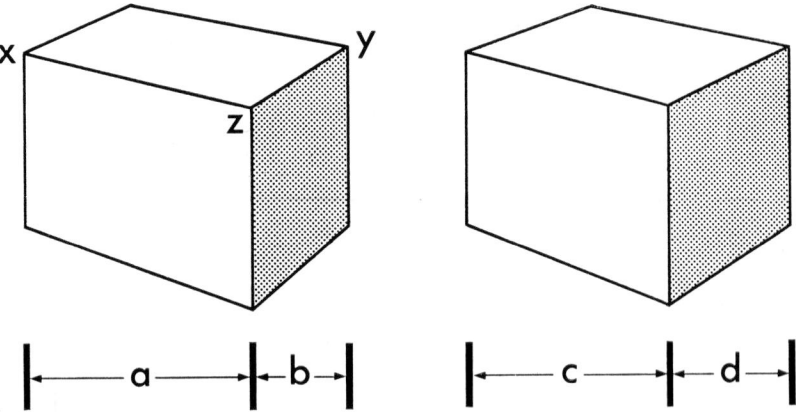

the distances a, b, c and d are horizontal dimensions of the block images — they are the horizontal separations of the vertical lines representing corners of the block. The separations "a" and "c" are comparable, and "b" and "d" are likewise homologous. Note that "a" and "c" are unequal, different, that there is a "disparity" between them, namely the amount of a-minus-c. Between "b" and "d" there is also a disparity, d-minus-b. These disparities, named in full, are *horizontal retinal-image disparities*. For short, we call them simply "retinal disparities." They are responsible for the fact that when the two images are "fused" into a binocular image of the block, the left side of the block slants away from us to the left, and the dotted face of the block slants less rapidly away to the right. The corner "z" is seen at a shorter distance than the corner "y" and the corner "x." *The block would appear thus even if the images contained no perspective.* The stereoscopic perceptions peculiar to binocular vision are *immediate, instantaneous* and do not depend in the least upon the presence of, or the "interpretation" of, any of the depth-cues which monocular vision can employ.

In our experimental comparison, above, of one-eyed and two-eyed viewing of a depthy scene, we tried to determine how much the injection of stereoscopic depth can add to the depthiness already present in monocular vision (with motion parallax excluded, that is).

Let us now see for ourselves that retinal disparity alone will generate depth in binocular vision, where no depth would be seen on any basis whatever in monocular vision with either eye.

In one of the hand stereoscopes provided, place the card that looks like this:

Looking through the instrument (which lets each eye see only its own half of the card, with accommodation and convergence in proper agreement), you will see two lines standing in space with the right-hand line nearer to you than the left-hand one. Neither monocular pair of lines embodies any depth cues. The whole of the depth between the "fused," binocular, lines is stereoscopic depth, and the whole basis of this is the retinal disparity of the monocular images — the difference in separation of the lines, in the two images thereof.

Put down the instrument and hold two pencils upright before your face, with the right-hand pencil somewhat nearer, in imitation of what you saw through the stereoscope, and closing first one eye and then the other, you will find that the *lateral* separation of the pencils is greater for your left eye than for the right eye. In your naked-eye binocular vision of the pencils, the retinal disparity being in favor of the left eye makes the left pencil appear farther. Since the drawings on the stereoscope card imitated the real retinal images of two real pencils of which the right-hand one is nearer, their binocular "fusion" caused the perception of just such a pair of "pencils."

In the binocular-fusion process, images of unequal width have somehow to be "forced" into union. One may say that it is this procrustean operation that generates the stereoscopic depth impression. This ability to combine unequally-wide images has its limits:

Hold your two index fingers in line with your nose, one at arm's length and the other about half that far from your face. Now bifixate the farther finger and note that the nearer one is "double"; bifixate the nearer finger and the farther one will double.

The diplopias just experienced are due to the fact that the retinal disparities of the configuration of fingers are too great to be overcome in fusion. Such diplopia, unlike that of a person who has a paralyzed eye-muscle, is perfectly normal and is hence called "physiological diplopia." In everyday binocular vision, many objects which are much nearer than the object of attention, or much farther, are seen diplopically while the object of attention is being seen singly because it is bifixated and its images are on corresponding retinal spots. We do not notice the doubled appearance of these too-near and too-far objects, simply because our attention is *not* on *them*.

Now that you are prepared to look for it, you will readily detect the physiological diplopias in the scene if you bifixate something halfway across the room, giving your *attention* not to *this* object but to nearer objects or farther ones. Covering and uncovering one eye repeatedly will make the diplopias very conspicuous.

Strangely, we can still directly perceive stereoscopic depth between objects when their real separation-in-depth is somewhat too great for us to be able to see both objects singly at the same time when either one of them is being bifixated. This was not established until recent years — formerly, it was taught that the moment one of two objects became diplopic, all stereoscopic depth between the objects would necessarily collapse.

Now, one of the two contributions stereoscopy makes to total space-perception is *stereoscopic visual acuity* — known, for short, as "stereo acuity." This is the term for one's ability to detect a tiny difference in the distance of two objects from the self. In monocular vision, "over-lap" can tell us which of two objects is nearer, but not how much nearer. Such clues as subtense and perspective enable an estimate of the distances to different points in space, but the estimates may be quite inaccurate. Motion parallax can make possible very accurate judgments of *large* differences in distance. But in monocular vision no cue or combination of cues can make possible the detection of such small distance differences as can be appreciated binocularly. What sets a limit upon the smallness of differences detectible is simply the smallest amount of retinal disparity capable of generating a stereoscopic-depth impression or percept. A series of stereoscope cards like the one you have seen, with increasingly smaller separations in the left-hand pairs of lines, could be used to measure a person's "stereo threshold." This value (the reciprocal of which expresses "stereo acuity") is the angular subtense at the eye of the *smallest* disparity that is detectible by reason of its being "converted" into appreciable stereoscopic depth. For a skilled observer in a laboratory situation, the stereo threshold may be as small as four seconds

(1/900 of one degree). A threshold about three times as great is allowable for an Air Force pilot.

A rough grading test of the percentage of stereopsis possessed by an individual is accomplished clinically with the Titmus stereo charts. Put on the polaroid glasses provided and see if you can reach "100 per cent stereopsis" by telling which of the rings "stands out" from the rest in all of the test target situations.

It must be emphasized that "stereoscopic vision" does not have to mean vision through a stereoscope. It only means vision *as if* through a stereoscope. You are seeing stereoscopically every day, just because you have two retinal images from each object and these images are not quite alike. A stereoscope is merely a device which makes it possible to give the two eyes separate images which have *not* come from the same object. Any device which does this (whether the material put into it generates depth impressions or not) is a "haploscope." But if our two eyes are fixating not the same thing but two separate things, we are seeing "haploscopically." If we try, we find that with a little effort and practice we can see haploscopically *without* a haploscope:

Put two coins, identical except perhaps for their dates, at the edge of the table and with about two inches between their centers. Make sure the coins are both "face up" and erect in orientation so that one is not tilted with respect to the other. Hold up a pencil between the coins and your nose, and bring the pencil slowly toward the nose, bifixating it constantly. You will be able to notice (without looking *at* them!) that the two coins become four — each one being seen in physiological diplopia. The "two middle coins" will slide together and become one when the pencil is about two-thirds of the way to your nose. If you find it difficult to perform this technique, try it this way: Place the coins as before, about fourteen to sixteen inches in front of you, but concentrate on the left hand coin. Place the pencil about five or six inches from your nose, and keeping your left eye covered, line up your *right* eye and the left coin so that the tip of the pencil "touches" the lower edge of the coin. Now keep the pencil and left coin still. Close your right eye and open your left eye and slide the right *coin* until it lines up with the pencil tip. (The coins should be about 2 to 3 inches apart.)

Now open both eyes and continue to concentrate on the pencil tip. You should see three coins; one clear one in the center (above the pencil), and one blurry one off to each side. When you are thus perceiving three coins and concentrating on the middle one, cautiously take the pencil down out of the field. Your two visual axes are now crossed, intersecting in space at the place where the pencil *was*. The left coin is imaged on your right fovea and the right coin is imaged on the left fovea, while each eye also sees a (non-foveal) coin off to one side. Since the foveas are "correspondent" and the foveal images are identical, they are binocularly fused — so, you see a binocular "coin" with a monocular coin at either side of it.*

Actually, the place where we would "theoretically" perceive the coin is the point of intersection of the visual axes. If you can hold the crossed coin-images fused while you put the pencil back at that intersection, you will find that the binocular image is "really" there, for with the point of the pencil you can seemingly scratch the edge of the binocular coin.

This method of "free vision" viewing (without the aid of an instrument) can be performed with *appropriate* stereograms** and is called "chiastopic" viewing (with the eyes "crossed"). By *appropriate* we mean the picture on the left must represent the right-eyed view.

With practice, stereograms can also be viewed without crossing the visual axes. In this case, the pair of pictures must be mounted with the left photograph on the left instead of on the right, as in chiastopic viewing. This type of "free vision" gazing at stereoscopic photos is called "orthopic" viewing (with the visual axes parallel).

---

*You may note here that the binocularly seen coin appears farther away than the monocular coins. This is not a simple matter, and the explanation is important: Such strong over-convergences (to cross the visual axes) causes a "size effect," an *apparent* reduction of subtense. Since coins cannot shrink, our perceptual apparatus may reject the possibility that the binocular coin is smaller, and the size-constancy phenomenon is invoked to persuade the mind that the coin, in order to keep its size, despite the apparently lessened subtense, must have moved away.

**A stereogram is a pair of drawings or photographs mounted on a card or plate for haploscopic presentation to the eyes, and embodying horizontal disparities capable of generating stereoscopic depth impressions. The term is synonymous with "a stereo pair of pictures."

In both chiastopic and orthopic viewing, each eye sees the picture "intended" for it, *i.e.,* its "correct" or corresponding view. However, if the views are reversed in either case, we encounter the phenomenon of pseudoscopy. Here, in effect, the two eyes are interchanged in the head and thus the directions of all retinal disparities are reversed.

Again view the stereoscopic card with the 2 sets of parallel lines. This time place the card in the stereoscope so that the wider spaced pair of lines is on the *right*; the left-hand line should now appear in front of the other, since the binocular parallax is reversed.

If retinal disparity were the only factor in the perception of relative depth, pseudoscopic viewing would make *all* far objects appear nearer and vice versa. But since, as we have studied, there are many other important depth cues, the brain is forced to decide which take preference. Sometimes, as for example, when a near object is obviously in front of a more distant one (*i.e.,* it markedly overlaps the contours of the distant one), the brain refuses to accept the contradictory impression it receives and the only result is an odd sensation of unreality. If there is no direct cue conflict, the relative depth of objects is governed by the "new" parallactic differences.

Following is a diagram and construction plan of a simple homemade "pseudoscope." When constructed, it will allow you to see common everyday scenes about you as if your eyes were interchanged. Remember, the brain does its very best to reconcile the contrary impressions it receives, and the result is often very curious.

Construction: Out of a piece of stiff cardboard, cut out the shape shown in the diagram below; the dotted lines show where a bend should be. The cardboard is folded up to form a square prism with sloping ends, and the edges are fastened with tape. Before you complete the folding, attach a piece of mirror to the inside of the end flaps. Test the instrument first and then fasten the flaps down permanently.

To use this pseudoscope simply look through the circular holes. The left eye looks straight ahead, but the light reaching the right eye is deflected by the two mirrors and comes from a position to the left of that seen by the left eye. Thus, the relative viewpoints of the right and left eyes are transposed.

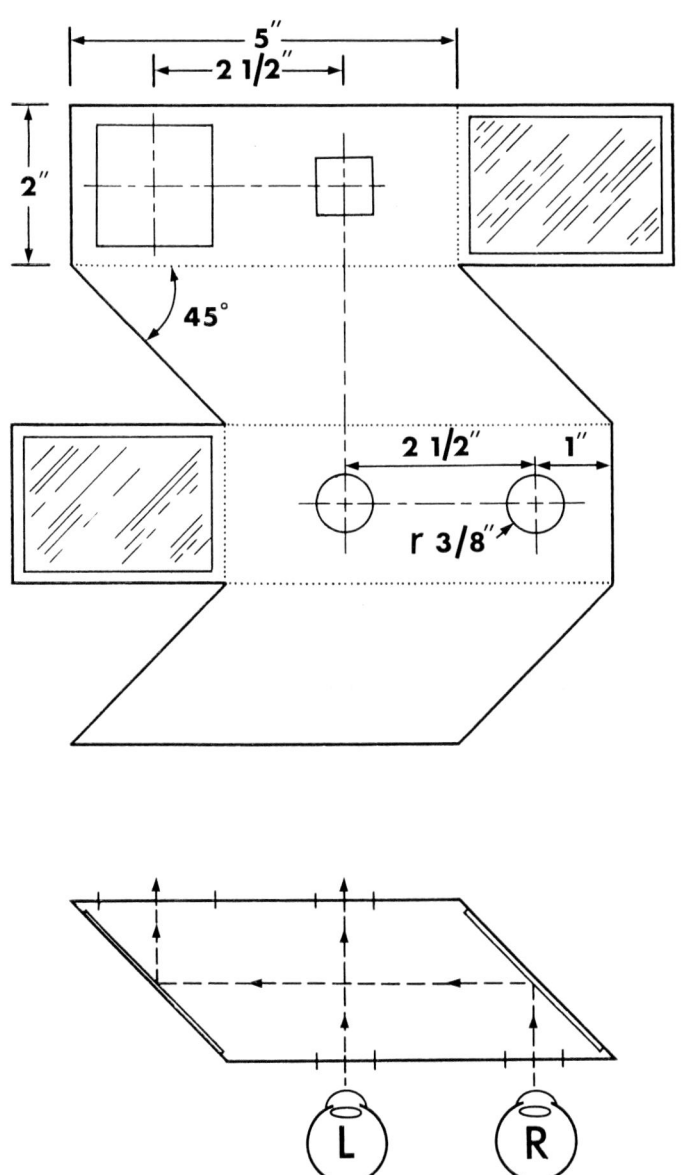

7. *Fusion and Some Alternatives*

What we have been calling, above, sensory fusion in binocular vision requires clarification. "Fusion" is the combination, in some sense of the word, of information from both retinas so that what is seen is seen in one place in space and also looks different from what either eye alone would see there. The fundamental nature of this fusion process has been debated for a century. Among the various notions about it, there stands at one extreme the idea of a physiological "final common path" or an anatomical "fusion center" — the idea that nerve fibers from both retinas synapse upon a single set of neurons, in which the excitations from both retinas as pooled, summated, blended together. At the other extreme stands Sherrington's idea that each monocular image is independently processed all the way to the level of consciousness, with the two images then combined into one by a "psychic act" of union. We cannot explore thoroughly here either of these extreme possibilities, nor give any time at all to some others that lie between them; but we can make a couple of observations which will indicate which extreme the truth is nearest to.

> From the supply table, obtain the neutral density filter. Look at a bright source of light, close one eye, and hold the filter over that same eye. Note the brightness of the light with the naked eye. Now open the other eye behind the filter so as to see the light binocularly. Does its brightness go up, stay the same, or go down?

The unexpected result of this experiment is called "Fechner's paradox." Opening the second eye increases the total stimulation of the visual system. If there is a binocular physiological final common path, brightness ought to go up. Instead, it goes down, to a level somewhere between the separate monocular brightnesses. Some sort of integration of the left- and the right-eyed intensities occurs, but it is no mere matter of pouring them both into a single hopper.

> Place in the stereoscope the card bearing a white and a black drawing of what appears to be a crystal.

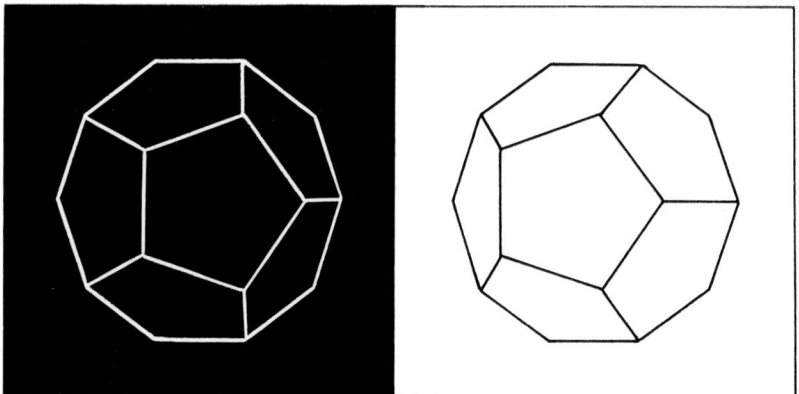

View this through the instrument and note that the binocular crystal is not a smooth, stable gray as it ought to be if there is a physiological final common path for binocular fusion. Instead, the crystal looks metallic as if it were made of dull silver or graphite. The appearance on its surfaces is called "lustre" and can *only* be obtained in binocular vision, when the lightness of an object is different for each eye. A real piece of polished metal always reflects more light to one eye than to the other, which is why it looks lustrous.

Some visual scientists consider such an experience of lustre to be a seeing of white and black in the same place at the same time. But whether this attitude is correct or not, it is at least clear that in lustre the two monocular intensities are being carefully *kept from* fusing in any physiological sense — for, if they were either summed or averaged, the binocular result could only be simple gray, which lustre certainly is not.

Substitute in the stereoscope the card bearing drawings of a pyramid as seen from above.

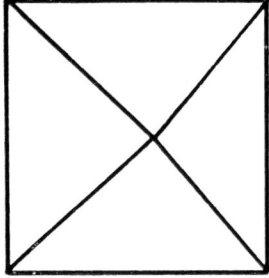 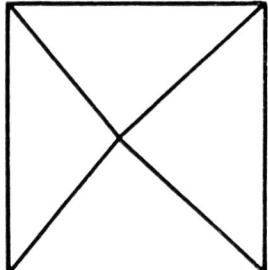

"Fuse" these and note that the binocular "pyramid" is depthy, three-dimensional. It is so, even though you may find that the base of the pyramid is diplopic when you are fixating the apex, or that the apex is doubled when you are fusing the left or right edge of the base.

Here, differing left- and right-eyed images are being combined, "fused," into a three-dimensional binocular image. But if this occurred in a physiological final common path, would not the binocular image look like the two monocular images in simple superposition? It does not, and such a combination could not look like a pyramid and could not look three-dimensional at all. Stereoscopic depth would not exist if the left and right images were not rigorously maintaining their identities right up to the point where their horizontal disparities are converted into depth. In short, we would not see stereoscopically at all if the binocular integration process really deserved to be called by the term "fusion."

It is a general rule that haploscopically-presented pictures or drawings such as those of the pyramid you have just seen will be capable of binocular combination if they represent left- and right-eyed views of an object that does exist or could exist. If they do not, then in binocular viewing of them any one of several things may happen, but the most likely result is something which further indicates that Sherrington was essentially correct, and that each image arrives in consciousness uncontaminated by the other — the two being combined at some still higher level of the visual system (*if* they are combinable). The usual result of trying to combine the uncombinable is called "rivalry":

> Now put into the stereoscope the card bearing round patches of diagonal lines which slant in different directions on the two halves of the card.

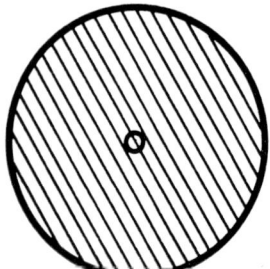 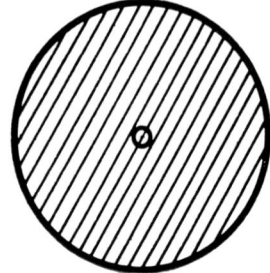

View this card long enough to be sure that you have seen every-thing happen that is going to happen. You should find that some of the time your consciousness is entirely monopolized by the left eye's image, that some of the time you see instead only the right eye's drawing, or you may see a patch of diagonal lines in one direction and a nearby patch of diagonals in the oppo-site direction, never a cross-hatched pattern, however; and, never for a moment do you see binocularly a pattern which con-sists of the whole of the one *plus* the whole of the other.

Rivalry did *not* occur with the "lustre" card, because there the left and right drawings did represent possible left- and right-eyed views of a possible object — a shiny object with highlights seen by one eye but not by the other. There is no possible real-life view that would provide the situation for rivalry to occur.

8. Visual Solidness

Most real solids appear visually solid and most visual solids are really (physically) solid. There are exceptions: A six-inch tumbler whose "bottom" was five inches thick would deceive us, for we should suppose it to be a glass of water; and a glass of milk is visually, perceptually, solid — only by experience do we learn that milk is a liquid. A piece of paper or even cardboard is not a visual solid because its thickness is negligible and we perceive it as two-dimensional, although, of course, it is physically a solid since it is neither a liquid nor a gas.

How much of visual solidity, corporeality, substantiality, is purely perceptual without benefit of learning, is hard to say. A liquid in a glass vessel is *assumed* to be a liquid simply because one knows that the only homogeneous-looking stuffs kept in glass vessels are liquids. It is truly *perceived* to be a liquid, even by an infant, if its surface is agitated. If the surface is still, it is directly perceived as a liquid only if it is transparent or translucent, and it must also have some color or turbidity. Is there really any *visual* difference between a glass filled to within an inch of the top with motionless water, and an empty glass with a thin disc of plastic stuck in it an inch down from the top?

Solid objects such as books and chairs are visually solid too. Are they as solid monocularly as they are binocularly? Yes, if they are perceived as being three-dimensional and not as being pictorial representations of books and chairs. We have learned above that objects can be thoroughly three-dimensional in monocular vision, if motion parallax is allowed — or even if it is not, provided geometrical perspective, illumination perspective, etc. are available cues. Is three-dimensionality alone enough to enforce a perception of solidity? Not with our glass of water, even in binocular vision. The glass itself is solid only via experience, because it is colorless; and the water in it cannot be *directly perceived* — hence, it "occupies no volume," "takes up no space," and could not seem visually to be a physical solid.

Look again at the "pyramid" card in the stereoscope. Here, on a pure basis of a single cue — retinal disparity — you have a percept which is inescapably three-dimensional. But, is the pyramid visually *solid*? Or is it a "wire model" of a pyramid, enclosing only empty space, and would you not expect to be able to pass a stick through it from side to side without encountering any resistance?

Clearly three-dimensionality by itself, even when it is stereoscopic, is not enough to provide perceptual solidity, for while it lays down the boundaries of a volume that has a particular size and shape, this volume has to appear *occupied* in order to appear solid. When we realize this, we realize at once that the reason why books and chairs appear solid is that they are not only three-dimensional, but opaque. So, of course, is our glass of milk, which is why it is *visually* equivalent to a solid cylinder of white plastic. One final and fascinating experiment should provide proof that the necessary-and-sufficient conditions for visual solidness are three-dimensionality and opacity.

Place two slide projectors side by side and parallel with their lenses a foot apart. Over the right lens install the red filter, over the *left* one install the bluish-green (*not* a pure green). Obtain one of the goggles with "lenses" of colored plastic. You now have an "anaglyphic" system, for each half of the goggles will let through to your eye only one of the two colored illuminations reflecting from the screen and the whole set-up can be employed as a haploscope. (This same phenomenon can be produced with a "polaroid" projection system instead of the anaglyphic one.) Hold fairly close to the screen any small irregular object (or, your empty hand will do), and stand where you are sure you can see *both* of its colored shadows *without* the goggles. Now, put on the goggles. Both colored shadows will turn black, and will fuse binocularly into a "solid" shadow.

In this demonstration, clear-cut corporeality is perceived, the components of which are stereoscopic depth (for which no learning is required) and the opacity provided by the black shadows (the perception of which, again, required no learning). Thus we find that a percept of solidness *can* be generated by the operation of only native equipment, and while experience may be necessary if some real solids are to be visual solids, solidity-perception can also have an immediate basis in nothing more than the contents of the two retinal images.

Previously it was stated that *binocularity* adds only a little to the capacity for spatial perceptions that exists in monocular vision. Also, fine stereo acuity was designated as one of the two contributions stereoscopy does make to space-perception. We can now see what the other contribution is: It is the ability to appreciate practically instantly, "at a glance," the three-dimensional modeling of a solid object, however unfamiliar, without need of previous experience, memory, groping interpretation of perspectives, or walking around the object in order to size it up (shape it up, rather!) through the medium of motion parallax. Without retinal disparities we can see just as three-dimensionally and solidly — but not with anything like so much speed and precision.

Basic Visual Optics

9. Accommodation

As any object approaches any optical system, the image formed by that system recedes away from the oncoming object. This fact holds for all objects and images, *i.e.*, they both move in the same direction. Thus, when any object comes *toward* the eye, the sharp image of it inside the eyeball "backs up" and the light rays may then strike the retina before they have converged to a point focus. The retina then bears a system of overlapping spots of light and the object "out of focus" is seen blurredly. If the object is of sufficient interest to demand detailed scrutiny, a process has to be instituted that will pull the image plane forward onto the retina, thus clarifying the image. This process is called accommodation, and in the eyes of different animals it is accomplished in different ways; sometimes by pulling the internal lens of the eye forward, sometimes by changing the shape of the lens; sometimes by even changing the length of the eyeball with the external muscles. The relatively large human eye has such a large "depth of focus" that it does not have to begin accommodating until the object comes closer than six meters (20 feet). This is why twenty feet is used as a standard for checking visual acuity clinically (Exp. No. 25).

The existence of a process of accommodation was first proved in 1619 by the classical "Scheiner's Experiment"; Lay a card on the table and, with a pin, prick two neat holes through it *side by side,* not as far apart as the diameter of your own pupil. The wider your pupil the more easily the observations can be made; so, although "focusing" your eye will constrict the pupil somewhat (see Experiment No. 13, Pupillary Reflexes), you can help matters by doing the experiment in a dim corner of the room. Obviously, there must be enough illumination for you to *see* through the pinholes in the card! The pinholes must appear to be overlapped somewhat when held close to the eye. You may have to make several pairs of holes to try. Press the card against the eye so that you are looking through both pinholes at once. Pick out a distant vertical line to serve as a far object, and hold the pin upright a few inches from the card to serve as a near object. Now look at the far object, and the near object will be doubled because two separate, blurred images of it are falling on the retina. Look at the near object (causing accommodation) and the light through both pinholes will form a single retinal image of it, while the far object will become double. Study the following diagrams until you are sure you understand why, and why this proves that an accommodation process must occur when one looks at a near object. Only a young person can make Scheiner's Experiment work, for with increasing age the power of accommodation decreases until by age forty-five there is so little left that: (1) if a person has never worn spectacles he must now adopt them for reading, and (2) if a person has been wearing spectacles, he now needs bifocals. When accommodation has become greatly reduced, one is said to be presbyopic ("old sighted").

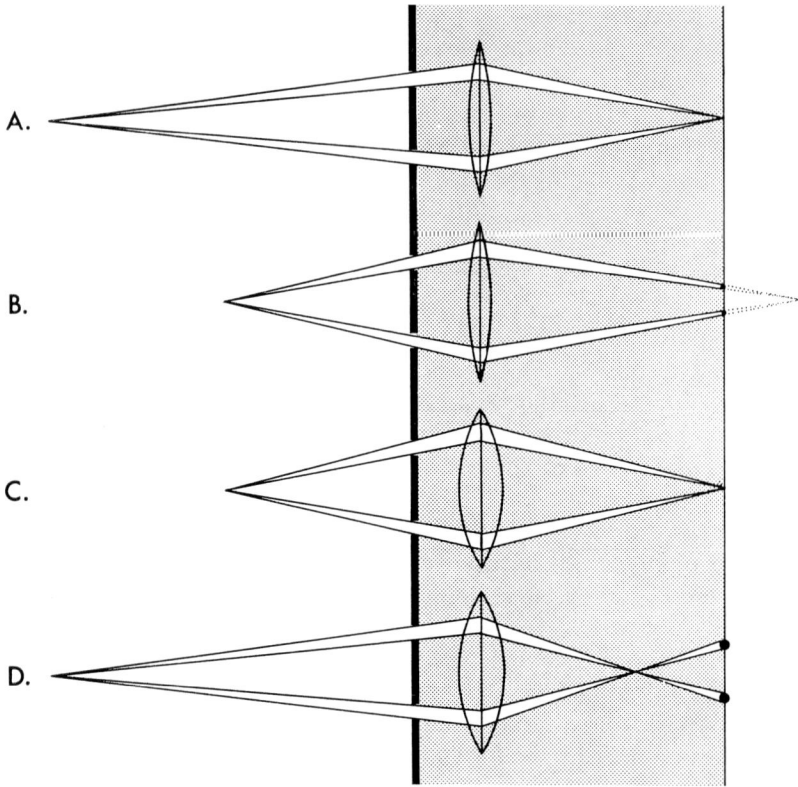

Figure A shows rays of light emanating from one *point* on a distant object. Only the rays able to pass through the double pinhole openings are focused on the retina onto one point.

Figure B shows that when the lens is focused for distance (unaccommodated), light rays from a near object would come to a point focus behind the retina, if the retina did not intercept them first. Since it does, two blobs of light are seen, instead of one.

In Figures C and D are shown the comparable optics when the lens is accommodating, thus increasing the power of the eye's optical system.

10. *Refractive Errors*

The cornea and lens together make up the optical system of the eye. To be ideal, their focusing power must bring light from some distant point into sharp focus onto the retina (with *no* accommodation to help it do so). This is "emmetropia"—the ideal state. However, if the *power* of the eye and the *length* of the eyeball are not properly matched for a given eye, a refractive error (or ametropia) is then present. Everyone knows that eyeballs differ in size and shape just as noses and ears do. Only seldom is the power perfect for the existing cornea-to-retina distance. More commonly, either the eyeball is relatively too long from front to back (myopic), or too short (hypermetropic—also, called hyperopic). Myopia is "near sightedness"; light rays from each point in a distant object are focused (by an optical system that is relatively too strong) in an image-plane which is *in front* of the retina; since they are not intercepted by a screen, these rays continue on and spread out again and form blobs by the time they strike the "too-distant" retina. Accommodation here (increasing the power of the optical system) would only make matters worse. If, on the other hand, the object is brought closer to the eye, its image will move backward, towards the retina. Eventually, a point will be reached when the object will form a clear image on the retina. That object is then at the "far point" of the myopic eye. Any more distant object is blurred and the eye can do nothing about it. If the object now continues to come closer, accommodation can help keep the image clear *on* the retina of the myopic eye, just as it does for the emmetropic. (Of course, the myopic eye will not have to exert as much accommodation as the normal for the same object distance.)

In hypermetropia, "far sightedness," the eye is "too short." Light rays from a distant object have not yet come to a sharp focus, when they strike the "too close" retina. These rays form blobs there. The hypermetropic eye can see far objects sharply only by accommodating (whereas an emmetropic eye would not have to). Obviously, a hyperope will "use up" all his available accommodative power before the object gets too close to his eye. His "near point" - the closest an object can be brought and seen clearly with *maximum* accommodation exerted—is farther away than an emmetrope's, whose is farther than a myope's (assuming all 3 eyes have identical total accommodative power).

For this experiment, obtain a +2 diopter lens and a −2 diopter lens. If you wear glasses regularly, keep them on, but for the purposes of this experiment pretend that you are emmetropic and that you do not need glasses. Cover one eye and put the convex +2 lens up to the other; you have now increased the power of your total optical system and are now artificially myopic. This lens pulls the image forward off the retina so that it is as if your eyeball were too long. Note that all distant objects are blurred, but that you can still see sharply anything close at hand. Keeping the + lens in place, put in the −2 lens in contact with it. This concave diverging lens pushes the image back where it belongs and renders you emmetropic. You have thus corrected your artificial nearsightedness with the minus spectacle lens. Clearly the treatment for myopia is a *concave* spectacle lens of the right strength. Look monocularly through only the −2 lens. This makes you artificially hypermetropic. It causes the sharp image to be formed too far behind the retina, so that it is as if your eyeball were too short. Note that you can still see distant objects sharply, although you are now having to accommodate to do so, but that an object approaching the eye becomes blurred long before it does if the −2 lens is removed (or the +2 lens is added to it to restore your emmetropia). The treatment for hypermetropia is the proper strength of *convex* lens. An uncorrected hypermetrope can get along somewhat better than an uncorrected myope for *distance* vision but cannot do close work as readily. Many a myope can do close work better without his spectacles than with them (even more easily than the emmetrope), since the myope does not have to accommodate as much. Before the use of spectacles became widespread, hypermetropes tended to adopt outdoor occupations, whereas myopes monopolized the scholarly vocations (such occupations as engraving and jewelry making).

A third common type of refractive error is "astigmatism." The usual reason for it is that the cornea has the "wrong" shape. The normal cornea has the spherical curvature throughout the central portion (which one actually looks through). To imagine an astigmatic cornea, picture to yourself a circular piece cut from the bowl of a glass teaspoon. Its radii of curvature are not all equal but have maximum and minimum values in planes at right angles to each other. This causes a characteristic retinal image blurring which is eliminated by a compensatory cylindrical spectacle lens. It is quite possible to be myopic in one meridian, and hypermetropic in another!

As we have seen, ideally *every* point in an object of regard is brought to a point focus on the retina. If the refractive error exists, (*any* kind of error), a "blur circle" is formed on the retina instead of a "point." The size of that blur circle is directly proportional to the size of the subject's pupil.

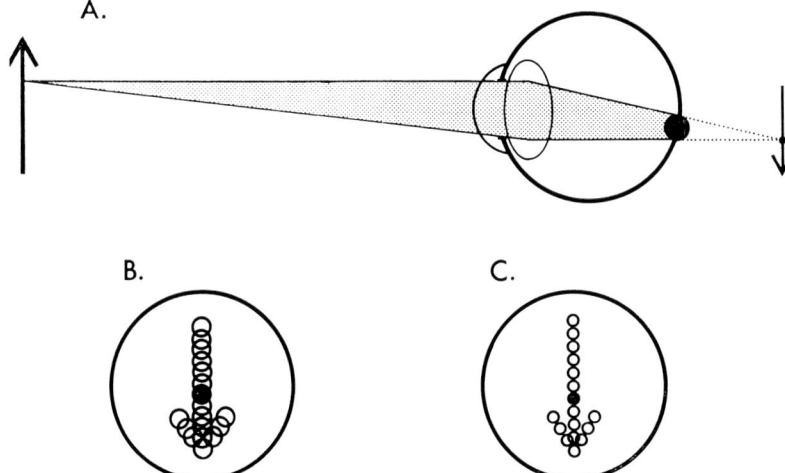

In Figure A, light from every point on the "object" is brought to a focus behind the hypermetropic eye, since its refractive power is too weak. What *is* on the retina is a blur circle (or a series of blur circles when the *entire* image is considered — Fig. B). If the pupil were made smaller, the diameter of that blur circle would decrease, and the retina would "see" an image more like the correct "point" image — Figure C. If a pinhole aperture were used immediately in front of this eye, it would act as an "artificial pupil", and the size of the blur circles would be correspondingly reduced. This is the reason many ametropic individuals (especially myopes) "squint"* (or squeeze the eyelids together) to see better, since in this manner they narrow their pupillary apertures.

*This is the lay use of the term, "squint." In ophthalmological "jargon," "squint" is synonymous with "strabismus," the presence of an eye muscle imbalance, as esotropia or "crossed eyes" (see Experiment No. 17, Eye Movements).

Repeat the first part of this experiment with the +2 and −2 lenses. Instead of correcting the induced refractive error by the opposite lens, look through a pinhole aperture and notice how the definition of the object of regard improves.

11. Light Sources and Eye Opacities

If a pinhole is held in front of an eye so that it is too close for the eye to focus upon, and a bright object background is present some distance behind the pinhole, the latter becomes a secondary source of light to the eye. The bright source behind is called an *extended source*. It can be considered to be composed of a very large number of point sources each emitting rays which can reach the pinhole from a number of different directions, thus making the pinhole itself appear to be a point source.

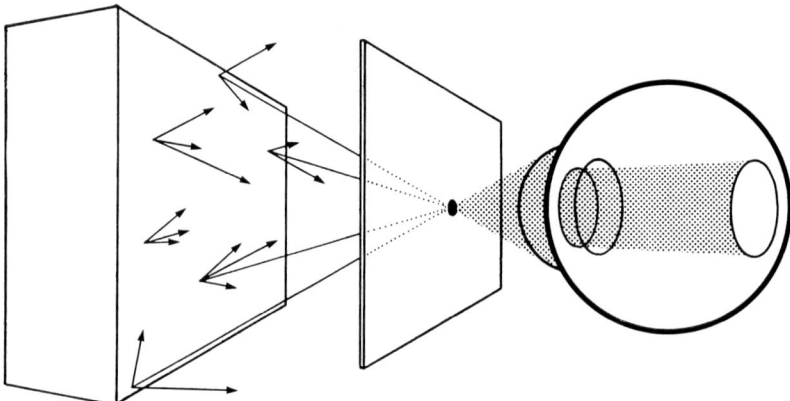

Only those rays from the pinhole which can get through the pupil of the eye will impinge on the retina, and form a blurry patch of light. The closer to the eye the pinhole is held, the larger the patch of light will be, and thus, the larger the pinhole will appear, with the maximum size appearing when the pinhole touches the cornea.

Any opacity between the pinhole and the retina will cast a shadow on the retina. Experiment No. 12 will discuss phenomena observed when the opacity is between the pinhole and cornea. Opacities in the lens, vitreous and even in the retina itself will cast shadows on the visual cells of the retina — (Experiment No. 20).

The most common opacities present, demonstrable in all normal subjects, are those "floaters" in the vitreous known as *muscae volitantes,* "floating flies." The name is derived from the elusive movements made by particles (remnants of the embryologic hyaloid vascular system and/or dense collagen fibrils) "floating" in the gelatinous vitreous when one attempts to follow them or move his eye about.

With a straight pin make a clean hole through a 3 x 5 card and hold the pinhole about two to three inches from the eye, and face the sky or a large, brightly illuminated wall, so that the pinhole will appear as a bright spot of light. Look quickly up, then down, then at the pinhole and notice the stringy, worm-like strands "floating" in the breeze. You are seeing the shadows cast on your retina by the vitreous floaters, but will also see sharply the shadows of *any* opacity from the cornea, lens or vitreous. If, instead of through a pinhole, you look directly at the entire bright, evenly illuminated background (which has no granular pattern at all), you can see a much larger field of floaters. Since the floaters are relatively close to your retina, the shadows cast are sharp. With such an "extended source," background opacities in the lens or pupil or cornea would *not* show up, as they might have when you used the pinhole source. The reason why opacities farther forward in the eye are invisible with an extended source are obvious from the following diagrams:

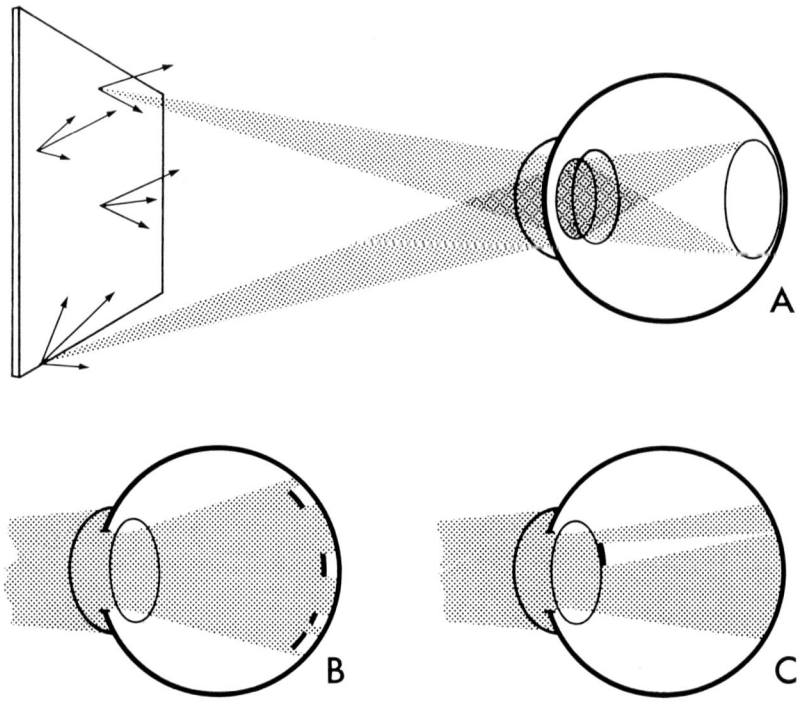

A. Since light from any point in the extended source can reach the pupil, a look at a brightly illuminated field gives a large brightly illuminated image, most of the eyeball being filled with light.

B. If an opacity is near the retina, the shadows are sharply seen.

C. A small opacity directly behind the lens, for example, will not cast a sharp shadow (umbra) on the retina, since some light from the extended source can still reach the spot in the retina where the shadow should be, thus blotting it out. This explains the severe annoyance caused by even very small opacities lying near the retina (the shadows cast being sharply defined) , and the "inconspicuousness" of much larger opacities situated more anteriorly in the vitreous or lens, such as early *cataractous* changes — opacities *within* the lens (a shadow in the latter case being only blurrily outlined, if at all visible).

12. *Inversion of the Retinal Image*

When you look at your partner, you see him right side up; but, on the retina, the optical image of your partner is upside down. This is not a paradox calling for some profound explanation. Anything that stimulates the lower part of your retina you perceive as "up," and anything imaged on the upper part you perceive as "down," and you were born able to perceive thus. It is of value and interest to do a simple experiment that shows that the retinal image must be inverted.

Use the same pinhole as in Experiment 11. Face a bright light and hold the card about three inches from the eye so that you see a pinhole as a bright dot. The pinhole again forms a secondary source of light rays entering the eye. Now hold the pin by its point, with its head up, and place it as close to the eye as you can. Raise it slowly upward and you will see framed in the pinhole a miniature pin, head descending down. The pin is too close to the eye for the light from the pinhole to form an image of the pin on the retina; instead, a *shadow* of the pin is falling on the retina; and, being a shadow, it is right-side up, like the pin itself. (It is perceived as being out in space in the plane of the pinhole.) Thus, you would perceive upside down anything whose retinal image was right side up. By holding the pin horizontal you can similarly demonstrate to yourself that a retinal image is not only inverted, but reverted, that is, has right and left interchange. Keep the pin still and concentrate on its visible image. Move the *pinhole* slowly a few inches away and then closer and note the change in size of the pin image, even though the pin itself is held still. How do you explain that the pinhead appears larger as the pinhole is brought closer to the eye?

If the pinhole is brought closer to the eye so that it stands at or near the "anterior focal point" of the eye's optical system (which is about 14 mm. from the cornea) you will still see a circular patch of the bright surface you are facing. It is not circular because the pinhole is circular, however; the circular boundary of the illumination is actually the retinal shadow of the edge of your own pupil. Light rays which pass through the anterior focal point and enter the eye are parallel to each other when they arrive at the retina, thus the retinal image is the exact same size and shape as the pupil.

Place the tips of both index fingers and one thumb together to create a little aperture a few inches from your face. Note that this aperture is triangular. Now bring the aperture slowly towards one eye and note that as soon as it arrives at the anterior focus it apparently becomes perfectly round. You are now really seeing the shape of your own pupil, unaffected by the shape of the opening of the light source, whether this be triangular or anything else. If you partly close the eye you will see your own eyelid margins and even eyelashes when they come opposite your pupil.

13. Pupillary Size and Pupillary Reflexes

Utilizing principles we learned in Experiment No. 11 (Light Sources and Opacities), we can construct a gadget for determining pupillary size to a degree of accuracy of 0.5 mm. When a pair of 1 mm. pinholes is held in front of the eye *in the anterior focal plane,* the following optical condition exists:

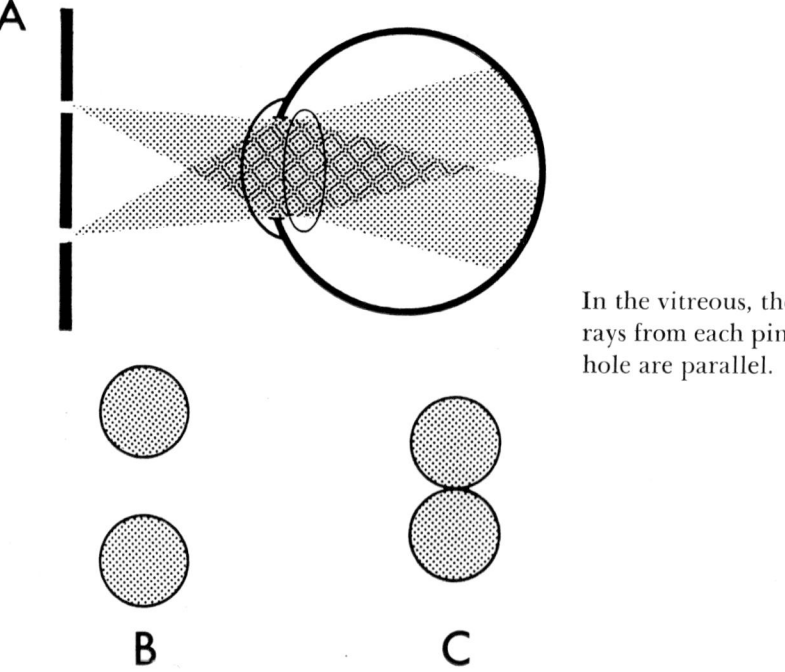

In the vitreous, the rays from each pinhole are parallel.

The observer will see two spots of light separated by a dark space — B. If two pinholes can be found that are separated just the right amount, the two visible spots of light will become tangent — C. When this condition is satisfied, the pinholes must be separated by a distance exactly equal to the pupillary diameter. Can you see why?

Pick up from the supply table the metallic plate with the paired pinholes and measure your own pupillary diameter in several different levels of illumination. Such an instrument, the Cogan entopic pupillometer, is useful as a quick, moderately accurate method of determining pupil size, for example, to measure the pupillary response to various drugs in pharmacologic experiments.

To measure the pupillary size very accurately, Drs. Lowenstein and Lowenfeld at the Columbia Medical Center have designed an infrared pupillography unit, a very sophisticated electronic instrument which simultaneously monitors the two pupil sizes to an accuracy of .05 mm.

The human pupil changes in size under many different circumstances and more often than not the response cannot be seen to have any importance for vision. The pupil is contracted by the sphincter muscle of the iris under parasympathetic control. The sphincter has to work against the elasticity of the iris tissues. When the pupil opens up, this is usually simply because the sphincter has relaxed. Relatively seldom does the antagonistic dilator muscle of the iris, which is under sympathetic control, contract slowly to open the pupil widely. We shall study experimentally only a few selected sample pupil reflexes; a valuable one, one of little value, and a completely valueless one.

Sit close to your partner facing him and hold one arm stretched out behind you with one finger up where he can see it. Watch one of his pupils closely while you bring the finger toward that eye. Repeat this several times moving the finger at different speeds. Under optimal conditions you will observe a contraction of the pupil when the fixation point comes closer than 30 centimeters. There will be a distinct latent period before the response actually shows.

This is the near reflex of the pupil. It is really a synkinesis rather than a reflex, for it takes place because accommodation is taking place, and it is the accommodation that has a stimulus of its own, not the pupillary constriction. In any event, it is a useful phenomenon, for the retinal image tends to blur through increased spherical aberration when the lens power increases, and the smaller pupil counteracts this; and the smaller pupil increases the eye's depth of focus which tends to become shallower as accommodation increases.

Have your partner sit facing away from any bright area such as a window. If he wears spectacles have him remove them. Sit where your face can be a few inches from his. Have him look into the distance over your shoulder. Shine a small bright spot from a penlight on his face away from one eye and repeatedly swing the beam slowly onto the eye and off again. Note that when the pupil constricts somewhat each time the eye is illuminated it slowly dilates again following removal of the light. Keep repeating this procedure, but watch the other eye and note that its pupil is also responding. Shade that eye with your hand, if necessary, to satisfy yourself that the penlight illumination is not reaching both eyes.

This is the "light reflex" of the pupil. It has two aspects; the constriction of the illuminated eye is the *"direct"* light reflex while the simultaneous constriction in the shadowed eye is a *"consensual"* reflex. Usually the contraction of each pupil in response to increased illumination is partly direct (because that pupil's eye is illuminated) and partly consensual (because the other eye is being illuminated). The retina is the receptor for the reflex, but the reflex arc travels no higher into the brain than the pretectal nuclei, and visual consciousness is not involved. The light reflex was the first reflex ever studied by Whytt, the discoverer of reflex action; it is still sometimes called Whytt's reflex. It is of little or no value for preventing over-stimulation of the retina itself by light. Since the decrease of pupil area reduces illumination of the retina by a factor which is tiny in comparison with the enormous range of light intensities to which the retina itself can adapt. The greatest importance of the light reflex comes when it is disturbed by brain lesions and the disturbance takes on diagnostic significance for the neurologist and neuro-surgeon.

Observe your own consensual light reflex in the following way: Hold the penlight in one hand and with the other hand hold very close to one eye a card with a pinhole in it. Recall from earlier in this experiment that the circular field seen through the pinhole really measures the pupil of that eye. Now shine the penlight beam into the other eye briefly and repeatedly. You will note alternate contraction and expansion of the field seen through the pinhole, due to the consensual light reflex of the pupil behind it.

The pupil can close about as far in the near reflex as in the light reflex but summation of the two effects can be demonstrated. There is also a consensual aspect to the near reflex, which you can look for, if you wish, by moving an object towards one eye while the other eye is shielded from seeing it.

Active contraction of the dilator or dilatator muscle occurs as a result of all sorts of central nervous events, particularly in various emotional states which involve widespread activity within the sympathetic part of the autonomic nervous system. Only one of the many dilatator reflexes is dependable enough to be studied in this laboratory exercise. It is the "pupillary skin reflex" and it is certainly useless.

Sit closely facing your partner and watch intently for dilation of his pupil while you give a quick pinch to the skin on the side of his neck, cheek or chin. You will have to pinch until it hurts to elicit a clear cut response. A latent period will be surprisingly long and the dilation itself sluggish. So repeat the procedure several times before you conclude that you have actually seen the phenomenon or that your partner does not exhibit it.

Visual Field and Eye Movements

14. Objective and Subjective Light

THE SO-CALLED ADEQUATE STIMULUS TO THE RETINA
IS RADIANT ENERGY WITHIN CERTAIN WAVELENGTH
limits absorbed inside the individual cells in the molecules of
special pigments (photopigments), which thereupon undergo
chemical change initiating the act of vision; the radiant energy
itself is the physicist's "light." The light "seen" is subjective; you
cannot show your sensation of light to anyone else. Physical light
(a stimulus) arouses psychological sensory light (a response—an
experience). But the very same kinds of light sensation can be
obtained from "inadequate stimuli" given to the retina. Most or
all of these certainly have no effect on the photopigments, but
bypass the visual cells and directly affect some of the retinal
neurons.

In a darkened corner of the room, close your eye; place a
fingertip at the outer corner of one eye and press it against
the eyeball, not too hard, and keep the fingertip wiggling. Note
that on the far side of the nose there, seemingly, is an incom-
plete bright ring that moves upward when the fingertip moves
down and vice versa. Any such sensory experience of light where
there is no physical light is a "phosphene." You should have
now seen a pressure phosphene. A blow on the head by a con-
trecoup on the eyeball generates an impact phosphene — "see-

ing stars." A mild current through the eyeball causes an electric-
al phosphene (colored in the case of the direct current, with the
color depending on the polarity). Movement of the eyeball
through a strong magnetic field gives a magnetic phosphene
probably due to eddy currents of electricity induced in the salty
intraocular fluids.

To a dark-adapted eye, x-rays arouse sensations of light which
should probably be classed as phosphenes. On the other hand,
when an ultra-violet light is shined into the eye and appears as
a "ghost-like" hazy blue glow, the retina is being stimulated by
visible light, into which the lens of the eye converts the ultra-
violet radiation by fluorescence.

15. The Visual Field

When both eyes are still and one eye is closed, it is as if the
seeing you, your "visual ego," were situated inside your head and
looking forward through a window of irregular shape. The contents of the window comprise the visual field, which is thus defined as the portion of external space visible to one motionless eye.

Observe one visual field as above. Now let the eye move in
various directions and note that many things become visible
which previously were outside the field. Your visual field is not
thereby being enlarged, but is merely being shifted about within
the totality of external space. If you turn the eye toward the
nose the visual field actually shrinks, for the nose encroaches
into it.

If you look intently at one point, that point "fixes your
gaze," hence is called a fixation point. The tiny spot in the
retina with which you are looking at the fixation point is your
fixing point. The fixation point is thought of as the "center" of
the visual field by common consent (although being noncircu-
lar, the field has no true center). The fixing point is at or near
the middle of the fovea centralis, which is thought of as being
in the center of the retina (although the retina also is not circular, but cup-shaped, and extends much further forward on the
nasal side of the eyeball than on the temporal side). An imagi-
nary straight line from the fixing point to the fixation point is
called the visual axis.

A vertical line through the fixation point cuts the visual field into a larger temporal and smaller nasal half and is called the decussation line. This line is never detectable in the visual field of a normal person; yet, owing to the partial decussation of the two optic nerves in the chiasm, everything to one side of the decussation line is registered in one half of the brain, whereas everything on the other side of the line is seen with the other half of the brain. On the retina itself, a vertical plane through the fixing point would separate the "nasal hemi-retina" (whose optic nerve fibers decussate "contralaterally" to the other side of the head) from the temporal hemi-retina (whose optic nerve fibers pass "ipsilaterally" to the cerebral hemispheres on the same side as the eye in question).

With both eyes open, steadily fixate a point straight ahead. By closing the right eye you will find that objects far to the right disappear because your left eye cannot see them.

This region on the extreme temporal side of the visual field of the right eye is roughly crescentic. There is a similar temporal crescent in the visual field of the left eye. Vision is monocular (one-eyed) in the temporal crescents, but between the crescents, the uniocular (separate-eyed) fields are overlapped and vision is binocular. In the "binocular field" both eyes are fixating the same spatial point; so the two decussation lines coincide. The entirety of a temporal hemi-retina of one eye and the large portion of the nasal hemi-retina of the other eye jointly view the same half of the binocular field and send their optic nerve fibers to the visual centers in the same cerebral hemisphere. Thus, the left half of the binocular field and the left temporal crescent are registered in the visual cortex of the right occipital lobe. At any point in that cortex where information arrives from a particular point in the right temporal hemi-retina, information also arrives from a particular point in the left nasal hemi-retina. These two retinal points would be said to be "corresponding points." If a point of light is imaged on each of them, you will see *one* spot of light in the external space.

Keeping both eyes open, place a fingertip against the lower lid of one eye and gently push that eyeball upward. Note that you will now see double. With each object in external space, the image of the object on one retina has been allowed to stay put, but the image on the other retina has been displaced off of the corresponding points or spots. The object can therefore not be seen singly; it is seen in two directions at once, hence, "diplopically."

Clinically, different instruments are utilized to map the visual field of any patient. One of these instruments is called a perimeter. It consists of a semicircular bar along which a small target may be moved, at all times equidistant from the pupil of the eye of the subject being tested. The subject places his chin in the rest provided for it and focuses one eye straight ahead, looking directly at the center of the curved rod. The target is moved by the operator along the circumference of the perimeter until the subject can no longer distinguish it (or, in the case of a colored object, its color), and this angle is marked on the chart fastened on the back of the curved rod. This method of perimetry is called "seeing to non-seeing" perimetry. The field mapped this way is always larger than that field mapped when the object is moved from the "blind" into the "seeing" retina. The *latter* is the preferable way of mapping a field; that is, the object should always be moved from the blind into the seeing area and the spot to which the patient responds as "seeing" is marked on the chart. The perimeter or semicircular rod is tilted to different angles and the procedure repeated. In this way a number of points are determined, which, when plotted on the chart supplied with the perimeter, establishes the periphery of visual field of each subject. In other words, the field of total vision is the area enclosed by this curve. Field defects or blind areas or "scotomas" may be present within the total field, even if the peripheral field is entirely "normal." Such scotomas must be checked for during the clinical use of this instrument. It would be instructive to map a visual field of one or more of the students in the group if time permits.

Another way of mapping field changes is by the tangent screen or campimeter. Here, however, only the *central* visual field is mapped; that is, an area about 30° away from the fixation point (as measured angularly at the pupil of the eye). The patient usually sits 1 meter away from a black felt screen, the patient intently gazing at a central fixation spot. The examiner moves a small test object, usually a white disk of about 1 to 3 millimeters diameter into the field until the observer notices it. A map of the patient's visual field so obtained is called a "central visual field." Clinically, it is of great use to ophthalomologists, especially in determining the characteristic field changes that occur in the disease, glaucoma. On the tangent screen, defects are greatly magnified as compared with those obtained on the perimeter. For example, a scotoma 2 cm. in size on the perimeter would be manifest as a field defect 6 cm. in size on the 1 meter tangent screen.

16. The Physiological Scotoma

In each monocular visual field there is a small area where any object actually present is totally invisible. It lies about 15 degrees to the temporal side of the fixation point and is the part of the visual field imaged on the head of the optic nerve, where there are no visual cells. In common-place vision, we are not aware of this so-called "blind spot," since the two optic nerve heads form non-corresponding spots in the two retinas. No external object is ever imaged on both of them at once. If it is imaged on one nerve head, it is simultaneously imaged on a sensitive retinal area on the other eye and is seen by that eye. But even if we close one eye and look at a blank wall, no blind spot is apparent for we see no black or "empty" spot on the wall on the temporal side of fixation. The wall looks the same all over, which is not to be expected, and requires special explanation.

Close or cover your left eye and hold this page at arm's length. Fixating steadily the cross printed below, bring the page slowly towards the right eye.

At a distance of about ten inches, the doll's head will disappear. When the page is somewhat closer, it will reappear.

Over the range where the head is invisible, its image is traversing the head of the right optic nerve. Note carefully; that when the head is invisible the area where you know it to be looks just like the surrounding blank paper.

Any area within the visual field where an object partly or wholly disappears is called a "scotoma." If the person is continuously aware of it, it is called a "positive" scotoma. Such a scotoma might be caused by a foreign body embedded in the vitreous humour where it could cast a shadow on the retina. A positive scotoma may be "absolute" (appearing in the visual field as a completely dark spot) or "relative" (forming a spot within which objects are seen but only dimly). The optic nerve head's scotoma is very different from a positive scotoma for its existence can be demonstrated only by a special experiment, such as the one above. It is an example of a "negative" scotoma by which is meant a scotoma that is "filled in" (by a little understood cerebral process) with the same kind of visual material that immediately surrounds the scotoma in the visual field. Since the nerve head scotoma, although it is, in a way, a defect, is something everyone has, it is called "physiological." Pathological scotomata of the negative type may be caused by small lesions of the visual cortex, geniculocalcarine tract, lateral geniculate nucleus, or optic tract. Scotomata, either positive or negative, are very common in migraine, and may serve as an advance warning ("aura") of the headache.

The filling-in process that makes a negative scotoma negative is surprisingly versatile. If in monocular vision you view a colored wall, the same color is seen even in the area of the physiological scotoma. If you look at a checkerboard, the pattern appears continuous.

With the left eye covered, look at the cross and head diagram with the right eye and position it so that the face disappears. Now shift your fixation up into the printed material. Knowing where the physiological scotoma is situated on the page, take note of the fact that its area is not empty, but is occupied by "imitation words." You cannot, of course, look at them (fixate them); so you are aware of the falsity only because of what you are learning here.

17. Eye Movements

The whole subject of eye movements is much too extensive for any complete experimental consideration here. Eye movements can be classified so elaborately and in so many different ways that one hardly knows where to begin to describe them. Here we will only make two simple distinctions; between movements which are voluntary and those which are involuntary, and between movements which are conjugate and those which are disjunctive.

> Have your partner face you and follow with his eyes the course of your finger which you move from side to side or up or down in his visual field.

Such voluntary or "willed" movements, since they are executed (or at least attempted) at command during a neurological examination, are called command movements by the clinician. Usually, however, voluntary movements are made at the whim of the individual to change his fixation from one point to another as he shifts his attention from one object to another. Such movements are seen only in organisms which, like man, have a small spot in the retina (a "fovea") particularly well constructed for seeing sharply. An animal whose retina is the same all over (no fovea) has no incentive to aim the eye at the object of attention, hence, does not perform voluntary eye movements.

> Have your partner face you and watch your nose while he shakes his head in the gesture "no" and nods it in the gesture "yes." Note that with each swing of his head his eyes swing in the opposite direction in their orbits. In consultation with him, you will find he was quite unaware that his eyes were moving for he did not have to will each movement in order to keep fixating your nose steadily.

Such reflex eye movements, purposed to keep the image of external space stationary on the retina in spite of movements of the head, are the most archaic of all eye movements. It was to carry out such "field-holding reflexes" that the eye rotating muscles were invented in the first place by the ancestors of the fishes. In man, there are reflex eye movements initiated by stimulation of the cristae in the semicircular canals of the ear, or initiated from the retina and mediated by way of the visual cortex. These latter reflexes are highly unusual among reflexes in general, for they involve consciousness of the stimulus and are set off (or not set off) by a given stimulus depending upon whether attention is being given to that stimulus or not. In this category are the eye movements involved in the "pursuit reflex" with which we effortlessly follow the movements of the bird in flight. Here, the only command given to the eye-moving apparatus is "follow that bird until I lose interest in it." No new command has to be given each time the bird changes direction or speed.

> Have your partner "follow" your finger while you move it slowly from side to side. Then hold the finger centered and move it slowly toward his nose while he continuously bifixates it. Note that at first his eyes were moving like a team of horses or like the front wheels of an auto, both of which turn to the left or to the right because they are interconnected by a metal tie-rod. Such movements of the two eyes are called "conjugate." When your finger approached the subject's nose, both eyes turned it, but not in the same direction; the left eye turned to the right while the right eye turned to the left. Such binocular movements are called "disjunctive."

Rarely is an eye movement purely conjugate or purely disjunctive. Both aspects are involved when we switch our attention from an object at one distance in one direction to another object at a different distance in another direction. The disjunctive aspect is called "convergence" even if it is asymmetrical (as when the bifixation point is straight ahead of one eye so that the other eye does *all* the turning.) Convergence occurs in the interest of keeping the two retinal images of the object of attention upon corresponding retinal points, so that diplopia will not occur. Increases or decreases of convergence occur automatically but there are no less than four tributaries to the river of nerve impulses flowing to the converging muscles (the medial and lateral recti). One of the four components of convergence is "tonic" (since the eyes are divergent in sleep, anesthesia and death). Another, "accommodative convergence," is synkinetic to accommodation. A third, "proximal convergence," is stimulated by conscious awareness of the nearness of the object. Any residual need for convergent effort is filled by a true reflex "fusional convergence" which is initiated at the cortex and for which the stimulus is the commencement of diplopia.

The separateness of the control of a disjunctive convergent movement of the eye from the control of an inward turning of the eye accompanying an outward turning of the other (a "conjugate lateral deviation") is easily demonstrated by a very interesting experiment.

> Stand or sit facing your partner. He will make the observation first and then you will exchange roles. Bring a finger slowly towards your nose in a straight line until it is at your "convergence near point," that is, as close as it can be without doubling. Now move the finger off to one side a foot or so, in a line parallel to your face, watching it continuously by turning your eyes without turning your head. Your partner will be able to note that after the eyes both turned in as far as the components of convergence can make them do, either eye can still be turned even further in toward the nose if it is called upon to take part in a conjugate movement to one side.

The convergence reflex, "fusional convergence," is readily stimulated in such a way that anyone can observe the results for himself. During binocular vision if the image on one retina is suddenly displaced sidewise on the retina there will be diplopia. If the doubled images are seen to come together promptly and unify again, the convergence reflex must be responsible, since there has been no change in the stimulation of the tonic, accommodative and proximal components:

> At the supply table obtain a 6Δ (prism diopter) prism, a glass wedge mounted in a metal ring. On the surface of the glass find a radial scratch which points to the base (thickest part) of the prism. Look across the room while holding the prism by its handle just beneath one eye, its base directed to either the left or the right. Bi-fixate something intently and attentively while you shove the prism up in front of the eye. Do you see double momentarily, and then singly again? Yank the prism down out of place. Is there a brief diplopia again? Turn the prism so that the base points to the opposite direction, and repeat. Is the diplopia produced any more readily with the

base towards the nose ("base in") or towards the temple ("base out")? Do the images unify any more promptly and readily in one case or the other?

Human eye movements would not need to be nearly as precise as they are if our vision were not binocular (and characterized by the correspondency phenomenon). Such team work is necessary to keep the retinal images of the object of attention always on corresponding points, and it is not surprising that imperfections can usually be demonstrated. During bifixation of a point, the fixing point in one fovea may look directly at that point, but the fixing point in the other eye may regularly miss it by a small angle. This is "fixation disparity," and is possible because interretinal correspondency is not so strictly point-to-point but what the images can be a little out of ideal positions and still be fused. The amount of fixation disparity varies among individuals and at different distances, etc., in the same person.

The maintenance of the proper convergence for seeing singly may put the neuromuscular apparatus under what, for want of a better term, may be called a strain. In young children, the oculomotor system sometimes gives up trying to maintain coordination, particularly if some special handicap is present. Squint ("Strabismus") then develops — only one eye fixates at all while the other turns conspicuously inward ("esotropia") or outward ("exotropia"). Most persons grow up to enjoy "binocular single vision," in which any stress there may be causes (at most) a latent tendency for one eye to turn out or in somewhat. If, while bifixating a distant point, each of your eyes maintains its aim even if it is briefly covered, you are "orthophoric." If, however, there is a deviation of one visual axis or both (greater than the extent of any fixation disparity present), you would be said to exhibit "heterophoria."

Here heterophoria is tested for at twenty feet. Toe the chalkline of the visual acuity test and use your letter chart as a target. Viewing it intently, hold your palm toward your eyes so that when the right eye is blocked, the left eye is not, and vice versa. Now move your hand to the left and to the right, so that you see the chart with one eye at a time in rapid alternation at the rate you find necessary for beta movement (see Experiment No. 28, Visual Movement). Watch for the top letter to "jump" from side to side (perhaps on a slant), no matter how hard you try to bifixate it in your alternocular vision. If it does jump, showing that it is in two rather different directions with respect to your two visual axes, then you do have some heterophoria, not necessarily enough to "worry about" but showing that your visual system is having to do something special all the time to keep your eyes "in line." By definition, heterophoria is a tendency to deviate, which is continuously kept under control.

If, during binocular vision of a *near* object, the individual eyes are similarly "dissociated" (that is, relieved of the necessity of bifixating and fusing,) inability to keep the eyes aimed as they had been is so common as to be physiological. Ordinarily the covered eye turns out, although it may turn in or it may turn out to an unusual extent, for in near vision there are factors at work other than the one responsible for any distance-heterophoria.

The heterophoria test described above is "subjective" since any deviation is evident only to the testee himself. Perform the (objective) "alternate cover test" as follows: Your partner sits holding an upright pencil before him at arm's length. Throughout this test he fixates it conscientiously to keep its image sharp. Stand beside his left knee and with a 3 x 5 card cover his left eye for a few seconds, now quickly swap the card over to the right eye and watch for the left eye to turn toward the pencil when it is uncovered. Any such turning shows that the left eye was deviating behind the cover; such deviation is loosely called "heterophoria at near" and can be objectively and accurately measured by finding strength of prism which when placed between eye and cover will make it unnecessary for the eye to turn when uncovered. This is called "neutralizing" the cover test, and is the way in which eye deviations are measured clinically, say as part of the preoperative evaluation of a "cross-eyed" child.

18. Protective Reflexes

The eyeball is protected from large missiles by the bony ridge under the eyebrow on the cheekbone. The eyebrow itself diverts the sweat which would sting the cornea and conjunctiva, since its salt content is much higher than that of the tears. The tear fluid keeps the living surface tissues of the eyeball moist and contains a valuable bacteriocidal enzyme (lysozyme). The lids serve chiefly to spread the tear fluid during periodic winking, a reflex action for which the stimulus is unknown — it is not related to the humidity of the surrounding air. The lids also take part in the actions which protect against mechanical or other insult.

Sit close to and facing your partner. With the corner of your handkerchief or bit of soft paper he touches the cilia (lashes) near the inner corner of the eye. Note that this sets off a powerful blink reflex. Recall that a sand particle or the like landing on the eyeball also sets off strong lid closure, accompanied by "tearing" purposed to flush away the particle. Irritant chemicals, as in smog, stimulate reflex tearing and may even cause blinking. These are all "sensory reflexes."

Gather around the instructor while he fires a photographic flashlamp. Be sure you are staring directly at the lamp before it fires. Prepare yourself to try to inhibit the blink that is stimulated and note whether you succeed. The act of blinking is an optical reflex since the retina itself is the receptor at one end of the arc. This response to bright light may seem valueless, but it reinforces a protective blink given to the infrared content of natural bright lights. The eye has no defense against ultraviolet radiation, but the delayed inflammation it causes (snow blindness, or welder's flash) stimulates strong reflex lid closure (perhaps giving better opportunity for healing).

Snuff a few grains of pepper from the palm of your hand to induce sneezing. Try to inhibit the strong blink that accompanies the sneeze. This blink is of doubtful value. It is *not* a reflex act in its own right, but just one of several synkinetic actions involved in the sneeze — a complex event. (Please observe normal hygienic precautions, when sneezing.)

Some lid actions are neither reflexes nor synkineses, and are not at all as automatic as they seem. Have your partner poke his fist quickly towards your eye, stopping just short of it. Note your blink reflex. Now tell yourself that you will inhibit that blink and repeat until you succeed. This response is believed to be acquired, not inborn. In keeping with this is the ease with which it is inhibited. It seems valueless since the lids can give no protection from a gross missile.

Adaptation and Brightness

19. Adaptation to Light Intensity

NO MAN-MADE LIGHT METER CAN CHANGE ITS OWN SENSITIVITY. IF ITS POINT MOVES A CERTAIN DISTANCE over a scale under a certain illumination, it will always move that same distance under the same illumination. A piece of photographic paper will always be darkened to the same extent by the same amount of light operating over the same length of time, or by any other intensity of light so long as the product of intensity and time is a constant.

The retina is vastly different, for its sensitivity is inconstant and depends upon its immediate past history. When the retina has been dimly illuminated (or in the dark) for awhile, it will respond to a feeble illumination and a moderate illumination will arouse a sensation of high brightness. But when the retina has been strongly illuminated for awhile, the lowest intensity to which it will respond may be 1,000 or 10,000 times that which would give a sensation before, and a moderate illumination will now look dim. Two opposite processes are involved, which are not defined in terms of the initial and final states attained, but only in terms of the *direction* in which the process goes. "Light-adaptation" is any decrease in the sensitivity of the retina (instigated by increasing in the intensity of illumination); "dark-adaptation" is any increase in the sensitivity of the retina (instigated by decrease in the intensity of illumination). We can distinguish "total dark-adaptation" as the state of maximal sensitivity to which the retina can attain when it is in complete darkness indefinitely; but there is no such thing as "total light-adaptation."

If the retina could not adapt, we should be blind in a dim light (which would appear to be "pitch darkness"), and we should be miserably dazzled by outdoor daylight. An important fraction of the range of adaptation is accounted for by changes in the concentration of the photopigment in the visual cells of the retina, which rises to a maximum in total darkness and is pulled down when intense illumination breaks down photopigment faster than it can be formed. But to a large extent, the processes of adaptation are based upon neurophysiological phenomena in the nerve tissue of the retina or even in cerebral visual centers.

If one has the necessary apparatus and the practiced skill, the best way to evaluate the adaptation state of the retina is to measure the "intensity threshold," the physical intensity of light that will merely arouse a sensation of light at the moment. By making such determinations repeatedly, the course of adaptation can be followed and expressed in a graph of threshold-intensity plotted against time.

Another method and the only one feasible here is to adjudge the brightness of sensation given by some fixed intensity of stimulus that is well above threshold level. Fold a piece of Kleenex into a 2" pad, apply to one eye, and over it tie a black "patch." This cover must be light-tight and is to be worn for thirty minutes; so before installing it, plan your work so as to keep busy doing experiments for which only one eye is needed.

When the thirty minutes are up, sit with your face a couple of feet from a gooseneck lamp, bent so that its light shines horizontally at your face. The covered eye is now practically totally dark-adapted. Your partner should provide himself with a watch having a second hand, and station himself alongside prepared to take down what you report to him. When he has taken note of the time on the watch and gives you a signal, quickly remove the patch and immediately begin looking at the light bulb, first with one eye and then with the other, using your palms for covers, and uncovering each eye for a couple of seconds at a time. Your initial task is to try to estimate how many times brighter the light looks at first to the dark adapted eye than it does to the light adapted eye. Your long term task is to try to decide when the brightness for the (formerly) covered eye is dropped to where it is no higher than the brightness for the other eye. This will afford a rough measure of the time required for light adaptation to the intensity of the lamp. Note how much less this is than the thirty minute period normally required for total *dark* adaptation. If, from time to time, you are able to report that the brightness for one eye is now about four times the brightness for the other eye, and now three times, and now two times, and if your partner records the time in which each estimate is made, you may be able to plot an interesting curve of the course of *light* adaptation.

20. Local Retinal Adaptation

More often than not, the state of adaptation is different in different areas of the retina at the same time. As we look about us, the images of different intensities are shifting over different parts of the retina. In fact, no one bit of the retina ever gets a chance to finish its adjustment to the intensity in any part of the whole retinal image, unless that image stands still for quite a while — which is a rather artificial situation.

Go to the slide projector and insert the slide showing a "negative." Cover one eye, project the slide and stare steadily at the X in the picture for at least twenty seconds. Have your partner now remove the slide so that the screen is simply flooded with light from the projector. Still looking at the screen with one eye, note that you see on it a "positive" image. If it tends to fade, firm blinking will revive it. If you approach the screen the image will shrink; if you back away it will enlarge.

You have just experienced a "negative after-image" in which the brightness relationships were opposite to what they were in the "inducing stimulus" (the direct image of the slide). From what you learned in the previous experiment you should have no difficulty in explaining why the illumination on the empty screen looks brighter to the retinal areas on which the dark parts of the projected picture were previously imaged. The change in size of the "positive" image with a change of your distance from the screen has nothing to do with adaptation itself, but is a demonstration of "Emmert's Law": The apparent distance of an after-image is directly proportional to the distance of the surface upon which it is projected.

21. Equal Final Brightness from Unequal Intensities

The process of light and dark adaptation are "perfectly compensatory" for changes of physical stimulus-intensity over a great range of intensity, if they are given time to run to completion. This means that when a high intensity looks less and less bright to an eye that is light-adapting up to that level, and when a low intensity looks brighter and brighter to an eye that is dark-adapting down to its level, the final brightnesses of the high and low intensities will actually be equal to each other provided, that is, that the high intensity is not too high nor the low intensity too low — the range over which compensation is perfect has limits, although these are at least in a 1000-to-1 ratio.

A clear implication of this is that if you should look very steadily at a pattern comprised of different shades of gray, such that all the different intensities in the retinal image were within the "perfect-compensation" range, the pattern would homogenize in a few minutes and its entire area would appear as one uniform gray. It is difficult to try to demonstrate this for a *routine visual scene** since each eyeball is normally in a state of continual fine, fast vibration (the "physiologic nystagmus") and no matter how steadily you may think you are fixating, your eye is not steady at all. However, there are two neat little demonstrations that will show you that if the image is kept steady on the retina there is a progressive dimming and subsequent disappearance of a visual field.

In the periphery of the retina, particularly at lower levels of illumination, the phenomenon is readily observed with the use of

---

*In a very elaborate laboratory setup, Riggs has shown that if the retinal image of visual space is well-stabilized (that is, the image is caused to move, perfectly co-ordinated with the physiological nystagmoid movements of the eye) the image seen does indeed fade, the field becoming homogeneous.

ordinary fixation, without the artificial stabilization referred to in the footnote. This observation was first described by Troxler (1804) and it carries his eponym.

Stare (both eyes open) at the dot next to the letter A from a distance of about 6-8". While fixating this dot as steadily as possible, note that gradually (after about 30 seconds) the group of dots above and to the left begin to fade, and eventually they can be noted to disappear. After they have "blanked out," if your gaze is then shifted down to dot B, the previously faded spots immediately vividly reappear from "out of nowhere."

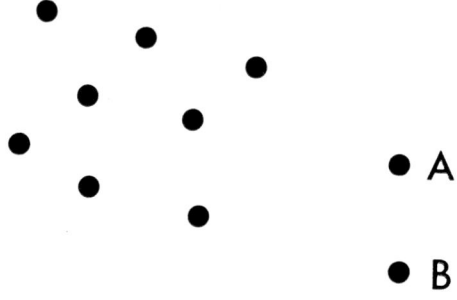

It just so happens that there is built into the eyeball itself another situation which will enable us to test the proposition that a pattern of higher and lower intensities on the retina will be invisible because of local adaptation, if the pattern *cannot* move the least bit with respect to the visual cell layer.

Examine a picture of the fundus of the eye as seen through the pupil with the ophthalmoscope. Study the arrangement of the retinal blood vessels in the picture, noting how the largest ones come away from the optic nervehead and curve over the retina giving off branches. The immediate neighborhood of the fixing point (center of the fovea) is left clear of vessels. All of these vessels are embedded in the retinal tissue, and lie between the incoming light and the visual cell layer (which is on the back of the transparent retina). Each vessel lets through less light than the tissue around it; so, on the visual cells right behind the vessel, all along its length, the illumination is reduced. This shadowing of the visual cells allows them to dark-adapt somewhat and increase their sensitivity so that the reduced light reaching them looks just as bright to them as if the blood vessels were not there. So, our whole pattern of retinal veins and arteries is normally invisible to us, despite the fact that it lies between the visual cells and the source of light.

Obviously, if we should illuminate the retina with light that strikes it from an unusual angle instead of coming straight in through the pupil, the shadow from every blood vessel would be shifted over a little so as to fall upon a line of visual cells which are not adapted to it. These visual cells would see the vessel as a dark line, and, simultaneously, a bright line would appear alongside where the displacement of the shadow had uncovered some dark-adapted visual cells. This slantwise illumination of the retina is easy to accomplish: Sit facing a dark area and close both eyes. Place the bulb end of a penlight directly against the upper lid of one eye as high up toward the bone as you can and wiggle the penlight slightly and continuously. It may help to keep your eyes turned downward in their orbits. The light is now shining through the lid and through the wall of the eyeball, and not through the cornea and pupil. You should see, apparently standing out in space before you, the whole pattern of the retinal vessels in much more detail than the posted picture. As the penlight jiggles, each vessel will be seen as a dark line, a bright line, or a combination of both. After its discoverer, this appearance is known as the "Purkinje vessel-figure."

Do not confuse the normal "adaptational invisibility" of the retinal vessels with the phenomenon of the negative scotoma (Experiment No. 16). The basis is very different in each case. Sometimes, however, a foreign object in contact with the retina fails to produce the expected positive scotoma because local adaptation evanishes it just as it does the retinal vessels.

22. Craik Blindness

This is a phenomenon so startling that you need reassurance that the procedure that produces it is harmless and that you need not fear that it will damage your eyes.

You and your partner can sit facing each other and perform the experiment simultaneously. Cover one eye light-tight with the palm of your hand. Place a fingertip against the other eye

at the outer corner of the lid opening, as you did in Experiment
No. 14, to evoke the pressure phosphene. Press the eye steadily
through the lid until you see the phosphene, but now increase
the pressure and maintain it until your partner's face begins
to fade. Within a few seconds you should see nothing whatever,
even though the eye is wide open and you know that there is
something there to see (your partner's face). As soon as you are
sure the eye has become entirely blind, remove the finger and
note that completely normal vision quickly returns. Now uncover the other eye.

The pressure on the eyeball squeezes all the blood out of the
retinal vessels and the nerve cells on the retina are quickly
brought to a functionless state. The visual cells are still receiving
light and their photochemical activity is unimpaired, but they are
disconnected from the brain so long as the abnormal pressure is
maintained. The name of the late K. J. W. Craik is attached to
this phenomenon. He did not discover it (it has been known for
almost a century), but he exploited it in his study of after-images.
By having a subject face a bright light, after first developing the
pressure blindness, Craik determined that the subject would later
see a negative after-image of light when the pressure was removed.
This showed that the physiological basis of the after-image must
be in the visual-cell layer and not in the brain, since no information about the inducing stimulus was being allowed to reach the
brain while the stimulus was present. You should attempt this
demonstration to yourself if you have time.

23. Brightness Versus Intensity

We have seen that in visual sensation the "final brightness,"
after complete adaptation, tends to be the same no matter what
the physical intensity of the light may be; but in the everyday use
of our eyes, insufficient time is allowed for complete adaptation.
When we casually look at one light or object after another we see
each one as having its "initial brightness," and the magnitude of
this is pretty directly determined by the physical intensity of the
light in the retinal image. If we look back and forth between two
lights of different brightnesses we see the initial brightness of each

light each time we look at it and the two brightnesses never do come to be equal.

When we talk about the relation between the subjective brightness of a light to its objective intensity, we are talking about initial brightness, with the state of adaptation of the retina assumed to be constant. Otherwise we could not even raise such a question as "What series of increasingly higher brightnesses will be given by this particular series of increasingly higher intensities?"

It was decided in the last century by the pioneer psychophysicist, G. T. Fechner, that brightness increases in proportion to the logarithm of the stimulus intensity. This statement is "Fechner's Law"; in another form it says that in order for brightness to increase arithmetically (steadily) the intensity has to be increased geometrically (more and more rapidly). A corollary is that if an intensity were to be increased steadily, brightness would rise more and more slowly. Fechner's law has been under critical fire ever since it was formulated but, nevertheless, it is common experience that we do get diminishing returns in brightness as we raise the intensity of the light.

This experiment is one which we cannot do here in the lighted room, but one which you can do at home, or which you can do in your "memory," or take on faith. In an overhead lampshade aimed down at a worktable bearing assorted objects, install a 25-watt bulb, then a 50-watt, then a 75-watt, and lastly a 100-watt bulb. Each time, evaluate the brightness of illumination of the table and contents. Are the brightnesses of things twice as great under the 50-watt lamp as under the 25-watt lamp? And twice as great under the 100-watt as under the 50-watt? This experiment is one which the light and power industry hopes the general public will never become familiar with. Your light bill is directly proportional to the wattage of lamps you are using; the brightness of your rooms at night is not.

Examine the posted plaque bearing a series of sample pieces of Munsel neutral papers; these are gray papers. Under pure white neutral illumination these grays are "visually equispaced"; their subjective intensities form an arithmetic series, and each sample appears to differ about as much from the next-lighter sample as it does from the next-darker one. The percentages of the incident light reflected by the samples (their "reflectances") are in an approximately logarithmic series, and so also are the intensities of the retinal images of the samples. If you are satisfied as to the subjective equispacing, you have before you a practical demonstration of the rough proof of Fechner's Law.

SECTION V

Acuity and Sensation-times

24. Intensity Discrimination
WHAT IS PERHAPS THE MOST IMPORTANT SINGLE
VISUAL FUNCTION IS THE ABILITY TO DETECT THE
difference between two intensities of light which are nearly equal.
Forgetting about color differences for the moment, it is clear that
when we see an object at all it is because the object and its background are different in brightness, which is another way of saying
that their physical intensities are barely detectibly different.

The extent to which an object and its background differ in
objective intensity is called the "contrast" of the object. For
example, in a white illumination, good-quality white paper reflects 80 per cent of the light and printer's ink reflects 5 per cent.
The contrast (C) of printed letters, then, is $C = \dfrac{80 - 5}{80} = 0.937$ or
93.7 per cent. The lowest contrast that the eye can detect measures
the "contrast sensitivity" of the eye and indicates how good intensity discrimination is. The function improves as the intensity
increases, and at high (but not dazzling) intensities even an un-
trained observer can be expected to see a difference between two
intensities, one of which is no more than one per cent higher than
the other. In research laboratories, discrimination of a difference
of only 0.4 per cent has been frequently accomplished. The

"world's record" is probably held by the highly skilled photome-
trists at the Bureau of Standards in France, who regularly detect
a difference of 0.1 per cent.

You can easily compare your own contrast discrimination with
that of your partner with a simple device invented over a century ago by Masson. Go to the rotary mixer (Figure 8, Experiment No. 30) provided and place on it the "Masson disc,"
which has a row of black spots along one radius (Figure 4A).
When this disc is spun so fast that the spots generate a set of
concentric rings, the effective intensity of the paper in each
ring is reduced in proportion to the angle occupied by the black
spot. The contrast between each ring and the paper just inside
the ring and just outside it is then:

$$C\% = \frac{360° - (360° - \text{spot angle})}{360°} \times 100 = \frac{\text{spot Angle}}{360°} \times 100.$$

Spin the Masson disc and note which is the largest ring you can
see; the angular size of the spot forming that ring is recorded
on the back of that disc. Calculate your "threshold contrast" in

Figure 4. Various rotating discs used in experiments. A. Masson disc—top
row center. B. Sectored disc—for Flicker. Top row right. C. Shrinking Spiral—
bottom row left. D. Expanding Spiral—bottom row right. E. Benham top—top
row left.

percent. (The simple formula given here ignores the facts that the reflectance of the disc paper is less than 100 per cent and the reflectance of the black spots is not zero.)

25. Visual Acuity

Visual acuity has come to be accepted as the broad term for the ability to make out fine details of the complicated pattern of external visual space. Although we were all taught that this ability is measured by a Snellen letter chart, "visual acuity" does have a strict definition. As a background to this experiment, we will define this term and give a description of the several different kinds of visual acuity and their measurement.

Most measurements evaluating various visual functions are made at threshold levels. If the capacity to be measured is a threshold intensity (of a colored light, for example), the reciprocal of this threshold is called a "sensitivity." On the other hand, if the threshold measurement is of a linear extent (or angular subtense* or areal extent), the reciprocal is spoken of as an "acuity."

Visual acuity as a term is unfortunately used with much laxity to cover many kinds of performance. The angular size (measured at the eye) of the narrowest single line which can be seen is the *minimum visible angle* and the reciprocal measures the *visibility acuity* for that target. If we place on white background two parallel black lines which can be moved closer and closer towards each other, such a target could be used to measure what is called "resolution acuity." Thus, when the lines can be seen to be two lines, they are being "resolved." When they are so close together

---

*Subtense: Threshold extents are customarily expressed as subtenses. The reason probably sees obvious. A one inch object at two feet gives the same retinal image size as that of a ten inch object at twenty feet, *i.e.*, the angular size of these two objects are identical, if measured at the eye.

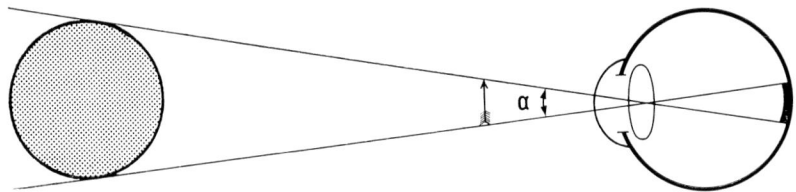

that they can barely be seen to be two lines and not one, they are being barely resolved, and their separation is the "resolution threshold." The reciprocal value of the angular separation of the two lines at this threshold is the *resolution acuity*. The smaller the threshold separation, the higher the visual acuity—as measured in this particular way. Continuing this on, the angular size of the smallest letters which can be read determine the *minimum legible* for the reciprocal of which there is no special name. The equiva-lent of objects is the *minimum cogniscible*. Then, there are other acuities: vernier (ability to line up two lines), stereo (depth dis-crimination), motion (just detectible) —all of which are the re-ciprocals of threshold *extents*.

Of all of these, only resolution *should* ever be called "visual acuity" without qualifying adjective. By international agreement (in 1909) visual acuity is the reciprocal of the threshold angular subtense of the gap in a black Landolt "broken circle" on a white background, and is given directly in "Snellen units" when the threshold is expressed in minutes of arc. "Clinically *normal* visual acuity" is considered to be 1.0 Snellen unit— the resolution *thres-hold* is assumed to be one minute.

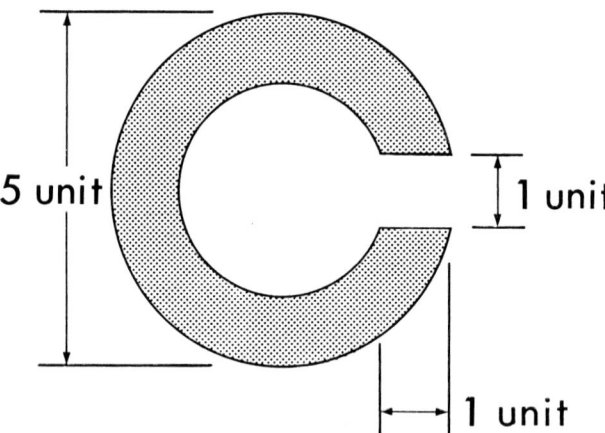

5 unit   1 unit

1 unit

This Landolt broken circle has been a favorite visual acuity target for research purposes, but is considered impractical for clinical use, where the Snellen block-letter chart is preferred. The size of the "Snellen letters" conforms exactly to the size of the corresponding Landolt "C." However, you should note that when an alphabetic chart is used clinically, it is really the *minimum legible* angle that is being measured. The pretense, however, is that one is measuring the *minimum separable* angle, the resolution threshold. Snellen himself made no distinction between the minimum visible, the minimum separable, and the shape-factor in legibility. When the letters were designed for the chart, the "stroke" (width of the black lines) and the white internal spaces were made equal to each other wherever possible, and were made always proportional to those in the line of letters in which these "critical details" subtended one minute of arc at 6 meters (or 20 feet). The supposition was that a letter would be legible only if its stroke was visible and its interspaces resolvable. (This assumption is obviously nonsense. The letter "V" is legible as a "V" and not an "A," since there is only one letter in the alphabet which looks like a triangle standing on one corner. The subject doesn't have to resolve anything. The same lack of a resolution challenge holds for *most* letters of the alphabet.) Snellen then expressed a subject's acuity by a *pseudo-fraction* with "20" (feet) as its numerator, and with its denominator the distance at which a clinically normal person (having a resolution threshold of one minute) would theoretically be just able to read the line of targets, which the subject at hand was just able to read at twenty feet. Thus, 20/30 expresses a subnormal acuity; 20/10 a supernormal one. To keep people from thinking of such ratings as true fractions, Snellen proposed that numerators should always be written in Arabic numerals and the denominator in Roman; his suggestion has not been followed. Because it hasn't, most people are led to the *false* conclusion that 20/40 "vision" is only half as good as 20/20!

Thus, alphabet letters are routinely used as acuity targets, not because they measure pure resolution acuity, but a mixture of this — shape-recognition, line-visibility, and other aspects of visual acuity. For this very reason, alphabet letters make our best test of "all round" seeing ability. Go to the line chalked on the floor twenty feet from the posted letter chart, and see how far down the chart you can read with each eye separately and with both eyes together. Have your partner station himself enough closer to the chart so that he can tell when you are making mistakes.

The lowest line at which you can correctly read more than half of the letters is your "threshold" as discussed above; if this happens to be the "15 foot line," your visual acuity would be rated "20/15," which means that you can read at twenty feet letters so small that the average person would have to be at fifteen feet to read them. Again, I caution you to remember these "Snellen ratings" are not fractions, even though they look like them. They should not be tampered with by dividing the "20" by 15, 20, 30 or whatever the threshold happens to be. Visual acuity is *not* independent of the distance at which it is measured; the Snellen rating contains a record of that distance.

It is only at the center of your retinal fovea—the neighborhood of your fixing point—that you have the high visual acuity you have just measured on the Snellen chart. The high-acuity area in your visual field is not much larger than your image of the full moon $(\frac{1}{2}°)$. Away from the fovea, visual acuity falls off so rapidly that you may be shocked to discover how rapidly:

> Have your partner face you at a distance of two feet and hold one arm straight out to one side. With that outstretched hand he now briefly holds up two, three, or four fingers. You, fixating his nose steadily, try to say how many fingers he is holding up. If you make errors, he should bring the hand in a few inches closer to his shoulder and repeat. How far to one side can his hand be, for you to be still able to count fingers?

> Finger-counting is a crude and liberal test of peripheral visual acuity. To get a still better idea of the tremendous superiority of the fovea, encircle with a pencil one word in the middle of a printed page, and note how close to it you must fixate before you would know what the word was if you did not already know. The average person has no idea that his visual acuity is not of foveal quality throughout his visual field; for, when he wants to look at anything, he aims the fovea at it by means of a voluntary eye movement.

Carefully analyzed, most kinds of visual-acuity performance (including visual resolution) can be seen to have their basis in intensity discrimination, where the intensities that must be discriminated are in the different parts of the *retinal image* of the target. It is common to say that resolution is nothing but a "special case" of intensity discrimination in which the special factor is the small size of the field (*i.e.,* the target).

26. *Visual Sensation-Time*

From the instant any illumination is thrown on the retina, an appreciable fraction of a second elapses before the ensuing sensation develops. This period of delay has been given more than one name; and different portions of it (which have names of their own) are the latent periods of distinct processes. For example, there is the time required for the photochemical effect of the light to build up, the time occupied by secondary chemical reactions within the visual cells, the time it takes impulses to travel along nerve fibers intraretinally, the time between visual cells and cerebral cortex, the delay at each synapse between nerve cell and nerve cell, and so on. We shall simply call the entire delay between stimulation and sensation the "sensation-time."

With simple means and only a few minutes' time, we could not hope to measure the actual sensation-time. But we can do something interesting that demonstrates an alteration of the sensation-time. The period is profoundly affected by intensity, being longer for a dim stimulus and shorter for a bright one.

Go to the supply table and obtain the gadget consisting of the white cylindrical slug of metal on a black string (Figure 5), and a neutral filter. Have your partner set the slug swinging on its string like a pendulum. The pendulum must swing always in a single plane (this is most easily accomplished if it is made to swing toward and away from the chest of the person holding it). You sit with your face about a yard from the pendulum, viewing it in a line perpendicular to its plane of swing, with both eyes open but with the filter in front of one eye. You will see the pendulum moving not in a plane, but in an elliptical or circular path. Swapping the filter to the other eye will reverse the direction of the slug in its path.

This is the "Pulfrich effect" or the "Pulfrich stereo-illusion." The underlying cause of the third-dimensional movement seen is the increase of sensation-time by the filter, which lowers the in-

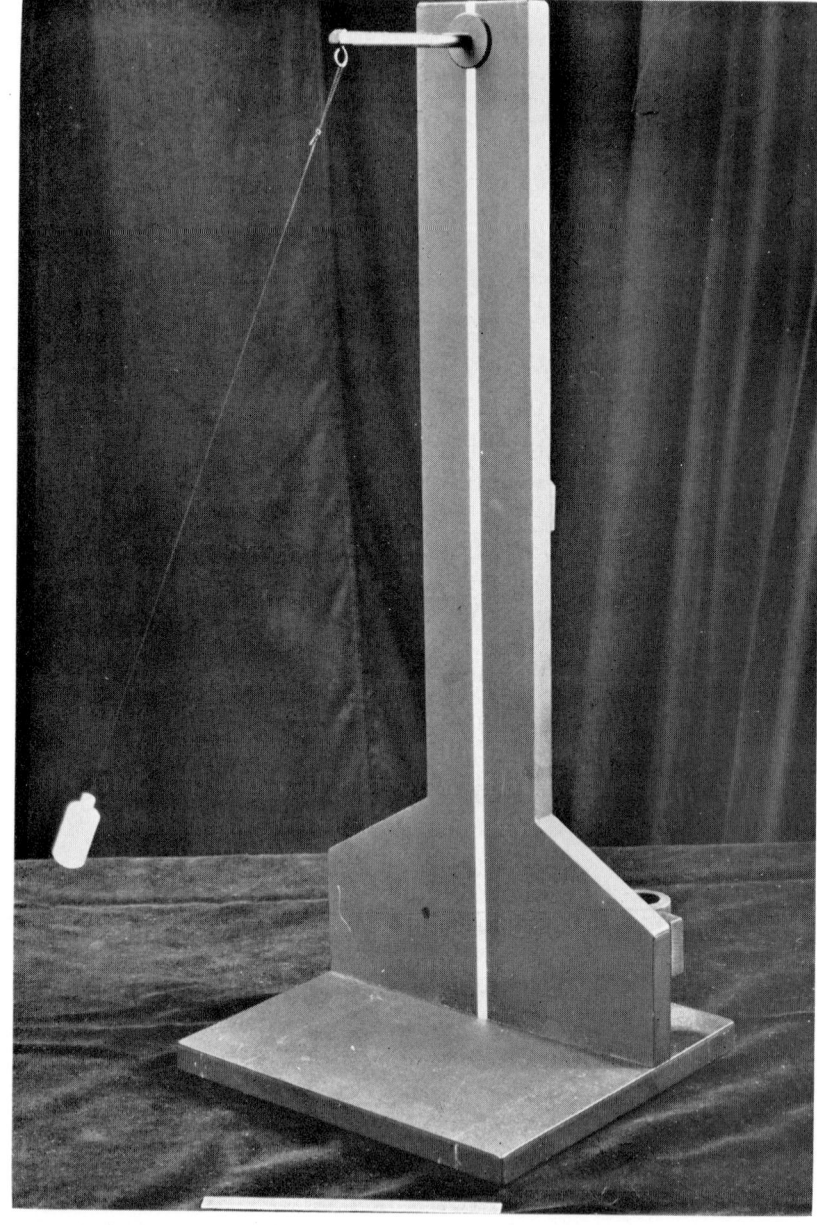

Figure 5. The swinging pendulum bob to demonstrate the Pulfrich "stereo" illusion.

tensity of the image on the retina behind it. At a given instant, when the pendulum bob is in a given real position, the naked eye is seeing it *behind* this position on its line of travel, but the filtered eye is seeing it still farther behind its real position. Examine the following diagram, showing the two eyes, the filter and the slug on its line of travel—going from right to left. Notice

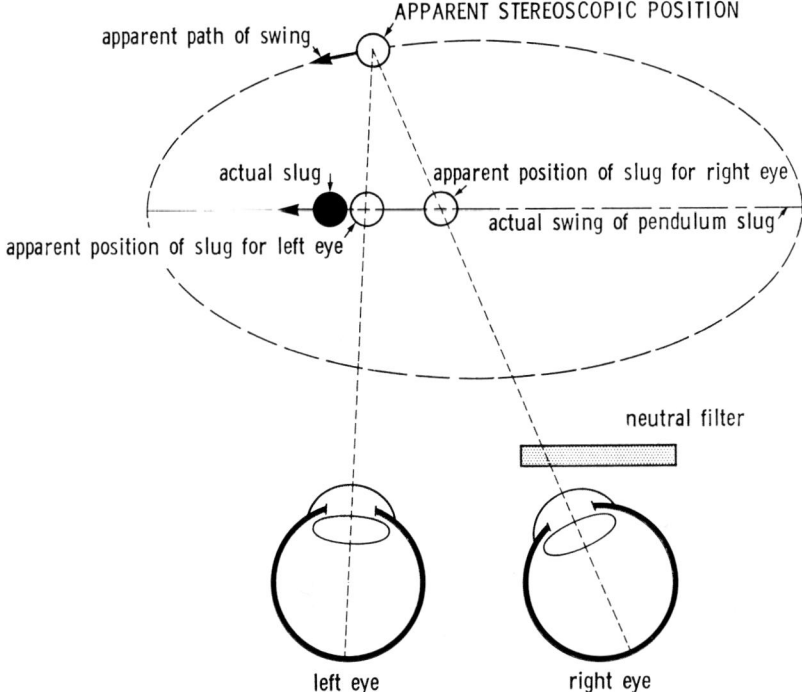

the apparent position of the bob *for each eye,* and the straight lines from the eyes through these positions (representing the visual axes). The apparent *binocular* position of the pendulum bob is shown. You should easily see why it appears to travel on a depthy course. Diagram for yourself the situation with the filter over the left eye, and the bob traveling from right to left, and check your conclusion as to direction of rotation by personal observation. Incidentally, there is no special virtue in the filter—any other means of dimming one retinal image will do, such as looking with that eye through a hole smaller than the pupil or half-closing the eye so as to "clip" the pupil with the upper lid.

An occasional observer will find that he gets the Pulfrich effect without a filter. Assuming his eyes are adapted alike, this betrays some asymmetry in the visual system, which may or may not be normal. Perhaps he should have his visual system checked by an ophthalmologist.

Something to do at home in the evening, if anyone in the house still smokes cigarettes: Take a freshly lighted cigarette with you to a dim place where you can just see the white shaft of the cigarette. Holding it upright in front of your face, shake it from side to side through a distance of a few inches at different speeds. You should find that the glowing end seems to jump loose from the cigarette and leads the dimly seen shaft by a large fraction of an inch, with the shaft catching up each time the cigarette comes to a halt and reverses its motion. Here again, differences in sensation-time for the bright "coals" and the dim shaft cause differences in their apparent locations while they are in motion.

27. Visual Persistence-Time

When an illumination or an image has been standing on the retina long enough to be seen, and is suddenly cut off, one continues to see it for a brief period—the period of the persistence-time of visual sensation. Just as it takes time for the sensation to develop (Experiment No. 26, Visual Sensation-time), it takes time for it to fade or "decay." This is not a mere matter of remembering the stimulus after it is removed. The basis of the "persistence of vision" is not psychological but physiological, partly even chemical (within the visual cells).

The persistence-time is of course affected by intensity, adaptation state, etc. It is long enough to be easy to detect, and to employ for the production of amusing effects. If it did not exist, certain important things would not be possible, such as television. But the "persistence of vision" is commonly credited with things it has nothing to do with. For example, it has nothing to do with making the movies "move."

In combination, the sensation-time and the persistence-time determine how fast the image of an object can move across the retina without the object's losing clarity and appearing as an elongated blur. Everyone has seen photos in which someone moved during the exposure and dragged his image across the film. Things would look like that to us all the time if an image in each of its positions on the retina did not generate sensations which grow quickly and decay promptly. It has been customary for many years to compare the plan of the eye with the plan of a photographic camera. The eye compares better with a television camera, for its pick-up surface (the retina) does not have to be sent out to be "developed"; and, the movement of an image across it at any reasonable speed does not produce an unintelligible blur.

The most direct demonstration of the persistence-time is the "immediate positive after-image." Hold a card in front of one eye and cover the other with a hand. See how quickly you can jerk the card sideways and back again, so as to uncover the eye for a brief moment. Do this cover-uncover-cover very briskly and crisply. Now do this a few times while facing the lit bulb of a table lamp. Each time the card comes back in front of the eye, you will briefly see the lamp on the card, or as if *through* the card. The duration of this appearance is the persistence-time (under the particular conditions of intensity and adaptation-state).

Another direct demonstration is one which you may have performed for amusement at some time. Children long ago discovered that if a live coal is fastened to the end of a wire and swung rapidly in a circle in the dark, it generates a gyrating arc of light which lengthens and closes into a complete ring when the speed is sufficient. The time then required for one revolution is the persistence-time under the conditions. In the use of the Masson disc (Experiment No. 24, Intensity Discrimination), an advantage was taken of this phenomenon.

"Flicker" is a very special visual experience, best considered here in connection with persistence-time since the latter is involved in flicker.

When a particular spot on the retina receives intermittent stimulation, the flashes of light may be perceived separately and counted, if the stimulus frequency (the flash rate) is low. If the stimulus frequency is carried high enough, the stimulus appears to be a steady, continuous one, and is said to be "fused." The lowest frequency that gives fusion is the "critical fusion frequency" and it is roughly proportional to the logarithm of the intensity (Ferry-Porter Law). In a sizable range of stimulus frequency just below fusion, flicker is experienced. The flicker sensation is indescribable and "must be seen to be appreciated"— particularly if the flicker area is considerable; for, it has a vague pattern (perhaps even showing color) and a characteristic pulsation. Contrary to popular belief, the *apparent* rate of this pulsation bears no relation to the *actual* flash rate of the stimulus, *i.e.,* the pulsation stimulus may flash 40 times per second, yet the flicker sensation experienced may be pulsating at the rate of only ten times per second.

Go to the rotary color-mixer and install the black-and-white sectored disc (Figure 4B). Note that its zones afford three different flash rates simultaneously. Spin it at slowly increasing speed. Note that at first you can count the alternations of black and white going through the fixation point. Even when you can no longer count the circles, you can still tell the direction of rotation. You are not experiencing flicker until you can no longer detect rotation but instead are seeing a pulsating pattern that stands still on the disc. At a still higher speed, the flicker will be quite suddenly replaced by a smooth gray. After "fusion" has thus ocurred, you will find that increasing the speed further will not produce any further change of appearance. Obviously, the rate of decay of the effect of each flash has a great deal to do with how soon the next flash must be given if the two are to "fuse."

No practical use of the phenomenon of flicker (which is not particularly pleasant) is made in everyday life. But there are some very practical situations in which flicker has to be considered, in the sense that it has to be kept from occurring, as it would be a source of annoyance. It was purely and simply the facts of flicker, together with the intensities of projector light-sources, that originally determined that motion pictures must be projected at least sixteen frames per second. At any lower frequency, some percentage of the audience would complain of flicker, especially in bright scenes. All *sound* motion pictures are projected at the rate of 24 frames per second, because of sound track requirements; 16 is usually enough to prevent flicker.

A stimulus may be intermittent but well above critical fusion frequency, and appear steady when viewed steadily, yet seem to flicker if the gaze sweeps across it. Any such "stuttering" of the picture is not genuine flicker and does not mean that the flash rate is not really high enough for fusion. Rather, it represents a spatial dispersion of the separate flashes upon separate retinal spots. It is just because all of the flashes are not falling on one retinal area, that each flash can be seen:

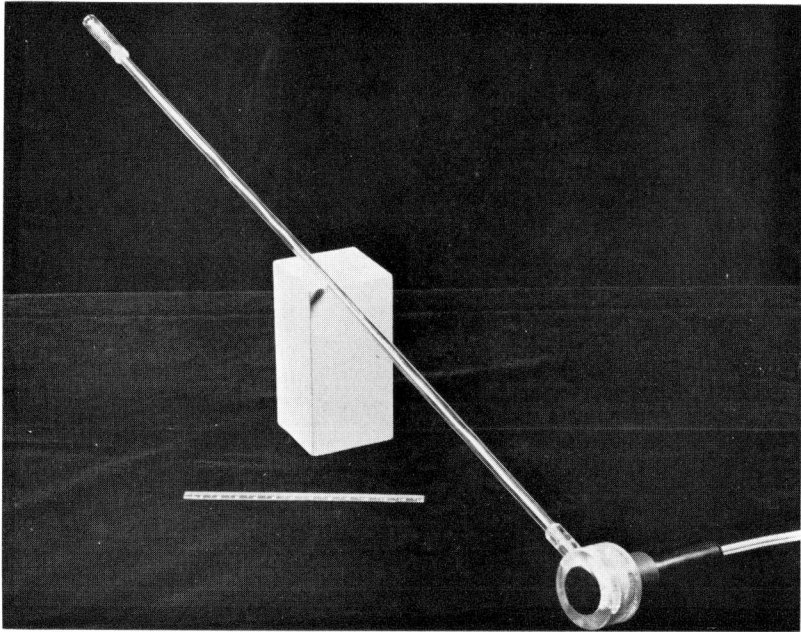

Figure 6. The neon lamp apparatus used to demonstrate "fusion" of an intermittent light source.

At the supply table, locate the tiny neon lamp on the end of a plastic tube containing a piece of lamp cord (Figure 6). Plug this in, hold the instrument by the handle, keep it still, and view it steadily. The red light will appear to be continuous. Actually, on 60-cycle current, it is flashing 120 times per second. While you stare straight ahead, wave the lamp from side to side and you will see these separate flashes. Remember, this is "false flicker" — the critical fusion frequency for a stimulus imaged at one place on the retina, having equal periods of light and darkness in its cycle, is *never* higher than 60 flashes per second. If the surroundings are not too bright, you can swing the neon lamp in a small circle and generate a ring of light which will be a "dotted line" (Figure 7) . You will then be able to tell whether the flashes last as long as the dark periods between them.

In the viewing of a television picture persistence-time enters in, in two ways. In its role as a nuisance, it forces the engineers to make the "frame rate" of the picture abundantly fast enough to avoid flicker. Persistence-time is at the same time a blessing, for without it television would not be possible at all. Each frame is laid down on the face of the viewing tube one "line" at a time from top to bottom, as if by a dot of light of fluctuating intensity which sweeps from one side of the tube to the other to generate each line-element of the picture. The bottom line must be generated within the persistence-time for the top line, so that the bottom of the picture will be seen before the top of the picture has had time to fade from the viewer's consciousness. (Of course, the "storage time" of the phosphors on the tube face helps here too.) You can see beautifully the fundamental basis of the viewer's end of the television system in the following experiment:

Go to a slide projector and aim it toward a dim corner — not at a screen. Put into it a slide. Locate the long white stick provided on the supply table. Hold a sheet of paper the size of this page a few feet from the projector, and have your partner focus the picture on the paper so that a sharp image of about that size is formed. Take the paper away, hold the stick by one end, horizontally, where the paper screen had been, and sweep it smartly down through the air so that it travels across the beam from the projector. You will see the picture in sharp focus, hanging in the air; the successive positions of the stick reflect successive line-elements, and the bottom one is seen before the top one has decayed; so, the whole of the picture is seen. By shaking the stick rapidly in the image plane you will be able to see the picture almost continuously.

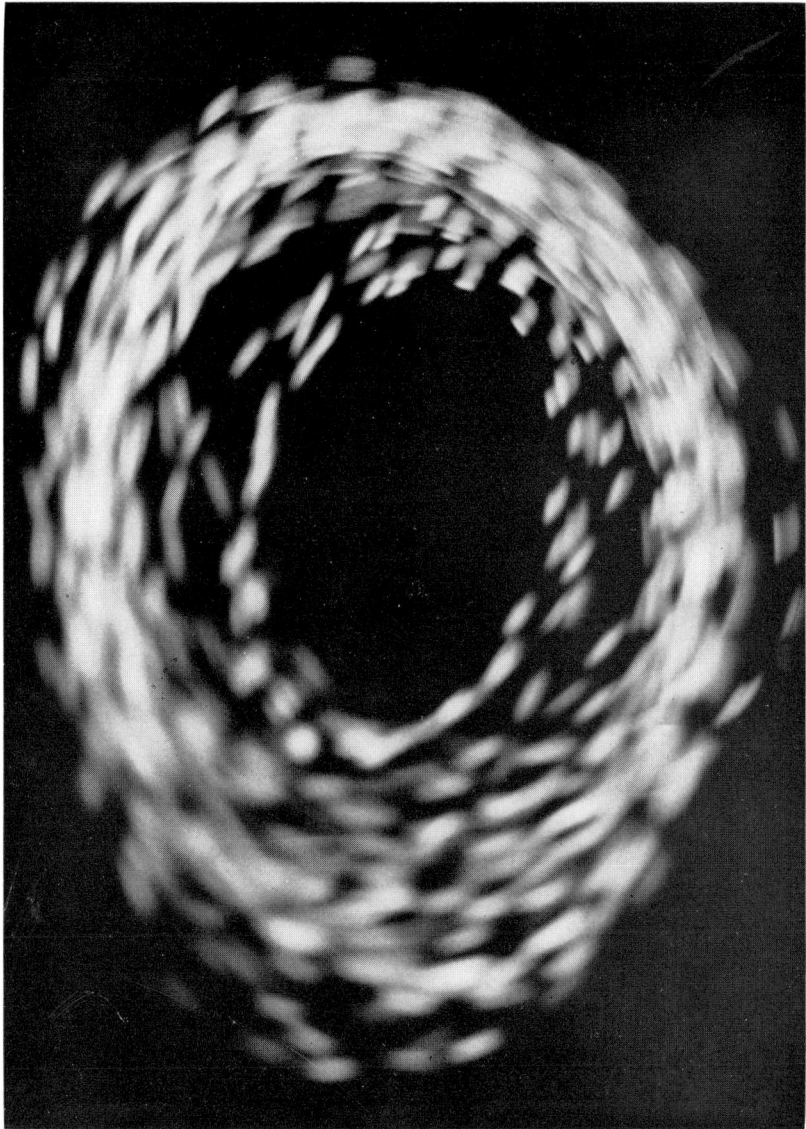

Figure 7. The "dotted line" is generated by a twirling intermittently flashing neon lamp.

28. *Visual Movement*

Any serious study of visual "real movement" is too complex for us to consider here. It would involve determinations of the minimum and maximum speeds at which an object could travel across the visual field and be seen as a moving object, of the smallest distance it would need to travel at optimum speed, of the effects of the size and intensity of the object on these values, of the effects of the presence and absence of stationary landmarks upon them, and so on.

It is important, however, to know the difference between the direct visual perception of motion and the mere knowledge, via the eye, that something must be moving.

> Find someone whose watch has a sweep second hand, and look at the watch for a few moments. The second hand travels fast enough for you to see it as a moving object, to see its "movingness." Now you know that the minute hand is also moving, but can you honestly say that you see it move? From time to time you are able to say that it is in a new position, and it is your eyes that are telling you so. But this is not the perception of visual movement, for you do not see the minute hand going from one position to another. On any very large clock, one may actually see the minute hand in motion. Never the hour hand, however.

It is also important to know that there are situations in which one directly perceives visual movement where there really is none. There is a good deal of "relativity" about visual movement, and one may readily see a moving object as stationary and attribute its movement to something else. When wisps of cloud are passing over the moon, one is very likely to see the moon as sailing along among motionless clouds. Probably, you are also familiar with the "railroad illusion." While sitting in a railroad car when the train on the next track begins to move forward, you are overcome with the peculiarly strong sensation that *your* car is moving *backward!* Even not counting this type of error, there are still several different kinds of visual "apparent movement." We shall study two samples: One, an important kind of apparent movement in which one "sees" an object actually changing its location;

and another, in which one has a strong visual impression of movement but without seeing the objects "getting anywhere."

Set two projectors side by side and in each one install a square metal "slide" with a ¼" hole, forming a small spot of light on a nearby screen. Focus these two spots side by side and overlapping a bit. Your partner, stationed behind the projectors, holds a square of thin black plastic over the front lens of each one and with these he uncovers the lenses alternately, briefly, crisply, and rhythmically so that the two light-spots appear on the screen alternately. He should try different rates of alternation while you try viewing the spots from different distances. You will soon hit upon a combination such that what you will perceive is a single spot jumping back and forth between two positions. You will actually see it seemingly in motion, forming a "blur" as it travels. This is "beta movement" in a simple form — the seeing of a continuous movement, where the object is really being exposed in fixed positions, its intermediate positions being supplied by your own brain. The "motion" just perceived was a "hopping" back and forth of a single spot of light. Such an apparent movement can take place along a curve or even around a corner, when the stimulus situation seems to "demand" it. It can also take place "in depth" if the two stimuli are disposed in depth. If the stimuli are semicircular (with the straight side of the stimulus-area common to both of them) the "movement" will take place in depth to "enable" one of the semicircles to "pivot" around the straight line onto the position of the other semicircle.

It is beta movement that makes the movies and television move. An object caught by the camera in a series of fixed postures appears to be in a smoothly continuous movement, when the eye sees the pictures in succession with proper timing. This phenomenon was employed in various entertainment devices long before film was invented and projected movies became possible.

When a really continuous movement is viewed only intermittently, as by a movie camera whose shutter opens periodically, or by the eye when the moving object is illuminated by a series of flashes, this process (of chopping up the motion into snapshots) is called "stroboscopy." A spinning wheel, stroboscoped at a correct frequency, appears to be standing still. Let the wheel's speed now change a little one way or the other, and "stroboscopic apparent movement" (really, nothing but beta movement!) will enter the situation and make the wheel appear to be turning slowly forward, remain still, or turn backward. Everyone has seen these phenomena in the wheels of a movie stagecoach. Stroboscopy by flashing illumination has practical uses in industry for studying the deformations of rapidly rotating objects and for measuring rotary speeds too fast for any mechanical tachometer to record.

There are many other types of "apparent motion" phenomena, most designated by other greek letters; for example, "delta movement," is sort of a reversed beta-movement that may occur when two spatially-separated stimuli are shown in succession, with the *second* stimulus brighter than the first, and "gamma movement" (which is obvious if you look for it in everyday life) —this is the *very* quick "growth," or "filling out" of the entire area of a broad light source (like any bowl-type light enclosure) that occurs when the light is first turned on; and the sudden shrinkage to a vanishing point (as if the light "pours down a drain") when it is turned off. Try to notice this for yourself the next time an opportunity presents itself.

We shall study now another type of apparent movement, called the "after image of motion." This was first noticed in Aristotle's time by a man watching a waterfall, who found that when he looked away, everything seemed to be rising up into the air—although "without getting anywhere." In the laboratory, this type of apparent movement is most easily elicited by watching a Plateau spiral:

> Go to the rotary color-mixer and install the disc bearing a black spiral (Figure 4C), titled "shrinking" spiral on the reverse side. Have your partner sit beside the mixer, facing you, to operate it at low speed. You sit two or three feet away and stare at the center of the disc for at least twenty seconds, timed by your partner. The speed should be such that you see the turns of the spiral as an endless parade of black rings shrinking inward toward the center of the disc. When the twenty seconds are up, your partner, still looking at you, stops the disc and you now fixate his nose. What you will see you can interpret as an apparent *outward movement* of the parts of his face from a com-

mon center — the after-effect of viewing the radially moving (shrinking) rings on the rotating disc. Next try changing to the "expanding" (Figure 4D) spiral disc and viewing it. After the same procedure the observer will note an apparent *shrinking movement* of the parts of the partner's face.

Try stimulating one eye only (the other being covered). After the stimulation, cover that eye and look at your partner's face with the previously covered eye. Is the "effect" transferable to the other eye?

Cover your left eye, and with your right eye fixate a spot just to the right of the spinning "shrinking spiral," so that the image of the spiral falls on the *temporal* half of your retina. (Be sure you understand this imagery). Continue to fixate this spot for about thirty seconds. Then quickly swap the cover to the right eye and with your left eye stare at your partner's *right* ear; repeat the above and this time stare at partner's *left* ear. Does his face seem to expand in both cases or only one of them? You should find that the "after image" transfer is possible only to the corresponding visual field of the opposite eye (in this case, when looking at your partner's left ear), and suggests that a basic *retinal* process as an explanation for this finding is most unlikely; the mechanism concerned is probably a property of the occipital striate cortex. However, the actual physiological basis of this startling and amusing phenomenon, has never been properly explained.

Color

29. Subjectivity of Color

As we approach the subject of color, the first and foremost fact to get in mind is that colors are not physical properties of lights and objects, but private and personal sensory experiences. We do not have color vision, but *colored* vision. We can show a "color stimulus" (a "colored" light, or an object that reflects that light) to another person, but we cannot show him what we see when we look at it. A "partially color-blind" man and a color-normal man may look at the same stimulus and get utterly different color sensations from it. That stimulus then "has" two colors at once; this is really no paradox since neither color is *in* the stimulus, but is in a human mind. Neither man is right and neither is wrong, for each has every right to his own sensations, and the "normals" are normal only because they are in the majority.

Perhaps the most convincing demonstration of the subjectiveness of color is one in which colors are seen, but without an obvious color stimulus. The "Benham Top" (Figure 4E) provides such a demonstration. The disc is half black and half white, with black arcs on the white half. Rotate this so slowly that the black arcs barely make complete rings (about 6 rotations per second). Note that each of the four sets of rings has a distinct color. Have your eyes about two feet from the disc.

Experiment with the placement of the gooseneck lamp, shining it on the disc from one angle or another to get the richest colors. The *optimal* lighting is critical and can only be found by trial and error. These colors are generated entirely within your visual system, as a result of the peculiar timing of the black and white stimulations the "top" gives to each point in the retina. What happens to the colors if the direction of spin of the top is reversed? If it is rotated clockwise, the innermost should appear dark blue, next, olive-green, then brownish, and the outermost yellowish-red. With counterclockwise rotation, the order of the colors is reversed.

Different observers agree fairly well with their color descriptions. If either the speed of the top is changed or the intensity of the illumination on it, the apparent color may be altered somewhat, but, in any case, a phenomenon of differing colors is conspicuously present. It is known that certain patterns of illumination arriving at the eye in broken spatio-temporal configurations can cause a vivid colored impression even when the light falling on the retina is *monochromatic*. The explanation for the perceived colors is not clear. The necessary conditions for this illusion seem to be the alternations of a uniform bright field, a uniform dark field and one which contains *sharp* spatial contrasts of bright and dark. It is known that there is a difference in the latencies of action (*i.e.*, time from the stimulation of the retina to perception of a colored image) of the different color vision mechanisms (the blue-sensitive pathway has a longer latent period than the red-sensitive mechanism). Perhaps the varied pulsing pattern falling on the retina, somehow develops the different latencies for each set of rings on the "top." Thus, a particular pulse spacing stimulates (at cortical level) an arriving "colored" stimulus. No physiological proof of this assumption (nor any other) is yet at hand.

30. Color Mixture

We do not have a separate type of visual cell to give us each different color sensation we can have. We have a very small number of types (three or four), each of which upon absorbing radiant energy "tries" to establish a particular kind of sensation — a particular, pure, huedness. These few basic sensory qualities (redness, greenness, blueness), are "components" which blend and interact to give us thousands of colors. With light of a given "spectral composition" (distribution of energy among its constituent wavelengths) serving as the stimulus, the components are aroused in some rank-order of magnitudes. No one visual cell can tell one wavelength from another — its response can vary only quantitatively, in accordance with the amount of energy it absorbs. The two largest components jointly determine the *hue* of the color seen; the multiple ratio of all components determines the *saturation* of the color (its *richness* of coloration, irrespective of which hue it happens to have). The intensity of the light of course determines the *brightness* of the color of a light, but not the *lightness* of the color of a reflecting surface. Under white illumination, the lightness (or darkness) of a surface color is determined by the *reflectance* of the surface. This property is not changed by changing the intensity of illumination.

We can mix two or more color stimuli so as to arouse the components in the same ratio that some other, single, stimulus does. That is, stimuli each of which has a unique color by itself can be mixed to afford still another color. If hearing worked in this way, we could strike two keys far apart on a piano, and instead of hearing those two notes we would hear only the note of some unstruck key between them. It is because color vision is componential that "color mixture" is possible. The major hues are red, orange, yellow, green, blue, and purple. If we think of purple as being adjacent also to red so that the hues form a circle, we can mix colors of two major hues to obtain any hue between them, so long as the two stimuli cannot be mixed to arouse all the components equally. In the latter event, the stimuli when mixed will comprise a neutral (white or gray) stimulus and are said to be complementary. Their hues will be found approximately opposite each other on the hue circle.

With only three "primary" stimuli fairly evenly spaced on the hue circle, all possible hues can be synthesized by mixing the primaries in pairs. Each two primaries will afford all the hues that lie between their own hues, on the hue circle. Any admixture of the third primary will always lower the saturation of a pair-mixture, and some particular mixture of all three primaries will be perfectly neutral, with saturation then zero.*

Go to the color mixer (Figure 8) and spin the disc which is part green and part blue. When each spot of retina receives these two kinds of light in rapid alternation, it is as if both kinds were continuously shining on the same visual cells. The mixture generates a new hue: a blue-green or "turquoise," which is neither blue nor green but intermediate between the two (or both-at-once, depending upon the point of view). Other proportions of green and blue would give all the hues between purest green and purest blue.

Now spin the disc which is part blue and part red. This will produce a purple. The purple series of hybrid hues ranging from violet (more bluish than reddish) to red-purple (more reddish than bluish) are mostly, we say, "outside the spectrum" since we can make all of them only by mixing long-wavelength light and short-wavelength light in various proportions.

Next, spin the part-red-part-green disc. The *hue* of the tawny color it produces is, unexpectedly, yellow. There is no such thing as reddish-green or greenish-red. These two components lose their identity in yellowness, which differs qualitatively from both of them. Yellowness in turn can blend with some extra redness to make orange, or with some extra greenness to make chartreuse. Various proportions of red and green in mixtures will therefore synthesize all the hues from red to green in the spectrum and on the hue circle.

Lastly, spin the disc bearing three primaries. It will generate a *perfectly neutral* gray if the only illumination upon it comes from an overcast north sky, and an *acceptable* gray under almost any "white" illumination. Each of the three primaries, in the amounts provided here, is perfectly complementary to the mixture of the other two. If any one primary were present in excess, it would introduce its hue into the sensation, with a saturation proportional to the extent of the excess.

---

*The color effects produced by the spinning discs will be "truest" in skylight. Pure fluorescent illumination will render the colors properly, but will stroboscope (see Experiment No. 28, Visual Movement) the discs and produce gyrating shadows. Pure tungsten lamp illumination would be too yellowish and show the desired effects very poorly if at all.

Figure 8. The rotary mixer for use in all disc spinning experiments.

31. Blackness

Blackness is not the same thing as mere darkness (which is the absence of light). It is a positive experience — at night, "the dark" never looks anything like black velvet. The color of a *surface* is always seen as having more or less of a "content of blackness" whenever it is a surface that sends less light to the eye than its surroundings do. The brighter "surround" is entirely responsible for the blackness seen as a constituent of the color of the area or object surrounded. One says that the blackness is *induced* into the area, by the brighter surround. Among common place objects, it is those with the lowest reflectance whose colors are contaminated with the most blackness, for the brightness of such objects is low relative to the brightness of the surround, and it is this *relative brightness* which we perceive as the "lightness" (or, "darkness") of the color; blackness induced into a blue area makes it navy blue; into green, it makes olive green; into orange, it makes brown. The color of a *light* could not be navy blue or olive green or brown; for, the light — for the very reason that it *is* a "light" — is brighter than what is around it, and the color of the light could not have any blackness induced into it. On surfaces, therefore, there is a whole family of blackness-containing colors that cannot exist in lights.

Place the two slide projectors side by side. In the slide recess of one, place the slide with the ½" hole through it. This will be the "spot" projector. In the other projector place the glass slide bearing the ½" disc of opaque foil, making this a "surround" projector. Shift the projectors on the table, and change the tilt adjustment of one of them, until the surround neatly fits the spot on the screen. Now, in the front of the spot projector, place first a light neural density filter. Follow this with a denser filter and then both together. Note that the spot becomes a gray disc — first a light gray, then a medium, lastly a dark gray. Each time, switch off the surround projector briefly and note that the gray disc turns back into a patch of light (bright, medium, or dim — certainly not "light," medium, or "dark"). When you switch the surround back on, you can actually watch the developing blackness invade the patch of light

and turn it into "a disc of gray material glued to the screen."
You can more easily demonstrate the "blackness," pouring by
induction, into the projected spot of light, if, instead of switch-
ing the "surround" projector on and off, you use your hand as
a partial shield directly in front of the "surround" projector
lens; this maneuver blocks off some of the light emanating from
the projector and can vary the intensity of light falling on the
screen from zero to full illumination. Place one of the neutral
filters in front of the "spot" projector and watch its "blackness
content" change as you vary only the surround illumination
with your hand. The physiological process underlying induction consumes an appreciable period of time. It is not known
for sure whether the process is retinal or cerebral.

32. Spatial Induction of Color

Just as bright whiteness can induce its "opposite," *i.e.*, blackness, so also a colored surround induces an opposite (complementary) color into whatever it surrounds.

> In front of the surround projector place, one at a time,
> every available color filter. Each time, adjust the brightness of
> the spot until the saturation of the induced color is maximal.
> The colors will be most convincing if one projector is displaced
> a bit so that the spot and surround no longer fit exactly. Note
> that the hue of the induced color is always essentially comple-
> mentary to that of the inducing color.*

This phenomenon can be "explained" physiologically only in
terms of certain theories of color vision (which do not necessarily
offer the best explanations of other color-visual phenomena). But
despite its mysteriousness it has immense practical significance,
particularly for women. Every growing girl learns empirically
that there are certain colors which she must not put next to her
face in the form of a high scarf or a droopy hat, else they will
"make her complexion look awful." The simple reason is that
skin-color looks wrong if certain other colors are induced into it

---

*Someone always asks how yellow and blue can be complementary, since mixing
yellow and blue *paints* gives green and not gray (as one would expect of complementary colors). The mixture seems green in the paint situation because green light
is the only kind that neither blue nor yellow paint *absorbs*, hence is the only kind
their mixture can *reflect*. It still remains true that a mixture of yellow and blue
lights is a white (or neutral) light.

and thus are mixed with it, and just this effect will be obtained from surrounds having complements of those undesirable additions. The color of almost anything we look at is altered somewhat by the colors of nearby things. What the "true color" of anything is, is a good question.

Induced colors are just as "real" as the colors given directly by obvious color-stimuli. Place the two projectors at least a foot apart, remove the slides, put a green filter over the front lens of one, and turn both on. If you hold a hand between the projectors and the screen it will produce two shadows, and your partner can easily cut the brightness of the white illumination until the pink shadow and the green one are equally saturated. The green shadow is optical and "objective" — the white light is blocked from the screen there, so that the green light naturally makes a green hand. But the pink shadow exists by virtue of spatial induction: It contains only white light, but this is rendered pink by the green light falling upon the *surrounding* screen area.

The basis for a startling "new" color vision theory recently proposed by Edwin Land of the Polaroid Corporation is in reality nothing new. The color phenomena he beautifully demonstrates can be fully explained on the basis of induction (or, "simultaneous color contrast" as it is officially called).

33. Color Blindness*

This rather poor term rarely means that the individual sees no difference between a color movie and a black-and-white one. Nearly all cases of color blindness are "partial," and sixteen out of seventeen of these are males—only 0.5 per cent of women are color blind. Almost everything that looks colored to the normal looks colored to the color-blind also. The difference is that where the normal sees tens of thousands of colors (*i.e.,* combinations of different hue, saturation, and brightness), the color-blind sees only hundreds. This means that many things that look quite different in color to the normal, look quite alike in color to the

---

*Since true *blindness* to colors is so rare the much-to-be-preferred term is color "deficiency" instead of color "blindness"; however, the latter is so widely used and accepted, we begrudgingly use it here.

color-blind. This is how it is that the common types of seriously color-blind people confuse certain shades of red with certain shades of green. To one type, they are all shades of yellow. To another type, they are all shades of green. In still another serious kind of deficiency (relatively uncommon), reds and greens appear "correct," but blue things look no different from green ones, and yellow does not exist (being replaced by gray).

Less serious color-vision deficiencies are characterized by a depression of saturation, and by the displacement of hues in one direction or another along the spectrum. In these conditions the individual can make all his colors by mixture only if he is allowed to use three primaries, but he does not make normal mixtures—he loads the mixture with an excess of one primary, usually green, less often red, very rarely blue. These "anomalous trichromates" number six men in every hundred. Only two others in a hundred are red-green confusers, who see only two hues in the whole spectrum instead of the normal 60 or 70. They have only two components, and can mix all the colors they see from only two primary stimuli. They are called "dichromates." There is not more than one green-blue-confusing dichromate in 13,000 people.

The seriously color-blind dichromate of each of the three chief types is sometimes lumped together with the kind of "animal" who most nearly resembles him, creating three main categories of defects: Protanoid (having more trouble with reds than other colors), deuteranoid (bothered particularly by greens), and tritanoid (having the most difficulty with blues and yellows). The commoner tests for color blindness make an attempt to detect all cases, and the better tests attempt to sort out the protanoids, deuteranoids, and tritanoids and/or to determine whether the defectiveness is "mild" or "severe" (corresponding to anomalous trichromasy versus dichromasy). Only in a research laboratory can every case of color deficiency be diagnosed with certainty, including the peculiar cases due to the inheritance of combinations of defects, etc.

> With the aid of your partner, take the H-R-R Test provided in the laboratory as strictly as possible according to the rules for it. Illumination from an overcast sky (but not direct yellow

sunshine!) can substitute well enough for the special artificial white light specified for the test. Each plate should be revealed to the testee for only two seconds, at a distance of thirty inches from his face. The test is invalid if these previous instructions are not rigidly adhered to. The observer's task is to say whether the plate bears a circle and/or triangle and/or cross. The first four plates in the book are legible to everyone and are for practice only to show the testee what is going to be expected of him. The next plate is "Plate No. 1." If no errors are made on Plates 1 through 6, the testee is considered normal and the test is over. If the testee does make errors here he should go on through the entire test. Examine the sample score sheet posted in the laboratory. If a team contains a deficient individual, the instructor will provide a fresh score sheet; but do not waste a score sheet on any normal individual.

The H-R-R Test is the newest and best of all tests of its kind. Its working principles are simple: For each type of anomalous trichromate, certain pastel colors are seen as having so little saturation that spots of these colors become "lost" among gray spots and cannot be seen to comprise any geometrical figure. For each type of dichromate there are strong colors of a particular hue which appear neutral and gray, because the locus of that hue (or of its complement) in the normal's spectrum is at the junction between the only two hues the spectrum contains for the dichromate. The dichromate sees no figure when the colored spots composing it appear gray to him; for, the spots of the background are also gray, for the dichromate as well as for the normal.

References

A SHORT LIST OF GENERAL REFERENCES TO WHICH
THE STUDENT CAN TURN TO OBTAIN ADDITIONAL IN-
formation on the experiments discussed follows:

1. Adler, F. H.: *Physiology of the Eye, Third Edition.* St. Louis, C. V. Mosby Company, 1959.
2. Brindley, G. S.: *Physiology of the Retina and the Visual Pathway.* London, Edward Arnold & Co., 1960.
3. Davson, H.: *The Eye,* Vols. I - IV. New York, Academic Press, 1962.
4. Davson, H.: *Physiology of the Eye,* Second Edition. Boston, Little, Brown and Company, 1963.
5. Helmholtz, H. von: *Treatise on Physiological Optics,* Vols. I, II, III, 1910. Translated by J. P. Southall. New York, Dover Publications, Inc., 1925.
6. Lancaster, W. B.: *Refraction and Motility.* Springfield, Thomas, 1952.
7. Linksz, A.: *Physiology of the Eye,* Vol. II, Vision. New York, Grune and Stratton, 1952.
8. Sorsby: *Modern Ophthalmology,* Vol. I. London, Butterworth, 1963.